South Vietnam

U.S.-Communist Confrontation in Southeast Asia

Volume 4

1969

South Vietnam

U.S.-Communist Confrontation in Southeast Asia

Volume 4

1969

Edited by Stanley Millet

FACTS ON FILE, INC.   NEW YORK, N.Y.

South Vietnam

U.S.-Communist Confrontation in Southeast Asia

Volume 4

1969

Published by Facts on File, Inc.,
119 West 57th Street, New York, N.Y. 10019.

Library of Congress Card Catalog No. 66-23943
ISBN 0-87196-236-5

9 8 7 6 5 4 3 2 1
PRINTED IN
THE UNITED STATES OF AMERICA

Contents

Foreword

THIS 4TH VOLUME of the FACTS ON FILE record of U.S. involvement
in the war in Vietnam covers that history for 1969, the year in
which the American conduct of the war was turned over to the
Nixon Administration.

The year 1969 marked another major turning point in the
struggle in Southeast Asia. The U.S. initiated its Vietnamization
policy, under which it began the withdrawal of American fighting
men from Indochina. The North Vietnamese leader Ho Chi
Minh, who had led his nation in its victorious struggle against
French colonialism, died during 1969. His death appeared to have
little or no effect on the North Vietnamese determination to win
the conflict with the U.S. and the Saigon regime. Peace negotiations continued in Paris, but there was little noticeable progress
toward peace. And men, women and children continued to be
killed on both sides.

As with most books in this series, this volume is based largely
on material compiled by FACTS ON FILE in its coverage of current world history. This book deals with events so controversial
that discussion of them evokes an emotional response from many
people. A sincere effort was made, however, to record these events
completely, dispassionately and objectively. The purpose here is
to provide the available facts of a situation in which there already
seems to be an adequate supply of opinion.

1

1969

The newly-elected Nixon Administration assumed power in the U.S. in Jan. 1969. Pres. Nixon soon began the slow but steady withdrawal of U.S. ground forces from Vietnam that came to be called "Vietnamization." The Viet Cong and North Vietnamese launched 2 offensives in South Vietnam during 1969. The Paris talks reached stalemate over the political issues involved in settling the war. Ho Chi Minh died, and leadership was reconstituted in North Vietnam. Pres. Nguyen Van Thieu continued to consolidate his political control over South Vietnam. Toward the end of 1969 Nixon was confronted by a strong Congressional opposition to his Vietnam policy and by a massive mobilization of antiwar forces in Washington. With 9,414 U.S. servicemen reported slain in Vietnam during the year, the number of Americans killed there since the U.S. became involved rose to more than 40,000 by the end of 1969.

NIXON SUCCEEDS JOHNSON

Johnson Administration Leaves

Coming to the end of his concluding term as U.S. President, Lyndon B. Johnson sent his 6th and last budget to Congress Jan. 15. Johnson proposed a $3¹/₂ billion reduction in spending for the war in Vietnam. He called for federal outlays totaling a record $195.272 billion in fiscal 1970 and estimated fiscal 1970 receipts at a record $198.686 billion. The resulting $3.414 billion surplus, the President said, was needed "to relieve the inflationary pressures in the economy and to reduce the strains that federal borrowing would place on financial markets and interest rates."

The anti-inflationary effect was listed by the President as one of three major goals of the fiscal 1967 budget. The other two goals: (1) Support "for our commitments in Southeast Asia" and "necessary improvements" in overall military capabilities; (2) "continued emphasis on domestic programs which help disadvantaged groups obtain a fairer share of the nation's economic and cultural advancements,"

The cut in Vietnam spending was the first since the U.S. got into the war. The war-area expenditures in fiscal 1970 were projected at $25.733 billion, a sum that included $336 million for economic assistance. The cut was attributed to a reduced need for ammunition (since Oct. 31, 1968), fewer aircraft losses (since the bombing of North Vietnam was halted) and the general scaling down of combat and of transportation and supply. Overall defense spending in fiscal 1970 was expected to rise by $541 million to a total of $81.542 billion.

The reduction of funds budgeted for the war was translated into plans to withdraw American troops from Vietnam, foreshadowing what became the Nixon policy of "Vietnamization." South Vietnam proposed Jan. 14 that U.S. troops start "a gradual, phased withdrawal [from South Vietnam] at the rate of 10 to 20,000 a month." Explaining the plan, Premier Tran Van Huong said South Vietnam was "confident" that it had the strength to fight the Communists with a diminished American force. Huong added: "We know that sooner or later American troops must withdraw. . . . If it is a gradual, phased withdrawal, we will have time to organize and make ourselves stronger. I see no harm in this withdrawal under such circumstances."

South Vietnamese Pres. Nguyen Van Thieu had suggested Jan. 1 that the government army "is ready to replace part of the allied forces" in 1969. He confirmed Jan. 18 that he had request-ed the withdrawal of some U.S. troops from Vietnam in 1969. But U.S. sources said the pull-out would likely be limited to no more than 50,000 men, not 150,000 to 200,000 as suggested by some Saigon officials. Thieu had discussed the matter Jan. 17 with Gen. Creighton W. Abrams, commander of U.S. forces, and Amb. Ellsworth Bunker. A U.S. official then said that Thieu had agreed with Abrams' view "that the withdrawals have to be linked to better training of the South Vietnamese forces and real improvement in the quality of the Vietnamese troops." A Saigon government statement Jan. 18 said Thieu had ordered Gen. Cao Van Vien, chief of the joint general staff, to confer with Abrams "to draft a program" for some U.S. troop with-drawal. The statement said that Thieu believed that govern-ment forces in 1969 must "share more of the burden of the war so that part of the American troops can return home ... to alleviate the burden for the people and government of the United States."

The South Vietnamese government Jan. 18 released the text of a letter in which Pres. Thieu had expressed "heartfelt gratitude" to Pres. Johnson for his "great decisive contribution" to South Vietnam. South Vietnam, the letter said, was "substantially stronger..., militarily as well as politically, and... it was mostly thanks to you that we have achieved these results." (Departing U.S. State Secy. Dean Rusk had defended the Johnson Administration's Vietnam policy at a Washington press conference Jan. 3. Rusk in-sisted that U.S. activity in Vietnam was "directly related to the national interests of the U.S." and was necessitated by "a per-sistent and determined attempt by the authorities in Hanoi to take over South Vietnam by force.")

(In another apparent move to "de-Americanize the war," it was officially disclosed Feb. 4 that South Vietnam would receive from the U.S. 60 jet fighter-bombers and 300 helicopters. The South Vietnamese air force was currently equipped with about 400 planes and 75 outdated helicopters. The new U.S. jet Saigon was to receive was the A-37, a twin-engine fighter-bomber with a maximum speed of 478 m.p.h. and a range of more than 1,400 miles. The U.S. Navy had turned over 60 heavily armed river patrol boats to the South Vietnamese navy by Feb. 1.)

Nixon Administration in Office

Richard M. Nixon was inaugurated Jan. 20 to succeed Lyndon B. Johnson as President. In his inaugural address, as in his election campaign, Nixon avoided specific reference to the war in Vietnam. Through its emphases on peace and an end to "confrontation," though cast in general terms, the inaugural address, however, suggested policies directed to the reduction of the impact of the war on the U.S. and, perhaps, the achievement of peace in Vietnam.

Excepts from Nixon's inaugural address:

. . . I ask you to share with me today the majesty of this moment. In the orderly transfer of power, we celebrate the unity that keeps us free.

Each moment in history is a fleeting time, precious and unique. But some stand out as moments of beginning, in which courses are set that shape decades or centuries.

This can be such a moment. Forces now are converging that make possible for the first time the hope that many of man's deepest aspirations can at last be realized. . . .

For the first time, because the people of the world want peace and the leaders of the world are afraid of war, the times are on the side of peace. . . .

The greatest honor history can bestow is the title of peacemaker. This honor now beckons America—the chance to help lead the world at last out of the valley of turmoil and on to that high ground of peace that man has dreamed of since the dawn of civilization. If we succeed, generations to come will say of us now living that we mastered our moment, that we helped make the world safe for mankind. This is our summons to greatness. And I believe the American people are ready to answer this call.

The 2d third of this century has been a time of proud achievement. . . . We have given freedom new reach; we have begun to make its promise real for black as well as for white.

We see the hope of tomorrow in the youth of today. I know America's youth. I believe in them. We can be proud that they are better educated, more committed, more passionately driven by conscience than any generation in our history.

No people has ever been so close to the achievement of a just and abundant society, or so possessed of the will to achieve it. And because our strengths are so great, we can afford to appraise our weaknesses with candor and to approach them with hope.

Standing in this same place a 3d of a century ago, Franklin Delano Roosevelt addressed the nation ravaged by depression gripped in fear. He could say in surveying the nation's troubles: "They concern, thank God, only material things."

Our crisis today is in reverse. We find ourselves rich in goods, but ragged in spirit; reaching with magnificent precision for the moon, but falling into raucous discord on earth.

We are caught in war, wanting peace. We're torn by division, wanting unity. We see around us empty lives, wanting fulfillment. We tasks that need doing, waiting for hands to do them.

To a crisis of the spirit, we need an answer of the spirit. And to find that answer, we need only look within ourselves. . . .

Greatness comes in simple trappings. The simple things are the ones most needed today if we are to surmount what divides us and cement what unites us. To lower our voices would be a simple thing.

In these difficult years, America has suffered from a fever of words; from inflated rhetoric that promises more than it can deliver; from angry rhetoric that fans discontents into hatreds; from bombastic rhetoric that postures instead of persuading.

We cannot learn from one another until we stop shouting at one another— until we speak quietly enough so that our words can be heard as well as our voices.

For its part, government will listen. We will strive to listen in new ways— to the voices of quiet anguish, the voices that speak without words, the voices of the heart—to the injured voices, the anxious voices, the voices that have despaired of being heard. Those who have been left out, we will try to bring in. Those left behind, we will help to catch up. . . .

As we reach toward our hopes, our task is to build on what has gone before—not turning away from the old, but turning toward the new. . . .

We shall plan now for the day when our wealth can be transferred from the destruction of war abroad to the urgent needs of our people at home. . . .

But we are approaching the limits of what government alone can do. Our greatest need now is to reach beyond government, to enlist the legions of the concerned and the committed. What has to be done has to be done by government and people together or it will not be done at all. The lesson of past agony is that without the people we can do nothing: with the people we can do everything.

To match the magnitude of our talks, we need the energies of our people— enlisted not only in grand enterprises, but more importantly in those small splendid efforts that make headlines in the neighborhood newspaper instead of the national journal.

I do not offer a life of uninspiring ease. I do not call for a life of grim sacrifice. I ask you to join in a high adventure—one as rich as humanity itself, and exciting as the times we live in.

The essence of freedom is that each of us shares in the shaping of his own destiny. Until he has been part of a cause larger than himself, no man is truly whole. . . .

No man can be fully free while his neighbor is not. To go forward at all is to go forward together. This means black and white together, as one nation, not 2. . . .

As we learn to go forward together at home, let us also seek to go forward together with all mankind.

Let us take as our goal: where peace is unknown, make it welcome; where peace is fragile, make it strong; where peace is temporary, make it permanent.

After a period of confrontation, we are entering an era of negotiation. Let all nations know that during this Administration our lines of communication will be open.

We seek an open world—open to ideas, open to the exchange of goods and people, a world in which no people, great or small, will live in angry isolation.

We cannot expect to make everyone our friend, but we can try to make no one our enemy. Those who would be our adversaries, we invite to a peaceful competition—not in conquering territory or extending dominion, but in enriching the life of man. . . .

And with those who are willing to join, let us cooperate to reduce the burden of arms, to strengthen the structure of peace, to lift up the poor and the hungry. But to all those who would be tempted by weakness, let us leave no doubt that we will be as strong as we need to be for as long as we need to be.

. . . I have visited most of the nations of the world. I have come to know the leaders of the world, the great forces, the hatreds, the fears that divide the world.

I know that peace does not come through wishing for it—that there is no substitute for days and even years of patient and prolonged diplomacy.

I also know the people of the world. I have seen the hunger of a homeless child, the pain of a man wounded in battle, the grief of a mother who has lost her son. I know these have no ideology, no race.

I know America. I know the heart of America is good. I speak from my own heart, and the heart of my country, the deep concern we have for those who suffer and those who sorrow.

I have taken an oath today in the presence of God and my conscience: To uphold and defend the Constitution of the United States. And to that oath, I now add this sacred commitment: I shall consecrate my office, my energies and all the wisdom I can summon, to the cause of peace among nations.

Let this message be heard by strong and weak alike. The peace we seek—the peace we seek to win—is not victory over any other people, but the peace that comes with healing in its wings; with compassion for those who have suffered; with understanding for those who have opposed us; with the opportunity for all the peoples of this earth to choose their own destiny.

Only a few short weeks ago, we shared the glory of man's first sight of the world as God sees it, as a single sphere reflecting light in the darkness. As Apollo astronauts flew over the moon's gray surface on Christmas Eve, they spoke to us of the beauty of earth and in that voice so clear across the lunar distance we heard them invoke God's blessing on its goodness. In that moment, their view from the moon moved poet Archibald MacLeish to write: "To see the earth as it truly is, small and blue and beautiful in that eternal silence where it floats, is to see ourselves as riders on the earth together, brothers in that bright loveliness in the eternal cold—brothers who know now they are truly brothers."

In that moment of surpassing technological triumph, men turned their thoughts toward home and humanity—seeing in that far perspective that man's destiny on earth is not divisible; telling us that however far we reach into the cosmos our destiny lies not in the stars but on earth itself, it our own hands, in our own hearts.

We have endured a long night of the American spirit. But as our eyes catch dimness of the first rays of dawn, let us not curse the remaining dark. Let us gather the light.

Our destiny offers not the cup of despair, but the chalice of opportunity. So let us seize it, not in fear, but in gladness—and "riders on the earth together," let us go forward, firm in our faith, steadfast in our purpose, cautious of the dangers; but sustained by our confidence in the will of God and the promise of man.

At his first news conference, Nixon told reporters Jan. 27 that foreign affairs had dominated his first week in office. He responded specifically to questions on Vietnam, China, arms control and nuclear-weapon strength and the Middle East. The President said that the Vietnam talks in Paris were "going to take time" and that "overly optimistic statements" were not "helpful." "Rather than submitting a laundry list of various proposals," he reported, "we have laid down those things which we believe the other side should agree to and can agree to . . ., matters that we think can be precisely considered and on which progress can be made." There was "a new team" in Paris with "new direction" and "a new sense of urgency," he declared. "There will be new tactics. We believe that those tactics may be more successful than the tactics of the past." It was "not helpful in discussing Vietnam to use such terms as cease-fire, because cease-fire is a term . . . that really has no relevance . . . to a guerrilla war. . . . When you have a guerrilla war, in which one side may not even be able to control many of those who are responsible for the violence in the area, the ceasefire may be meaningless."

Henry Cabot Lodge had been named by Nixon Jan. 5 to succeed W. Averell Harriman as chief U.S. negotiator at the Paris talks on Vietnam. Harriman resigned as of Jan. 20, inauguration day of the Nixon Administration. Lodge, 66, Nixon's running mate in the 1960 Presidential campaign, had served as ambassador to South Vietnam in 1963-4 and 1965-7. During his term in Saigon, Lodge had formed a close friendship with Nguyen Cao Ky, currently South Vietnam's vice president and chief adviser to the South Vietnamese delegation to the Paris talks. Lodge had expressed doubt about achieving peace in Vietnam through negotiations. The most likely end to the fighting, he had said, was that the enemy eventually would decide to "fade away." But in a statement issued after his designation Jan. 5, Lodge upheld the Paris talks as "a hopeful forum for the definition of the interests of all parties involved and for the design of agreements to meet those interests."

These other members of Nixon Administratsion team at the Paris talks were also named Jan. 5: Lawrence Edward Walsh, 57, a New York lawyer and deputy attorney general in 1957-60, as deputy chief negotiator to replace Cyrus R. Vance, who was remaining temporarily after Jan. 20; Marshall Green, an Asian affairs expert, assigned on temporary duty to assist the negotiating team while retaining his post as ambassador to Indonesia; Philip C. Habib, a deputy Assistant State Secretary who was a political officer for Lodge in Saigon, retained in his current role as an expert adviser at the talks. Lt. Gen. Frederick C. Weyland was named Feb. 11 to be military adviser to the chairman of the U.S. peace talks delegation in Paris.

Nixon had announced Jan. 4 that Ellsworth Bunker would be retained "for a period of time" as U.S. ambassador to South Vietnam.

Quiet on Battlefields

Against this background, the battlefields in Vietnam were relatively quiet during the early days of 1969. The Viet Cong's unilateral 72-hour New Year's truce ended Jan. 2. Intermittent fighting, however, had taken place between the period 1 a.m. Dec. 30, 1968 and 1 a.m. Jan. 2, 1969 as the allied forces refused to recognize the ceasefire and alleged that the enemy had repeatedly committed battlefield violations. At the start of the ceasefire Dec. 30, 1968, North Vietnamese troops in the allied southern sector of the demilitarized zone (DMZ) had fired on a U.S. observation plane but missed. The U.S. command listed the attack as the 47th "significant incident" in the zone since the halt in the U.S. bombing of North Vietnam Nov. 1, 1968.

The South Vietnamese government announced Jan. 7 that it had complained to the International Control Commission about continued Communist violations of the DMZ. The complaint said that since the bombing halt there had been 840 cases in which North Vietnamese soldiers, weapons or new fortifications had been observed in the buffer strip.

The establishment of a 150-mile U.S. naval patrol along the South Vietnamese-Cambodian border was announced Jan. 5. It extended from the Gulf of Siam to the city of Tayninh, 58 miles northwest of Saigon. The border patrol, carried out by more than 100 vessels, was designed to protect Saigon from attack. Navy boats had started patrolling about 50 miles of waterway along the border from the Gulf of Siam in mid-October 1968; the surveillance was further widened in December, and the final link was extended to Tayninh. The latter region was the scene of most of the action: more than 50 clashes had occurred, and 22 arms caches had been uncovered.

Among combat developments reported in early 1969:

● 12 Vietnamese civilians were killed and 16 wounded when a Viet Cong mine exploded Jan. 2 under a U.S. Army truck on a road in Quangnam Province, 35 miles south of the U.S. military base at Danang. 2 U.S. soldiers were wounded.

● The launching of 2 strong allied sweeps Jan. 2 was disclosed by the U.S. command Jan. 5. Little enemy resistance was encountered in either operation. In one drive, a force of 5,000 U.S. Marines and South Vietnamese pushed through an area around the former U.S. stronghold at Khesanh in the north. The troops, ferried in by helicopters, found ammunitions dump and a destroyed Soviet-made truck. In the other operation, in the south, a combined U.S. Army and Navy force searched a major Viet Cong supply route in the Plain of Reeds west of Saigon. Patrol boats, armored monitors and landing craft carrying infantrymen of the 9th Division turned up 5 arms caches on the Vamcodong River. The caches—concealed largely in sunken metal drums—contained about 50,000 rounds of small-arms ammunition and about 800 rocket grenade and mortar rounds.

● The Viet Cong Jan. 11 carred out widespread mortar attacks on at least 24 South Vietnamese cities, towns and military bases, mostly in the Mekong delta. At least 17 persons, including 7 U.S. soldiers, were killed; 155 persons, 11 of them Americans, were wounded. The heaviest assault was directed at a South Vietnamese training center near Mytho in the delta. 93 men were wounded by 21 mortar rounds. A 9-man U.S. patrol was wiped out in a Viet Cong ambush one mile southeast of Dongtam, the largest U.S. base in the delta. 5 U.S. soldiers and a South Vietnamese scout were killed. 3 U.S. soldiers were wounded.

● A Viet Cong force Jan. 13 made an unsuccessful attempt to overrun the U.S. Army's 164th Aviation Group base at Cantho in the delta, 75 miles southwest of Saigon. 3 helicopters were destroyed and 15 damaged by satchel charges attached to the aircraft. 8 U.S. soldiers were killed and 15 wounded in repelling the infiltrators after they had penetrated the base's barbed-wire defenses. At least 5 Viet Cong were killed.

● U.S. and South Vietnamese forces launched a 2-pronged drive Jan. 13 against an estimated 800 Viet Cong on Cape Batangan, 340 miles northwest of Saigon, it was disclosed Jan. 15. One force of 2,500 U.S. Marines landed on shore in helicopters and assault boats (this was described as the largest beach assault since the Korean war), while at least 1,000 U.S. troops and 500 government soldiers advanced overland to the cape from the west. The allied units made little initial contact with enemy forces but were reported Jan. 18 to have seized more than 1,200 suspected Viet Cong and to have killed 32 Viet Cong. U.S. authorities Jan. 22 reported the finding of 56 Viet Cong with 100 women and children in an elaborate tunnel complex. By Feb. 7 the U.S. Navy described the operation as a success; it said that enemy forces surrounded by the allied troops had been "forced against the sea." The report said 200 Communist soldiers had been killed and 251 members of the Viet Cong political structure and 131 sympathizers captured.

● A 50-truck U.S. convoy was attacked by the Viet Cong Jan. 14 as it approached Tayninh, 58 miles northwest of Saigon. Only 2 trucks were damaged in the ambush, but 7 Americans were killed and 10 wounded in nearly 7 hours of fighting. The Viet Cong force was thrown back with a loss of 122 killed.

● 2 U.S. vessels were blasted by a Viet Cong mine Jan. 17 on the Cua Viet estuary, a main supply line leading to the U.S. Marine command at Dongha. One barge sank, and a landing craft was badly damaged. The blast killed 5 sailors and an unidentified U.S. civilian aboard the landing craft.

● 2 U.S. sailors were killed and 14 wounded Jan. 21 when a rocket hit their tank landing ship at Vungtau, southeast of Saigon. 6 other rockets struck the city, but no damage was caused.

● A U.S. naval patrol boat Jan. 21 sank 45 small basketlike boats south of Danang. 10 men in the boats were killed and 24 captured. The U.S. craft had opened fire when 125 of the wicker boats, spotted in a restricted area, broke for the beach after being challenged. A U.S. spokesman said the boats had not been definitely identified as Viet Cong.

● An abandoned village 7 miles northwest of Quangngai, occupied by a hostile force of 200 men, was overrun by U.S. troops Jan. 23. The village had been surrounded by 800 American troops since Jan. 20. Intensified attacks by tanks, artillery and planes finally forced the enemy to flee. The hostile force was suspected of planning to use the village as a base for a drive against nearby Quangngai in February.

● The 1,000th U.S. helicopter of the war was shot down Jan. 25 in fighting at a village about 35 miles northwest of Saigon. The aircraft was one of 2 sent to suppress fire from 3 machineguns, which accounted for the lost plane.

● 7 U.S. Marines were killed Jan. 26 while clearing mines near Quangngai. The men were riding in a vehicle used to blow up minefields by hurling explosive charges into them but the vehicle itself was blown up when a charge went off prematurely.

● North Vietnam and the U.S. traded mutual charges of violations of the demilitarized zone. Hanoi claimed Jan. 26 that U.S. artillery in the southern part of the DMZ had fired Jan. 24 on parts of the northern sector of the zone. U.S. planes had bombed several villages Jan. 25 in North Vietnam's Nghean Province, Hanoi said. U.S. military officials reported that 15 North Vietnamese troops observed moving near the eastern end of the DMZ Jan. 28 had been fired on by U.S. artillery and that 9 of the enemy troops were killed. North Vietnamese mortars opened fire Jan. 28 near the center of the buffer strip and wounded 7 U.S. Marines in South Vietnam just below the DMZ.

● The North Vietnamese Foreign Ministry charged Jan. 27 that 6 U.S. B-52 bombers had raided North Vietnam Jan. 23 and 24, "doing extensive damage to civilian areas and killing and wounding civilians." The ministry said the planes had dropped bombs on the Botrach district of Quangbinh Province, 30 miles north of the demilitarized zone, committing "by far the most serious act of war" since the U.S. had suspended the bombing of the North Nov. 1, 1968. The U.S. State Department Jan. 27, denying Hanoi's charge, said "we have not resumed the bombing of North Vietnam."

● The Viet Cong announced Jan. 29 that its forces would observe a truce to mark the Tet (lunar new year) holidays Feb. 15-22. South Vietnamese Pres. Nguyen Van Thieu said Feb. 1 that he agreed in principle to the cease-fire, but "that depends upon the situation between now and Tet."

● 500 North Vietnamese Feb. 1 attempted to overrun a U.S. artillery base 43 miles northwest of Saigon, but the defenders repelled the assault in a 5-hour fight. Helicopter gunships, fighter planes and artillery aided in throwing back the onslaught. One 'copter was shot down. In fighting elsewhere Feb. 1, allied forces killed 245 troops. In the largest of these encounters, South Korean marines killed 23 soldiers near Hoian, about 300 miles northeast of Saigon.

● The U.S. and South Vietnamese commands reported Feb. 6 that 3,190 Viet Cong and North Vietnamese had been killed Jan. 26-Feb. 1. This was the highest Communist fatality toll since the week of Sept. 15-21, 1968, when 3,380 were reported slain. In the Jan. 26-Feb. 1 period, 198 U.S. soldiers and 242 government troops had been killed.

● 2 U.S. civilian employes were killed and a 3d seriously wounded Feb. 7 when Viet Cong troops attacked their jeep about 19 miles east of Saigon with a rocket grenade. A U.S. military communique said Feb. 9 that 3 other U.S. civilians apparently had been abducted by the Viet Cong there at the same time. Their Volkswagen was said to have been found "abandoned and ransacked." All 6 men were employed by Lear Siegler, Inc., a U.S. concern with an Army aircraft-maintenance contract.

● A government spokesman reported Feb. 8 that South Vietnamese troops had overrun a Viet Cong camp Feb. 7 in the Mekong delta, 55 miles south of Saigon, and had freed 30 civilian prisoners, killed 43 Viet Cong and captured 21.

● The South Vietnamese government reported Feb. 9 that government marines had found "the biggest heavy-weapons cache" ever discovered by the South Vietnamese army. The cache, uncovered 60 miles north of Saigon, included 15 wheel-mounted, 51-caliber anti-aircraft machineguns of Chinese Communist make, a 122-mm. rocket launcher plus 200 rockets and 39 mortars.

● A U.S. military communique disclosed Feb. 12 that a major Marine drive had been launched Jan. 22 in an area 19 miles southeast of Culu in northern Quangtri Province. The U.S. Marines were said to have killed 57 Communist troops through Feb. 10. Marine losses totaled 18 killed and 63 wounded.

In observance of Tet, the lunar new year, the Viet Cong unilaterally declared a week-long truce Feb. 15-22. Allied troops suspended fighting for 24 hours Feb. 16-17. A U.S. military spokesman reported Feb. 18 that there had been no major fighting during the Feb. 16-17 cease-fire but charged that Communist forces had initiated 196 incidents. Casualties had resulted in 84 of the engagements. Combat fatalities in the 24-hour truce period had totaled 8 Americans, 4 South Vietnamese and 151 Communists, the spokesman said. 94 U.S. troops and 51 government soldiers were wounded. One of the heaviest engagements fought during the Viet Cong's Tet truce took place in the Mekong delta Feb. 20-21 and cost 99 Viet Cong lives. U.S. troops, in a sweep of an area 45 miles south of Saigon lost 6 men killed and 8 wounded.

Allied agreement to observe a holiday truce had been announced by the South Vietnamese government Feb. 15. Speaking to government airmen at the Tansonnhut Air Base outside Saigon, Pres. Nguyen Van Thieu recalled the Communist Tet offensive of 1968. He said: "We will not permit the Communists to repeat their treacherous attacks during Tet this year. Therefore, I am asking you to accept some more efforts and sacrifices by staying alert." As Thieu spoke, heavy military precautions were being taken in Saigon to prepare for a possible enemy onslaught. Elements of the U.S. First Infantry Division had moved closer to the city, and several government battalions were placed on duty in the capital.

American casualties, however, remained relatively high. U.S. authorities reported Jan. 30 that the killing of 190 U.S. troops in the period Jan. 12-18 had brought the American combat death toll in Vietnam since Jan. 1, 1961 to 31,181. Communist fatalities in the 8-year period were estimated at 438,937.

Paris Talks Expanded

Prior to the change in U.S. Administrations, U.S. and North Vietnamese delegates in Paris had announced agreement Jan. 16 on holding expanded talks on the Vietnam war. South Vietnam and the National Liberation Front participated in the first session of the broadened conference on substantive issues Jan. 18, and the 4 parties quickly reached agreement on procedures for further negotiations to end the war.

The final accord leading to the 4-party parley had been reached at 2 meetings held outside Paris Jan. 15 and earlier Jan. 16 by Cyrus R. Vance, deputy head of the U.S. delegation, and Col. Ha Van Lau, the North Vietnamese deputy. The principal stumbling block that had held up the start of the expanded talks for 10 weeks was removed when the 2 men concurred on the type of table that was to be used at the conference. The 4 delegations were to sit at a circular table (diameter: 13 feet $1^1/_2$ inch) without name-plates, flags or markings. 2 rectangular tables (measuring about 3 feet by $5^1/_2$ feet) were to be placed 18 inches from either side of the delegations' secretarial staff.

Subsequent statements on the agreement Jan. 16 continued to reflect the controversy over U.S.-South Vietnamese demands for a 2-sided conference (allies and North Vietnam), which would have implied non-recognition of the NLF as a separate delegation, and Communist insistence on a 4-sided meeting, which would have suggested recognition of the front as an independent delegation. A statement issued by the South Vietnamese delegation said that it had made "all efforts toward conciliation compatible with the concept of a meeting of two sides." South Vietnamese Foreign Min. Tran Chanh Thanh said in Saigon that the agreement "is the nearest we can get to the 2-sided formula we have been fighting for, and it looks like a victory if you look back at the demands of North Vietnam." W. Averell Harriman, outgoing chief of the U.S. delegation, told reporters that the U.S. and South Vietnam would always regard the peace talks as a "2-sided conference," regardless of claims that it was 4-sided. Harriman added: "We did not give in, and we did not expect them to give in. Meanwhile, we can go ahead and do business." Harriman said the accord on the table was "a decision all could agree to" and was not the suggestion of one person.

A statement issued by Pres. Johnson Jan. 16 expressed pleasure with the Paris agreement. He said the U.S. "must pursue peace as diligently as we have fought aggression. And this year we have made steady progress toward the peace we all devoutly pray for."

Hailing the seating compromise, Pres.-elect Nixon said Jan. 16 that his administration would pursue the peace talks "with energy and purpose." It was revealed Jan. 16 that Nixon had supported Johnson's efforts to break the deadlock by directly informing the South Vietnamese that he favored a compromise. At a closed session of the Senate Foreign Relations Committee Jan. 15, State Secy.-designate William Rogers indicated that he had been contacted by State Secy. Dean Rusk and asked to elicit Nixon's support for a new seating proposal. Nixon concurred and authorized a message to be sent to South Vietnamese Pres. Nguyen Van Thieu through Amb. Ellsworth Bunker. Rogers also directly contacted South Vietnamese Amb. Bui Diem and informed him that the Nixon Administration wanted a settlement of the deadlock. The contacts reportedly occurred Jan. 10 and 11.

Tran Hoai Nam, chief spokesman for the NLF delegation, said at a news conference in Paris Jan. 17 that the front would participate in the expanded talks as a "fully independent and equal party." The NLF, he said, "has its own position and attitude, being one of the delegations."

The conferees reached agreement on 15 to 20 procedural

questions at the Jan. 18 meeting. Among major agreements: (1) the delegates' statements would be translated first into French and then into English or Vietnamese; (2) the round table seating arrangements with the 2 side desks would be retained; (3) the question of an official name for the subsequent plenary sessions would be left open (the allies called them the Paris Meeting on Vietnam whereas the Communists dubbed them the Paris Conference on Vietnam); (4) each delegation would select liaison aides who would be in contact with the other negotiating parties; (5) no single document would be issued to state the procedural rules agreed on.

An agreement to hold the first plenary meeting Jan. 25 was announced Jan. 21. The date had been proposed at a meeting of Henry Cabot Lodge, Harriman's successor as chief of the U.S. delegation, and Pham Dang Lam, head of the South Vietnamese delegation. It was accepted by North Vietnam and the NLF. Lodge had arrived in Paris Jan. 20 to assume his new duties. Lodge had told Harriman on the latter's return to Washington Jan. 19 that "the entire country is in your debt for getting the negotiations started."

U.S. Proposes Restoration of DMZ Neutrality

At the first plenary session of the expanded talks Jan. 25, the U.S. proposed that the neutrality of the demilitarized zone between North and South Vietnam be immediately restored. The plan was advanced by Henry Cabot Lodge "as a practical first step on the road to peace." Lodge proposed that the DMZ should be: "Free of all regular and irregular military and subversive forces and personnel, military installations, military supplies and equipment; an area in which, from which, and across which, all acts of force are prohibited, a zone temporarily separating North and South Vietnam pending their reunification through the free expression of the will of the people of the North and of the people of the South; an area the same in size and definition as that provided in the 1954 Geneva accords; subject to an effective system of international inspection and verification."

Lodge suggested that both sides "publicly declare their readiness to respect the provisions of the 1954 Geneva accords relating to the DMZ and abide by those provisions." He said the U.S. was prepared to develop the details of its DMZ proposal "into a practical move toward peace."

Lodge called attention to the "shortcomings of existing methods" of international supervision as carried out by the International Control Commission (ICC) established by the 1954 Geneva agreements. "One of our principal tasks," he continued, "will be to work out more effective ways of supervising any agreement. . . . We believe that the nations of the area, which have the most crucial interest in peace and stability in the region, should be involved in the system of monitoring of the agreement at which we arrive." (U.S. officials in Washington Jan. 26 quashed speculation that Lodge was suggesting that China be included in expanded international supervision of a Southeast Asian settlement. The officials explained that Lodge's statement was similar to those made by other U.S. negotiators at the start of the Paris talks in May 1968. Previously, U.S. diplomats had suggested that the ICC be expanded to include such Asian countries as Thailand, South Korea and Cambodia.)

Chief North Vietnamese negotiator Xuan Thuy's reaction to the U.S. plan for the DMZ was disclosed by the Hanoi delegation's spokesman, Nguyen Thanh Le, at a news briefing after the plenary meeting. Le recalled that in the past the North Vietnamese negotiating team had "criticized and rejected these fallacious arguments. Minister Xuan Thuy demanded that the U.S. first put an end to its war of aggression." Le charged that U.S. allegations about military activity in the DMZ were "simply aimed at misleading public opinion about the aggressive character of the United States in Vietnam, which slanders the North for having, so it says, aggressed against the South."

Although Le's statement said that the North Vietnamese and NLF delegations had "rejected" Lodge's proposals, a somewhat more qualified statement on the front's position was given to newsmen by NLF spokesman Tran Hoai Nam. Commenting on NLF chief negotiator Tran Buu Kiem's remarks at the plenary session, Nam said: "We have made some observations and have judged that Mr. Lodge's proposal is not correct and that it was made with the intention of getting around the 'correct' problems which could bring about a political solution to the South Vietnam problem. And as we have said before, we completely reject this way of posing the problem by the American delegation."

In a prepared statement delivered at the plenary meeting, Kiem had charged that the U.S. was pursuing "an extremely perfidious and cruel policy" in Vietnam. Washington, he asserted, had "established in South Vietnam an extremely tyrannical ... administration of valets, using them as an instrument to suppress the hopes of the South Vietnamese people for peace, independence, democracy and reunification." Kiem charged that the U.S. had extended the war to North Vietnam to "escape from its defeat in South Vietnam," but had failed. "To avoid heavier defeats," Kiem suggested that the U.S. "end its aggression, withdraw all American and satellite troops from South Vietnam, allow the people of South Vietnam to settle their own affairs without foreign interference."

Thuy contended in his prepared statement for North Vietnam that "while the United States speaks of 'goodwill and peace,' it continues its reconnaissance flights over North Vietnam and its bombing raids against many populated centers" in the North. Thuy reaffirmed the Communists' position: The NLF was "the organizer and the leader of the South Vietnam people against U.S. aggression ..."; it had liberated 4/5 of South Vietnamese territory with a population of 11 million people; it "possesses mighty armed forces, and has set up democratically elected administrative establishments in almost all regions"; the NLF "is the authentic representative of the South Vietnam people"; the NLF delegation at the conference "is an independent one, equal in rights to the other delegations and competent to settle all problems regarding South Vietnam."

South Vietnam's chief negotiator, Pham Dang Lam, insisted that his government was "the only qualified representative of the people of South Vietnam." His statement to the plenary session said that Saigon had sent a delegation to the Paris conference "with the main objective of putting an end to the war of aggression brought about, directed, and kept up by the Hanoi administration." Lam maintained that the conference was "a meeting between 2 sides—. . . of North Vietnam and its auxiliary organizations in the South—and the side of the victim of aggression," South Vietnam. Lam said Saigon demanded that North Vietnam: end its "armed aggression" against South Vietnam; restore the DMZ; stop the infiltration of men and supplies into South Vietnam; evacuate its forces from the South; "refrain from interference in the internal affairs of South Vietnam"; respect the Geneva accords of 1954 and 1961, "which it has signed"; "accept an effective international control."

South Vietnamese Vice Pres. Nguyen Cao Ky said in Paris Jan. 27 that he would be willing to hold "private talks with the other side if they are willing" to enter them. Ky would not specify whether he was proposing private talks with North Vietnam or the NLF or both. Ky said that such talks could be conducted in Paris "or anywhere else." Ky's proposal was rebuffed by the North Vietnamese delegation Jan. 28. The North Vietnamese asserted that "now that the 4-party conference in Paris has opened, each delegation that has something to say may do so."

At the 2d plenary session in Paris, North Vietnam and the National Liberation Front Jan. 30 rejected the U.S. proposal to restore the neutrality of the DMZ as a first step toward peace. Xuan Thuy charged that the proposal was only a scheme to conceal "American aggressive designs." Thuy insisted that "only on a political basis can we settle military questions. Therefore, both the political and the military problems have to be solved" at the conference. Thuy and the NLF also rejected an American suggestion, raised at the first plenary session, for a mutual troop withdrawal from Vietnam and an early exchange of prisoners.

Henry Cabot Lodge said at the Jan. 30 session that the U.S. and South Vietnamese delegates had submitted the DMZ question for early consideration "because it is an important problem, which readily lends itself to a solution." The question of the DMZ "will be, in effect, a pilot project which will enable us to form a pattern for constructive work together," Lodge said.

Communist demands that political questions be discussed at the Paris talks had been rejected Jan. 27 by South Vietnamese Foreign Min. Tran Chanh Thanh in Saigon. He insisted that "our political internal affairs are not discussable at an international conference. If the North Vietnamese try to intervene in South Vietnamese internal affairs at Paris, we in turn will ask that internal affairs of North Vietnam also be discussed."

The NLF delegation Jan. 28 rejected Pres. Nixon's statement, made at his news conference the previous day, that Lodge's proposals on the DMZ, on troop withdrawal and on prisoner exchange were "matters that we think can be precisely considered and on which progress can be made." These specific steps "that can be taken now" were preferable to "submitting a laundry list of various proposals," Nixon had said. In rejecting the President's views, the front statement accused Nixon of attempting "to mask the aggressive designs" of the U.S. in Vietnam. The NLF reaffirmed the position that the U.S. must accept the political demands of the front and North Vietnam. Hanoi's 4-point program and the NLF's 5 points stressing Communist dominance were the only "correct basis for a political settlement of the Vietnam problem," the statement said.

The negotiators made no progress at the 3d and 4th plenary sessions Feb. 6 and 13. During both sessions North Vietnamese and NLF delegates again rejected the U.S. proposal to restore the DMZ's neutrality as a first step. The Communists reiterated demands that political questions be discussed first and that the U.S. negotiate directly with the NLF.

Lodge said after the Feb. 13 meeting that he did not "expect much to come out of these public meetings." This remark added to the speculation that U.S. and North Vietnamese delegates had been meeting in private in an attempt to break the conference deadlock. The reputed secret contacts were first reported Feb. 6. The meetings were said to have been conducted on a low working level, with no senior delegates participating. U.S. and Communist officials were noncommital when asked to comment on the report. The French Communist Party newspaper *L'Humanite* reported Feb. 12 that U.S. and North Vietnamese delegates had conferred privately several days previously. The newspaper said the U.S. officials had complained about an alleged Communist rocket attack on Hué and about the presence of Communist forces in the DMZ. The North Vietnamese rejected the protest, the newspaper said. The French newspaper *Le Monde*, reporting Feb. 14 on the secret meeting, quoted a North Vietnamese source as saying that Col. Ha Van Lau, Hanoi's deputy chief delegate, had shown "displeasure at being troubled for so little"—the American protest. The outgoing U.S. deputy chief delegate, Cyrus Vance, and his successor, Lawrence Walsh, were said to have delivered the protest. A North Vietnamese source said the complaint was a U.S. "pretext" for attempting to resume private contacts with the North Vietnamese delegation.

But Nguyen Trieu Dan, a spokesman for the South Vietnamese delegation, had said Feb. 13 that "to our knowledge, there are no such contacts" between the allied and Communist sides.

Vice Pres. Nguyen Cao Ky, political coordinator of the South Vietnamese delegation, had reiterated in Paris Feb. 3 that he was ready to "hold private talks now" with the Communists if "they want to talk privately with me." He insisted, however, that the "first" topic of such discussions deal with "how to end the war of aggression by North Vietnam." As for "internal political problems, our president and government will discuss them" in South Vietnam, Ky said. Ky declared himself "ready to make more concessions, in any field, if we are sure to reach results." Ky made the statement to newsmen after conferring with Lodge and visiting U.S. Sen. John G. Tower (R., Tex.). Ky Feb. 9 again expressed willingness to meet with the Communists. In an interview aboard a plane returning him to Saigon, Ky said: "If after the withdrawal of North Vietnamese troops" from South Vietnam, "the Viet Cong want to come and talk about a political settlement, we will talk with them. . . . If Hanoi and Washington can arrange to withdraw their troops, we can solve those problems ourselves, in an Asian manner." On his return to Saigon later Feb. 9, Ky said in an airport interview that if the Paris talks "are to be fruitful, then both sides should show goodwill. . . . In the last few months we have made . . . concessions and shown enough goodwill. Now we are waiting for the other side to make some sign of goodwill." Ky called France a "hostile country" and said that Saigon's agreement to hold the talks in Paris was a "big concession."

South Vietnamese Pres. Nguyen Van Thieu had said Feb. 6 that Saigon would not withdraw from the Paris negotiations until a settlement was reached. His statement was in answer to a newsman's question as to whether South Vietnam would quit the talks if the Communists continued to refuse to discuss military issues before political problems. Thieu said Saigon "knows how to be patient in peace talks. We will go step by step until the end."

Le Duc Tho, political leader of North Vietnam's delegation, left Paris Feb. 10 for Hanoi. Denying that he was taking a new U.S. offer, Tho said his flight was one of "work and routine." Tho said Nixon's administration was "pursuing the same policy as the administration of Pres. Johnson. There is absolutely no difference between them."

There was no apparent movement toward breaking the allied-Communist impasse in the 5th plenary session held Feb. 20. But Lodge asserted Feb. 26 that he believed "some progress" was being made. He said: "These things move along in a way that's rather hard to define. Some groundwork is being laid, and I think something will come of it." Lodge made this statement after conferring with Nguyen Cao Ky, who had returned to Paris from Saigon Feb. 25. A spokesman for Ky, commenting on Lodge's optimistic statement, said: "I don't know personally of any progress in the talks."

SPRING OFFENSIVE

By the end of Jan. 1969 the National Liberation Front and North Vietnam apparently had concluded that the new Nixon Administration was no readier to meet their terms for peace than had been the Johnson Administration. The Viet Cong thus announced Feb. 2 that it would "push forward with a general offensive and widespread uprisings" in South Vietnam. The declaration said the purpose of the drive would be "to completely foil all schemes of the United States' aggressive war and smash at its perfidious and roundabout contentions at the Paris conference." The statement said the first 2 plenary sessions of the Paris talks had shown that the U.S. "still maintains its obdurate stand of aggression" while it "feverishly steps up the war and keeps piling up barbarous crimes against the people."

The Viet Cong threats of a new offensive followed several weeks of reports that the Communists appeared to be preparing for a major push in the Mekong delta or against Saigon.

Viet Cong/North Vietnamese Attacks

Communist forces launched a major offensive throughout South Vietnam Feb. 23. The offensive followed by one day the expiration of the 7-day truce the Viet Cong had proclaimed for Tet. In a coordinated series of shellings and ground assaults, Viet Cong and North Vietnamese troops struck simultaneously at Saigon and about 115 other towns and military targets. They pounded at least 18 provincial capitals, 28 district towns and 60 military bases. In the first 15 hours of fighting, about 100 U.S. soldiers and 1,000 Communists were reported killed. South Vietnamese military casualties were reported light. But government officials reported Feb. 25 that in 3 days of mortar and rocket attacks the Communists had killed 52 civilians, wounded 263 and destroyed 123 buildings. 12 civilians were said to have been kidnaped.

Downtown Saigon was hit by 7 rockets in the first 2 hours

of fighting, and there were clashes on the outskirts of the city. 3 more rockets struck the heart of the city later Feb. 23. This was the first shelling of Saigon since Oct. 31, 1968. Among other major cities hit were Danang, Pleiku, Mytho, Bentre and Vinhbinh. Danang appeared to have suffered the heaviest assault; several rockets hit the center of the city and the U.S. Marine base on Marble Mountain just outside Danang. The U.S. airfields at Kontum and Nhatrang were also shelled.

The attacks eased Feb. 24; only 60 allied military targets were shelled. The heaviest ground fighting occurred 20 to 40 miles northwest of Saigon along the traditional infiltration routes leading from the Cambodian border. In 3 separate engagements, troops of the U.S. 25th Infantry Division killed an estimated 259 North Vietnamese soldiers. 2 U.S. positions just south of the demilitarized zone came under heavy ground assault Feb. 25. In one of the attacks, 36 U.S. Marines were killed after North Vietnamese suicide troops with explosives tied to their backs blasted holes in the barbed wire of the camp's defense perimeter. This permitted other troops to break into the base, and hand-to-hand fighting ensued. The U.S. losses were described as the highest in a single battle in South Vietnam in nearly 6 months.

Allied military sources reported that Communist combat fatalities in the offensive totaled 7,200 by Mar. 3. 325 U.S. and 572 South Vietnamese soldiers were killed in the same period, the sources said. A South Vietnamese spokesman Mar. 3 reported 160 Vietnamese civilians killed and 545 wounded.

Among major developments in the offensive:

• Saigon authorities asserted Feb. 25 that they had thwarted a Viet Cong plan to follow up the shelling of Saigon with a ground attack. The plan was blocked by the capture of 43 members of an underground cell in Saigon's Cholon district and the arrest of several students. About a dozen of the alleged Viet Cong agents captured in the raid were presented before a news conference.

• Viet Cong troops carried out heavy ground assaults against 2 major installations in the Saigon area Feb. 26. At Cuchi, 20 miles northwest of the capital, commandos penetrated the perimeter of the base of the U.S. 25th Infantry Division by cutting through 10 barbed wire fences. The force, estimated at 80 men, destroyed 9 large transport helicopters, killed 13 Americans and wounded 50 in the $3^1/_2$-hour operation. Viet Cong losses totaled 31 killed. In the 2d engagement, 20 miles northeast of Saigon, a North Vietnamese battalion of 200 to 300 men fought to within a mile of the big U.S. airbase at Bienhoa. An estimated 150 North Vietnamese were slain in 16 hours of fighting, the U.S. command said. Allied losses were reported to be light.

• In another clash Feb. 26, U.S. Marines killed 84 enemy soldiers in a 5-hour battle 22 miles southwest of Danang. American losses totaled 8 killed and 29 wounded. More than 50 towns and military bases came under Communist shelling during the day.

● A force of about 100 men was spotted by U.S. troops Feb. 27 near Lolu, 6 miles from the center of Saigon. This was the first time an enemy force had moved that close to the capital in 6 months. A U.S. 18th Infantry Division battalion was reinforced by 5 additional companies after failing to dislodge the enemy from rice paddies. With helicopter gunships joining in the renewed attacks, the fighting continued through the early hours of Feb. 28, and the Communist units were routed. 6 enemy bodies were found.

● South Vietnamese Pres. Nguyen Van Thieu said Mar. 1 that "there has been complete failure" in what the Communists called "their 4th offensive." Thieu said he believed that the Communists "no longer have the ability to sustain offensives, and if they continue to launch them, they will be defeated."

● Saigon was hit by 4 Communist rockets Mar. 3. 12 civilians were killed and about 30 houses destroyed by the resultant fires. In the ground fighting, about 500 U.S. Marines repelled a strong North Vietnamese attack on an artillery base 3 miles south of the demilitarized zone and about 15 miles west of Dongha. 13 Marines were killed and 22 wounded as the defending force threw back repeated North Vietnamese charges. The bodies of 20 North Vietnamese were found after the battle.

● Viet Cong rocket and mortar shells Mar. 4 hit a prison for South Vietnamese civilians at Dien Bien, 10 miles south of Danang. 5 prisoners were killed and 20 wounded.

U.S. and South Vietnamese forces launched 2 separate major drives in South Vietnam—in the Ashau Valley Mar. 1 (not disclosed until Mar. 23 for security reasons) and around Saigon Mar. 18—to counteract the post-Tet offensive. Viet Cong and North Vietnamese troops, however, continued to press their drive with widespread ground and rocket attacks against military and civilian centers throughout South Vietnam. U.S. military bases were the most frequently hit targets as particularly strong pressure was exerted around Saigon and Danang.

At least 3,000 U.S. and South Vietnamese soldiers were committed to the operation in the Ashau Valley, considered North Vietnam's principal infiltration route into South Vietnam's northern provinces. In the first 3 weeks of the campaign, aimed at easing the Communist threat to Hué and Danang, troops of the U.S. 101st Airborne Division were reported to have killed 60 Communists. U.S. losses were placed at 23 killed and 53 wounded. A similar U.S. Marine drive in the Ashau Valley in February had resulted in the killing of 1,405 North Vietnamese regulars and the seizing of nearly 500 tons of supplies.

The allied Saigon-area drive, Operation Atlas Wedge, was directed largely against the French-owned Michelin rubber plantation at Dautieng, 40 miles northwest of Saigon. Communist troops had entered the area in force at the start of their offensive Feb. 23. Allied officials regarded the Communist presence there as a stopping place on their way to attack Saigon. An allied force of 2,400 men, using tanks and armored troop carriers, swept the plantation Mar. 19 and reported killing 114 of the enemy. The allied offensive, however, had not yet succeeded in coming to grips with the main force of the Communist troops around Saigon. Operation Atlas Wedge required the removal and resettlement of 2,500 Vietnamese plantation workers and their families from hamlets in the northern part of the rubber fields to create a free-fire zone. (The Communists had used the Michelin property as a rest and refitting camp for the past 20 years. The French plantation owners at the end of World War II had worked out an agreement with the Communist guerrillas, then known as the Viet Minh, to pay taxes to the Communist fighters in exchange for being left alone to operate their business.)

Washington Reacts

On the opening day of the Viet Cong offensive, Pres. Nixon Feb. 23 ordered an investigation to determine whether the drive violated the agreement that had led to the halt in the U.S. bombing of North Vietnam and the Paris talks. He asserted that a tacit condition both sides had accepted for halting the bombings was that the Communists would not shell major population centers in South Vietnam.

The launching of 2 other offensives by U.S. Marine units in the northern provinces was diclosed by U.S. officials in Saigon Apr. 4. The first drive had started Feb. 22, at the beginning of the post-Tet attacks, in the northwestern corner of South Vietnam near the DMZ. Several Marine battalions swept an area about 10 miles northwest of the abandoned U.S. base at Khesanh in search of North Vietnamese troops that had been attacking American artillery bases. In the 2d sweep, begun Mar. 31, more than 6,000 Marines were searching for North Vietnamese troops and rocket crews in an area about 30 miles south of Danang. The order for a full investigation of the offensive called for gathering data on the types of weapons used, the number of rounds fired, targets and casualties.

White House sources said the President had no intention of

ordering immediate retaliatory air raids against North Vietnam even if the Communist drive appeared to suggest a new pattern of attack. When first commenting on initial reports of the offensive, Nixon, then aboard his plane en route to Europe, said that "the key word is shelling, because if that happens it requires some action on our part." The President noted that, according to information then at his disposal, the Communist attacks on South Vietnamese cities appeared to be by "grenades and small arms." Subsequent reports, however, confirmed heavy Communist shelling.

At a press conference Mar. 4, on his return from a trip to Europe, Nixon said, in response to questioning on Vietnam, that the Administration was "examining" the new enemy offensive against the cities to see if its "magnitude" was in violation of the understanding reached for the bombing halt. "Technically, it could be said that it is in violation," Nixon held. "Whether we reach the conclusion that the violation is so significant that it requires action on our part is a decision we will be reaching very soon if those attacks continue at their present magnitude ... We have not moved in a precipitate fashion, but the fact that we have shown patience and forebearance should not be considered as a sign of weakness. We will not tolerate a violation of an understanding" nor "attacks which result in heavier casualties. ..." Defense Secy. Melvin R. Laird toured South Vietnam Mar. 6—10 on a fact-finding mission for Nixon. On arriving in Saigon Mar. 6, Laird charged that the recent attacks on South Vietnamese cities was an "ominous" violation of the U.S.-North Vietnamese "understanding." "I want to state unequivocally that if these attacks continue unabated, an appropriate response will be made," he warned. Laird conferred Mar. 8 with U.S. Amb. Ellsworth Bunker and Gen. Creighton W. Abrams, commander of the U.S. forces in Vietnam. The 3 men then met with South Vietnamese Premier Tran Van Huong and Pres. Nguyen Van Thieu. At a news conference at the U.S. base at Danang Mar. 9, Laird said that according to briefings he had been given by allied military and diplomatic personnel, the results of the post-Tet offensive "have not been great, as of today." But he warned again that if "indiscriminate shelling of population centers" "is going to continue to any extent, a response will be made by the forces here in Vietnam." (He also said he would ask Congress to increase the budget for the Vietnam war by $70 million in the next fiscal year. The

additional funds, he said, would finance a build-up of South
Vietnamese forces. "If we are going to be in a position where,
through the building up of the South Vietnamese forces, we can
relieve American service personnel from combat here, we must
fully fund that effort," Laird said.)

Laird Mar. 9 toured the I Corps area, comprising South Vietnam's 5 northernmost provinces. At a stopover in Hué, he conferred with Maj. Gen. Ngo Quang Truong, commander of the South
Vietnamese First Infantry Division. Laird later said he had been
"very impressed" with the improvement he saw in the effectiveness and training of South Vietnamese forces. Despite these improvements, Laird said, the time had not yet come to replace
Americans with South Vietnamese soldiers. He explained: "This
is not the time to discuss troop withdrawals. Not when there's an
offensive being conducted by the enemy and while we are engaged
in very important discussions in Paris where the No. 2 item on
the agenda is mutual troop withdrawal." The No. 1 item on the
Paris agenda, Laird pointed out, was the U.S. proposal for restoring the DMZ's neutrality.

Speaking at a news conference in Washington Mar. 14, Pres.
Nixon referred to his consultation with Laird the previous day on
the latter's return from a Vietnam inspection trip: he said their
decision to continue the current level of combat rather than a retaliatory response was "very close." Nixon said that in view of the
Communist offensive, "there is no prospect for a reduction of
American forces in the foreseeable future."

Asked about his warning Mar. 4 that an "appropriate response" to the offensive would be forthcoming if the offensive continued, Nixon said "it will be my policy to issue a warning only
once, and I will not repeat it now." "My response has been measured, deliberate and, some think, too cautious," he said. "But it
will continue to be that way, because I am thinking of those peace
talks every time I think of a military option in Vietnam."

A cautious evaluation of progress in the Paris talks and a decline in U.S. combat deaths from the 453 total 2 weeks previously
were cited by Nixon at his Mar. 14 press conference as factors in-
fluencing his restraint in response to the enemy offensive. He said
the Paris negotiators were making "very limited progress" toward
secret talks. "I think that is where this war will be settled," he
declared, "in private rather than in public." The President rejected criticism that the enemy offensive might have been provoked

by the U.S. military pressure in Vietnam since the bombing halt
in Nov. 1968. "For the past 6 months the forces on the other side
have been planning for an offensive," he said. "Under those circumstances, we had no other choice but to try to blunt the offensive." "Any escalation of the war in Vietnam has been the responsibility of the enemy," he declared. "If the enemy de-escalates
its attacks, ours will go down. We are not trying to step it up."
These same factors—the level of enemy activity and progress in
the peace talks—plus the "ability of the South Vietnamese to defend themselves in areas where we now are defending them,"
would be the determinants in any decision to withdraw U.S.
troops, Nixon said.

Sen. George S. McGovern (D., S.D.) attacked the Nixon Administration on the Senate floor Mar. 17 for continuing the "tragic
course" of the Johnson Administration in Vietnam. McGovern
described the past policy as one "of military attrition and moral
disaster." McGovern especially criticized the U.S. failure to seek
"a military disengagement" after the Paris talks had begun. "We
have pursued the opposite course," he said. "While the North
Vietnamese responded to our bombing halt by withdrawing 22
full regiments from South Vietnam, we were preparing a great
extension of our own offensive operations in the south. Air, Marine
and ground engagements increased in number and intensity."
He asked whether the current Viet Cong offensive was "designed to
trigger a general escalation of hostilities by all combatants" or was
"a response to our own offensives over the last 5 months."

"We are still committed to the preservation of the current
regime in Saigon by means of American blood and military
power." McGovern charged. "We are trying to win, on the battlefield and in Paris, what the Saigon government long ago lost
beyond all recall: the allegiance of its own people and the control
of its own land." McGovern repeated his proposals that the U.S.
should withdraw half its troops in Vietnam and concentrate the
remainder around easily defended installations while intensifying
the peace effort in Paris.

McGovern's attack was not joined, as such attacks had been
in the past, by other Senate critics of U.S. policy in Vietnam. In
an interview later Mar. 17, Senate Democratic leader Mike Mansfield (Mont.), a critic of the Johnson Administration's Vietnam
policy, said Nixon should be given "a further chance" to develop
his policy in Vietnam. "My belief is that the President still wants

a reasonable peace," he said. "But he doesn't have too much time, and I see no sense in shaving that time any closer." Mansfield did support McGovern's criticism of the continuation of U.S. search-and-destroy missions after the bombing halt was announced. The effect of the continued U.S. pressure, he said, was to "set off the act-react syndrome in the Vietnam war despite the fact that North Vietnam withdrew [after the bombing halt] 3 divisions into Cambodia and Laos." Senate Democratic whip Edward M. Kennedy (Mass.) agreed Mar. 17 that Nixon should be given more time. He said he thought the President had "shown some restraint" in not escalating in response to the attacks.

Reaction in Paris

The Communist offensive drew sharp rebukes from U.S. officials at the Paris talks. U.S. spokesmen questioned whether the attacks, particularly the shelling of population centers in the South, violated the U.S.-North Vietnamese understanding that had led to a halt in the U.S. bombing of the North and to the Paris talks.

Speaking at the 6th plenary session of the Paris negotiations Feb. 27, Henry Cabot Lodge warned the National Liberation Front and North Vietnam that the shelling of Saigon and other cities "clearly complicates our task" in Paris. Lodge said: "Such attacks bring you no military advantage. They bring down upon you a universal condemnation and disappoint the world's hope for peace." The offensive raised the question of whether the Communists sincerely desired peace. "The consequences of these attacks are your responsibility." "There is no question that the understanding which was made clear to the North Vietnamese representatives, prior to the stopping of the bombing on Oct. 31, remains in force." Lodge's latter statement was in response to the Communist contention that there were no conditions attached to the U.S. bombing halt. Xuan Thuy, head of the North Vietnamese delegation, charged that the Nixon Administration was "more stubborn and perfidious than the previous one in intensifying the war."

The North Vietnamese Foreign Ministry Feb. 25 had issued a statement defending the offensive. It said that "the South Vietnamese people have the right to fight against the United States aggressors at any place on Vietnamese territory. That is the Vietnamese peoples' inalienable right of self-defense." The ministry denied that Hanoi had violated any agreement with the U.S. in regard to the bombing halt. It charged that it was the U.S. that had committed a breach of faith. The statement said that North Vietnam had agreed to the 4-party conference in Paris "with a view to seeking a political solution" to the war but that the U.S., "by continued encroachments on the sovereignty and security" of North Vietnam, had violated its pledge. The North Vietnamese Communist Party newspaper *Nhan Dan* charged Feb. 25 that reports that Hanoi had reached an understanding with the U.S. on halting the bombing of the North were a "blatant and shameless lie." Washington's contention to this effect, the newspaper said, was "a pretext for prolonging and expanding the war" by charging violations by "the Vietnamese people."

A U.S. State Department statement Feb. 26 discounted *Nhan Dan's* statement as intensified propaganda to accompany the Communist drive. The statement insisted that the U.S. and North Vietnam had reached an understanding on the conditions under which the U.S. would maintain the bombing halt. It was "an understanding which they know very well and we expect them to live up to," the U.S. statement warned. The State Department Feb. 27 reaffirmed its stand: "We are satisfied that the other side did then and does now understand our position, . . . and we expect them to live up to the understanding." State Secy. William P. Rogers asserted Mar. 3 that the shelling of Saigon that day would not "succeed . . . in putting any additional pressure" on the U.S. to grant political concessions in Paris. He said that the 3d rocket attack on Saigon in 9 days "is a renewed reminder of the callous attitude with which the enemy regards the lives of innocent noncombatants." Rogers asserted that "the consequences of these attacks are the responsibility of the other side and clearly raise the question as to its true desire to work for a peaceful settlement of the conflict." A State Department spokesman said the "consequences" referred to by Rogers could be "both political and military."

Tran Buu Kiem, chief NLF negotiator in Paris, said at a French Communist Party rally Mar. 3 that the Viet Cong/North Vietnamese offensive was a "stern answer" to "the intensification of the war by the Nixon Administration." Kiem said the Communist operation would "foil the ambition of the Americans to negotiate from a position of strength."

At the Mar. 6 plenary meeting in Paris Lodge warned the NLF and North Vietnamese that "the consequences of these attacks are your responsibility." He reminded the Communist delegates that "the understanding, which was made clear to the North Vietnamese representatives, prior to the stopping of the bombing, remains in force."

Tran Buu Kiem asserted that despite Nixon's "copious honeyed words of peace," his Administration "does nothing but continue and intensify its war of aggression in South Vietnam." And Xuan Thuy, chief North Vietnamese delegate, said that demonstrations that had greeted Nixon on a European tour the previous week proved that "the peoples of the world are determined not to tolerate the aggressive and cruel actions of the United States in Vietnam."

The Mar. 6 session was adjourned after 4 hours, making it the shortest meeting since the expanded talks had started Jan. 25. Pham Dang Lam, head of the South Vietnamese delegation, had requested the adjournment because, he said, "an atmosphere favorable to useful discussions does not exist."

At the Mar. 13 session, Lodge asserted that the Communist offensive was an effort "to terrorize the civilian population into submission" in South Vietnam. Tran Buu Kiem replied that if the U.S. "commits new adventurous acts of war under the pretext of 'appropriate response', it will bear full responsibility for the consequences."

Hostilities Continue

The fighting occasioned by the post-Tet offensive continued through March and into April. Saigon and other cities were shelled, and sporadic but sharp clashes took place throughout South Vietnam. U.S. forces briefly invaded Laos and the demilitarized zone. Throughout this period, heavy casualties were suffered by both sides. *Among military actions reported:*

• Shelling of Saigon Mar. 6 which claimed the lives of 22 civilians and wounded 35 others. At least 7 rockets struck the city, most of them landing in a densely populated slum neighborhood.

• A force of 300 to 500 North Vietnamese attacked 2 U.S. infantry encampments near Kontum in the Central Highlands but was repelled with the loss of 89 lives. No American casualties were reported. Government troops were said to have killed 66 Communists in the northern province of Quangtin and 32 in the Mekong delta's Chuongthien Province.

• U.S. ground forces Mar. 7 threw back attacks against 3 American positions around Saigon—2 in Tayninh Province and the other near Dauthieng in Binh-duong Province. The heaviest of the attacks occured in Tayninh at a U.S. artillery base near Phukhuong, 54 miles northwest of Saigon. Viet Cong attempted to penetrate the base's defence perimeter. Repulsed in a 5-hour clash, they suffered 154 men killed. U.S. losses totaled 14 killed and 30 wounded.

● The incursion of a force of about 100 U.S. Marines into Laos was reported by U.S. military sources Mar. 8. The action, involving the seizure for about a week of several hilltops just south of Dongha, South Vietnam, was part of Operation Dewey Canyon, a major allied operation launched late in January. The operation, which was ending, had resulted in the death of about 1,400 enemy soldiers, about 125 U.S. Marines and several dozen South Vietnamese infantrymen. More than 400 tons of enemy arms were captured. Military sources said that the brief U.S. military move into Laos, a violation of Laotian neutrality, was aimed at protecting the flanks of a Marine force maneuvering along South Vietnam's northwestern border.

● About 50 mortar shells hit military and civilian targets in South Vietnam Mar. 7. The heaviest assault was directed against a U.S. Marine camp and a nearby civilian settlement outside Anhoa City, 23 miles southwest of Danang. 14 civilians were killed in the 130-round mortar barrage. U.S. casualties were reported to be light.

● Hue came under rocket attack Mar. 10 for the first time since the start of the offensive. 2 civilians were killed and 5 wounded in the explosion of 7 rockets near a medical school, in a high school playground and outside Hue's power plant.

● Communist mortar and rocket attacks decreased substantially Mar. 11 with about 10 shellings reported, compared with the recent daily average of 35.

● A U.S. infantry unit camped at a helicopter landing field 3 miles northeast of Phukhuong came under attack Mar. 12 by a force of 500 to 600 men. 5 Americans were killed and 20 wounded.

● The U.S. command reported Mar. 12 that its artillery had fired twice into the DMZ the previous day, killing at least 14 North Vietnamese soldiers and knocking out 3 enemy machinegun positions. In the first incident, U.S. guns opened up after an American reconnaissance plane was fired on while it was flying a little over 300 yards north of the southern section of the DMZ. The shelling killed at least 4 enemy soldiers and silenced the machineguns. The 2d American barrage, in which 10 North Vietnamese were killed, came after 15 North Vietnamese soldiers were seen $2^1/_2$ miles north of the southern edge of the DMZ.

● A U.S. Marine force moved about one mile into the southern section of the DMZ with armored vehicles Mar. 15. It was the first American strike force sent into the buffer strip since Nov. 1968. Fighting broke out after a Marine patrol in the zone spotted enemy rocket emplacements in the DMZ firing into South Vietnam. After a 3-hour fight about 3 miles northeast of Giolinh, the enemy retreated. The bodies of 10 North Vietnamese were then found in the area. While the DMZ clash was in progress, a U.S.-South Vietnamese force was ambushed by a North Vietnamese unit 6 miles south of Giolinh. 5 South Vietnamese soldiers, 6 Americans and 4 civilians were killed in the ambush.

● The North Vietnamese Foreign Ministry Mar. 16 accused the U.S. of bombing North Vietnamese territory and denounced the U.S. incursion into the DMZ.

● Communist activity during daylight hours Mar. 15 dropped to its lowest point since the start of the offensive but picked up sharply at night with 65 mortar and rocket attacks throughout South Vietnam. The number of shellings was the highest for any night of the post-Tet drive. Most of the assaults were against U.S. military installations; casualties were reported light. Several civilians were injured in the 2d shelling of Hué and of Gocong and Bentre in the Mekong Delta. Ground fighting was negligible.

● Troops of Thailand's Black Panther Division killed at least 109 Viet Cong and captured 4 Mar. 16 at Locninh, 35 miles from the capital, Thai supreme headquarters announced in Bangkok Mar. 17. The communique said elements of the 12,000-man division had inflicted the losses on the enemy as they attacked a regimental camp from all sides.

● U.S. forces fought 6 significant engagements in the Saigon area Mar. 17-19. U.S. military spokesmen said the actions took place in the area north and northwest of the capital between the Communists' Cambodian border sanctuaries and Saigon. In one clash lasting several hours, U.S. troops, helicopter gunships, artillery and jet strikes killed 28 men of a 250-man Viet Cong force 6 miles northeast of Dautieng. 35 Communists were slain by U.S. troops 5 miles northeast of Tranbang, 25 miles northeast of the capital.

● Communist forces Mar. 19 fired 10 rockets into Danang, killing 11 Vietnamese civilians and wounding 23 persons, including 3 U.S. military personnel.

● Heavy ground fighting erupted just south of Danang Mar. 19, according to South Vietnamese reports, and 116 Viet Cong soldiers were killed in 3 battles with government soldiers. The heaviest engagement was fought at Dienban, 10 miles south of Danang. The Viet Cong infiltrated the city, and fighting raged in the streets all day before the Communists were forced to retreat into the countryside with a loss of 50 men killed.

● 65 mortar and rocket attacks were mounted throughout South Vietnam Mar. 20. The U.S. command reported that 34 of the attacks were against U.S. military positions. The heaviest attack was directed against the U.S. airbase at Chulai, 55 miles south of Danang. The base reported light to moderate damage. U.S. air bases at Banmethout and Pleiku in the Central Highlands also were hit.

● One of a string of U.S. artillery bases protecting Saigon came under heavy Communist assault Mar. 21. The fire base of the First Cavalry Division, about 45 miles northwest of the capital, first was bombarded with mortars and rocket-propelled grenades, then was attacked by infantry using tear gas. The 250 American defenders blocked the attempt to penetrate the base's defense perimeter. 18 Americans were killed and 12 wounded. 3 Viet Cong were slain.

● According to U.S. military intelligence sources, 10 North Vietnamese regiments were reported Mar. 22 to be massed on the southern border of North Vietnam, just above the DMZ. Elements of 3 of these divisions were said to have moved into South Vietnam in recent days.

● Allied military authorities Mar. 24 reported an increase in ground fighting the previous 24 hours throughout South Vietnam. At least 265 Communist and 7 allied soldiers were said to have been killed in moderate to heavy clashes. The ground action was accompanied by 35 Communist rocket and mortar attacks on allied forces and population centers.

● The launching of an allied counteroffensive near the DMZ Mar. 15 was disclosed March 24. A force of about 3,000 U.S. Marines and South Vietnamese took part in the operations, called Maine Crag. The purpose of the drive was to block a North Vietnamese threat to allied bases along the northern frontier and to cut North Vietnamese supply lines from Laos into South Vietnam. Thus far the Marines were said to have killed 43 North Vietnamese troops and to have captured 2 prisoners and 129 rifles.

• A U.S. Army unit 50 miles northwest of Saigon came under heavy mortar and ground assault Mar. 25. 8 Americans were killed and 17 wounded, but the defenders held their positions. 2 Communist bodies were found after the incident.

• North Vietnamese forces suffered heavy losses in 2 ambushes of U.S. military convoys near Godauha, 45 miles northwest of Saigon, Mar. 25 and 28. In the first incident, Mar. 25, North Vietnamese forces were thrown back with 85 men killed. U.S. losses totaled 2 dead and 4 wounded. In the 2d engagement, an American supply convoy of more than 100 vehicles was attacked by North Vietnamese troops positioned on both sides of the road. About 20 tanks and armored troop carriers leading the convoy were fired on. The forward armored column turned off the road and drove into the enemy fire, while the remainder of the convoy sped through the gap. In the day-long battle that ensued, 46 North Vietnamese were reported killed.

• Heavy fighting raged in the northern provinces Mar. 27-30. About 120 North Vietnamese soldiers and 14 Americans were killed in a clash near the DMZ Mar. 27. In the Mar. 29-30 clashes, government forces were said to have slain 50 enemy soldiers about 20 miles south of Quangngai, while U.S. troops killed about 70 Communists in the area of the Mar. 27 skirmish.

• Saigon came under sporadic shelling Mar. 29-31, while heavy ground fighting occurred the night of Mar. 30-31 northwest of the capital. In one of 6 engagements, U.S. troops were said to have killed more than 100 Viet Cong near Dauthieng and Phukhuong. U.S. authorities reported Mar. 31 that 6,000 Communists had been killed in the provinces around Saigon since the start of the post-Tet offensive. Another 2,000 Communists, however, posed a serious threat to the capital a few miles to the southwest, the American officials said.

• A force of 600 North Vietnamese soldiers suffered heavy losses in an attack Apr. 4 on a U.S. artillery base near Godauha, northwest of Saigon. The U.S. defenders, supported by artillery and air strikes, drove off the attackers, killing 81 of them. American casualties totaled 4 killed and 13 wounded.

• U.S. infantry units suffered heavy losses from 2 separate Viet Cong attacks Apr. 5 and 7. In one encounter, Apr. 5, an American patrol came on a Viet Cong force 28 miles west of Kontum in the Central Highlands. 8 U.S. soldiers were killed and 17 wounded. The attacking force was driven off by artillery and air strikes; the bodies of 23 Viet Cong were found. In the 2d clash, Apr. 7, 11 Americans were killed and 13 wounded in a Viet Cong attack on a camp 6 miles southeast of Baoloc, about 100 miles northeast of Saigon.

The casualty reports, particularly those issued weekly by the U.S., reflected the intensity of the fighting.

The U.S. military command said Mar. 6 that during the first week of the post-Tet offensive 453 Americans had been killed (this was the highest weekly death toll since May 1968) and 2,593 wounded. The U.S. casualties exceeded the number suffered during the first week of the 1968 Tet offensive, when 400 Americans had been killed. South Vietnamese and Communist casualty figures for the first week of the 1969 drive were lower than for the comparable period of the 1968 offensive. The U.S. command reported that 6,752 Communist and 521 government troops had been killed the previous week. This compared with 13,118 Communist and 1,032 South Vietnamese soldiers slain during the first week of the 1968 offensive. Commenting on these losses, a U.S. high command officer said "the military significance of the figures is clear. The enemy has concentrated his attack on American installations and managed to kill significantly more United States soldiers this year while losing less than half the men he lost last year." (The South Vietnamese national police reported March 6 that during the first week of the new offensive 249 Vietnamese civilians had been killed in shellings and terrorist attacks. In addition 660 were wounded and 86 had been kidnapped. Since Jan. 1, 1,009 civilians had been killed by the Communists, 2,078 wounded and 1,885 abducted, the report said.)

The U.S. command reported Mar. 13 that combat deaths in the 2d week of the offensive totaled 336 Americans, 259 South Vietnamese and 4,063 Communists. The U.S. command reported Mar. 20 that 351 Americans had been killed Mar. 9-15, the 3d week of the offensive; 325 South Vietnamese soldiers and 4,137 Communists had been killed Mar. 9-15.

By the end of March, according to figures released by the U.S. command Apr. 3, American combat deaths in the Vietnam war exceeded those suffered in the Korean conflict. The death of 312 U.S. troops Mar. 23-29 raised the total of American fatalities in Vietnam since Jan. 1, 1961 to 33,641, compared with 33,629 U.S. soldiers killed during the Korean war (1950-3). Communist and South Vietnamese fatalities Mar. 23-29 were 4,314 and 357 respectively.

During what appeared to be the high point of the offensive, the National Liberation Front Mar. 19 urged its forces in South Vietnam to inflict heavy casualties on allied troops in a final, all-out war effort. The statement, broadcast over NLF radio and dated Mar. 7, had been read by Nguyen Huu Tho, the front's chairman, at a meeting of NLF leaders somewhere in South Vietnam Mar. 18. The session was attended by high-ranking NLF leaders, representatives of various South Vietnamese provinces, delegations from Saigon and Giadinh, various peace movements and Viet Cong soldiers who had distinguished themselves in the current offensive. The statement appealed to the South Vietnamese people in the cities to join the NLF in a national uprising to force the withdrawal of U.S. troops from South Vietnam and to topple the Saigon government. The NLF called on neutral governments and liberal groups throughout the world to support the front's cause. The broadcast boasted that the NLF had "scored continual victories" since the start of the 1968 Tet offensive. The statement charged that President Nixon "talks of peace yet continues to use every means to widen his aggression, ... rearming the Saigon government forces and giving greater backing to the Thieu-Ky-Huong authorities." Pledging total victory soon, the broadcast asserted that "we will continue with our holy war."

North Vietnamese Pres. Ho Chi Minh was reported Mar. 16 to have lauded the current Viet Cong offensive in a message to NLF Chairman Tho. Ho urged that the drive be pressed "vigorously and hard till the United States puppets are completely defeated."

In an overall assessment of the results of the offensive, and apparently marking its official termination, the Viet Cong's Liberation News Agency claimed Apr. 1 that the current campaign had "shattered" strategic plans drawn up by Gen. Creighton W. Abrams, commander of U.S. forces in Vietnam, after the 1968 Tet offensive. The agency, news organ of the NLF, said the post-Tet drive had turned Abrams' defensive strategy of "avoiding losses and reducing expenses" into a "fiasco" and had "ruined American illusions." The agency said: American strategy was based on 3 defensive "sanctuaries": (1) north and west of Saigon involving half of the U.S. force in Vietnam; (2) the Danang area, from north of the Thubon River to the foot of the Hill of Clouds, with a strongpoint at Anhoa; (3) an area stretching from Hué to the west of Highway 12, with mobile strongpoints in the Ashau and Cocave regions. These "sanctuaries" had been used by U.S. forces to launch raiding and "cleaning-up" operations around the cities. But American strategists were surprised when, as a result of the current drive, the U.S. "lines of concrete and steel were pierced and United States losses reached the level of the spring of 1968." The intensity of the attacks had forced the Americans "to pull back to consolidate their sanctuaries" and had made the "accelerated pacification program burst like a soap bubble."

U.S. paratroopers had been sent in to the Hué and Danang regions to replace Marines "who were bogged down in the mountainous zones to the west of these cities."

Allied sources in Saigon had said Mar. 28 that the offensive was having little effect on the government's pacification program. They claimed that in only a few of the country's 44 provinces the government drive to extend military security, oust Viet Cong political agents and build roads and schools had been disrupted. But the Liberation News Agency scoffed at announced American intentions to turn over more combat responsibility to South Vietnamese forces. "If the United States Army cannot deal with the offensive, what will the puppets do when they are left to themselves?" it asked.

A separate communiqué issued by the NLF April 1 said that the offensive had thwarted "American plans" to prolong the war and to extend it into Cambodia and Laos. The communiqué expressed determination "to strengthen our military solidarity with the Cambodian government and people, who ... are struggling courageously against the odious provocations of American imperialism."

Offensive Subsides

Reduced casualty reports in early April indicated that the post-Tet offensive was ending. Combat deaths during the period Mar. 30-Apr. 5 dropped to a record low, according to figures released by the U.S. command Apr. 10. Those listed as killed in battle during this period·were 222 Americans, 246 South Vietnamese and 3,220 North Vietnamese and Viet Cong.

Although battlefield reports continued to reveal occasional sharp clashes during the remainder of the month, Viet Cong activity was reduced largely to rocket and mortar attacks. *Among actions reported:*

● U.S. infantrymen Apr. 8 ambushed a Viet Cong force near Benluc, 17 miles southwest of Saigon and killed 47 Communist soldiers.
● Communist forces Apr. 10 launched 45 mortar and rocket attacks against military installations and populated centers throughout South Vietnam. The heaviest assaults were centered on Vinhlong, 60 miles southwest of Saigon, and on Tayninh, 55 miles northwest of the capital. Vinhlong's market place was struck by 100 mortar rounds. 15 persons were killed and 103 wounded in the attack. Tayninh's military headquarters compound was pounded by about 80 mortar and rocket shells, touching off explosions in an ammunition depot. The blasts killed more than 80 government soldiers. Hanoi radio claimed Apr. 12 that 100 U.S. and South Vietnamese soldiers had been killed in the

Tayninh attack.

● Troops at a U.S. infantry camp 33 miles northwest of Saigon Apr. 15 threw back a 1,000-man North Vietnamese assault and killed 198 of the enemy. A U.S. Army spokesman said that 2 North Vietnamese battalions had come "from the direction of the Cambodian border" to carry out the attack. 13 Americans were killed and 3 wounded in the 2-hour clash.

● Elements of the U.S. 11th Armored Cavalry Regiment were ambushed Apr. 18 when they came on a hidden North Vietnamese base camp near Phukhuong, about 50 miles northwest of Saigon. At least 82 Communists and 7 Americans were killed in the day-long battle that ensued.

● Following 3 days of relative calm, Communist forces carried out heavy rocket attacks against civilian and military centers Apr. 20. One of the targets hit was a South Vietnamese army training center at Lamson, 21 miles north of the coastal city of Nhatrang; at least 35 soldiers were killed and more than 175 wounded, most of them inductees. A U.S. Marine helicopter base outside Danang also was hit; 2 Marines were killed and 46 wounded.

Talks in Paris

While the spring offensive took place in South Vietnam, discussions in Paris remained stalemated, and the U.S. continued to urge private talks among the parties.

On the final day of a visit to Paris during a European trip, Pres. Nixon met Mar. 2 with leaders of the allied negotiating teams. No details of the discussion were made available, but participants indicated that they had agreed that confidential talks were necessary to achieve early progress toward peace. Nixon met privately with South Vietnamese Vice Pres. Nguyen Cao Ky and U.S. chief negotiator Henry Cabot Lodge. Ky, who had publicly advocated a resumption of the bombing of North Vietnam if the post-Tet offensive were not halted, said he and Nixon had discussed "many new approaches" to the talks, but he gave no details. He denied that he had raised the issue of bombing North Vietnam. He called the issue "a Vietnamese question that we have to discuss among Vietnamese."

In the course of a news conference on his trip, Nixon said Mar. 4 that the talks in Paris had entered Phase 2—"hard bargaining on the major points of difference" after both sides had presented their positions. The U.S. would employ "a variety of approaches," Nixon said, and he was "encouraged" that Ky had indicated to him "his desire to attempt to find and explore new approaches at the conference table, rather than simply resign ourselves to a military decision."

During March, the U.S. and South Vietnam continued to

press for private talks as the means to break the impasse. The National Liberation Front and North Vietnam condemned the allied suggestions as deceitful, but they did not seem to reject the idea completely.

Nixon, speaking at a luncheon of the National Association of Broadcasters in Washington Mar. 25, said it was "our conviction and our belief that it is through private talks with the North Vietnamese and others involved [in Paris] that real progress towards peace will be made." The President said he had instructed his aides to "say nothing" about such meetings. "If private talks are to be private, they must be private." "To disclose when, where and what and how would not serve the interests of peace," Nixon said.

South Vietnamese Pres. Nguyen Van Thieu said Mar. 25 that his government had advised the NLF and North Vietnam that Saigon was ready to enter unconditional, private talks with them in Paris, either separately or together. "The first private meeting has not been scheduled yet, but we are working on it," Thieu said. He pointed out that "in the private talks, anyone could raise any question, and we might consider any problem that arises. Private talks will help in some way to bring fruitful results and solve what we cannot solve in the official talks." Thieu said it was possible that Vice Pres. Ky would conduct the private talks, if and when they took place. Thieu was asked whether the private talks would involve only Saigon and the NLF or all 4 sides. He replied:

"Either way, it makes no difference, because in private talks we do not consider any more the problem of 2 sides, or 4 sides. . . . We could talk with Hanoi with the presence of the NLF, either with 3 groups or 2, it makes no difference."

The Communists assailed the allied suggestions at a briefing session following the 10th plenary session of the Paris peace talks Mar. 27. Tran Buu Kiem, head of the NLF delegation, charged that Thieu's statement had been dictated by the U.S. "This is not a serious act but a maneuver of the Nixon Administration aimed at covering up its policy of intensifying the war of aggression in South Vietnam," Kiem said. Kiem reiterated previous demands that the U.S. "must hold direct talks" with the front. An NLF statement issued in Hanoi called Thieu's proposal a "treacherous maneuver" "aimed at hiding the warmongering attitude of the Americans." Xuan Thuy, head of the North Vietnamese delegation, denounced Thieu's proposals as "tricks to calm down public opinion."

Henry Cabot Lodge, chief U.S. negotiator, had said Mar. 20 that "some progress" had been made at the 9th plenary session that day. Speaking to newsmen at the conclusion of the meeting, Lodge said: "If you define progress as meaning, were we swapping firm offers with each other—no, we were not." But the discussions had resulted in a "better understanding of each other's positions and the facts," Lodge said. Lodge's optimism was not shared by Nguyen Thanh Le, spokesman for the North Vietnamese delegation, who said that the talks had "not progressed in any way."

It had been reported in Paris Mar. 16 that allied and Communist negotiators were informally discussing ways of starting secret talks in order to break the impasse. One plan reportedly under discussion called for modifying the formula of plenary meetings once a week; working committees of the 4 delegations would take up specific military and political questions while the chief delegates would restrict public statements and comment on the course and content of the meetings.

In testimony before the Senate Foreign Relations Committee Mar. 27, State Secy. William Rogers left 2 Vietnam issues up to the enemy: (1) He said the U.S. could act very quickly to withdraw its troops from South Vietnam if North Vietnam would agree to simultaneous withdrawal. (2) He said the prospect of secret peace negotiations was up to the other side—"If they're serious about peace—if they want to talk about it, we're ready. The only way we can start negotiations is if they show up and are willing to negotiate." "We're prepared, if the other side is prepared, to have a withdrawal over a very short period of time," Rogers said. "I don't want to get involved in actual time limits." This statement was made in response to a question from Sen. Albert Gore (D., Tenn.) about a report that a Rogers aide had remarked privately to a group of businessmen that "the American people will be bought off with phased withdrawal—50,000, 60,000 a year, I believe was mentioned." Rogers said the reported remark "does not represent my thinking," and "it would be unrealistic and unwise to be talking about a phased withdrawal over any such period."

On the matter of internal politics of a future South Vietnamese government, Rogers said Saigon "has made clear its willingness that all political elements . . . who are prepared to renounce violence, and put their views peacefully to the populace for a decision, should be assured of their right to participate fully in the political process under the national constitution." He stressed that the U.S. "wouldn't have any veto power, and we don't want any," on the matter of political terms, especially terms for holding elections.

Following the Apr. 3 plenary meeting, North Vietnamese officials denied a statement made by Defense Secy. Melvin Laird that day that secret talks had started and that there had been "some sign of progress." It was not clear whether Laird meant that discussions were being held between the combined U.S.-South Vietnamese and North Vietnamese-National Liberation Front delegations or whether he was referring to South Vietnamese Pres. Thieu's Mar. 25 offer to hold private talks with North Vietnamese and NLF negotiators. A report from Paris Apr. 3 said that "direct secret talks" between Saigon and NLF representatives had begun.

The North Vietnamese officials called the reports of secret talks "pure invention." An NLF spokesman asserted that there was "absolutely no meeting" between his delegation and either the U.S. or South Vietnamese in Paris or elsewhere. The NLF and North Vietnamese delegations at the Apr. 10 meeting denounced the Nixon Administration for spreading "rumors about 'private meetings.' " The Communist delegates also charged that the Nixon Administration was "trying to make believe that it has a 'program for the peaceful settlement' of the Vietnam problem." They called this a U.S. trick "aimed at soothing the criticism" of the American people.

Allied proposals for mutual troop withdrawal from South Vietnam were rejected at the Apr. 17 meeting by North Vietnam and the NLF. At the Apr. 24 meeting, Pham Dang Lam, head of the South Vietnamese delegation, declared that the Saigon regime "never advocates the annihilation of those who are now bearing arms against the government" of South Vietnam. A Saigon delegation spokesman later quoted Lam as having added that South Vietnam did not demand the surrender of the guerrillas. He said South Vietnam "only demands that the Viet Cong abandon violence in order that they, along with other citizens, may participate in the democratic political life within the legal and constitutional framework and in a spirit of great national unity and national reconciliation."

Peace Plans

During the following months the parties to the dispute issued elaborate "proposals for peace" encapsulating their current positions for the termination of the war.

The first of these proposals was that the Saigon regime. Pres. Nguyen Van Thieu Apr. 7 made public a 6-point plan to end the war. Speaking at the opening of a new session of the Saigon parliament, Thieu called for: (1) a halt to Communist aggression; (2) withdrawal of North Vietnamese troops and their cadres from South Vietnam; (3) withdrawal of North Vietnamese bases and staging areas in Laos and Cambodia; (4) South Vietnamese adoption of a policy of national reconcilication; (5) reunification of North and South Vietnam by the free choice of the peoples of both areas through democratic processes; (6) an effective system of international control and guarantees against "the resumption of Communist aggression." Pending reunification, Thieu said, North and South Vietnam could examine the possibility of economic and cultural exchanges "together with other intermediary measures of peaceful co-existence." He promised that if North Vietnam ceased all aggressive actions and designs against South Vietnam, Saigon would "ask its allies to remove their forces" from the South. Thieu said he would soon call a conference of all leading political figures in South Vietnam to establish 2 parties—one, headed by himself, representing the government, and an opposition group. Thieu pledged full political rights for former Viet Cong members once peace was achieved.

A 10-point plan "with a view to ending the war in South Vietnam and contributing to peace in Vietnam" was presented by the National Liberation Front May. 8 at the 16th plenary session of the Paris talks. North Vietnam gave its full support to the plan. Although many of the points apparently restated previous NLF policy, the U.S. and South Vietnam May 9 expressed cautious interest in some aspects of the proposal. The plan, presented by Tran Buu Kiem, head of the NLF delegation, called for the unconditional withdrawal of U.S. and allied troops from South Vietnam under "international supervision," the holding of free elections and the ultimate establishment of a co-alition government, the restoration of the neutrality of the demilitarized zone, the exchange of war prisoners, the eventual reunification of North and South Vietnam and the application of the 1962 agreements on Laos.

Henry Cabot Lodge, U.S. chief delegate, confined his immediate reaction to the NLF plan's call for a U.S. troop pullback. Commenting after the meeting, Lodge said the U.S. was opposed to an American withdrawal from Vietnam "without any mutual action" on the part of North Vietnam. State Secy. William P. Rogers said May 9 that the NLF peace plan "contains some clearly unacceptable proposals, but there are elements in it which may offer a possibility for exploration." He said the NLF plan would be studied "carefully in the hope that it represents a serious response to the proposals put forward by South Vietnam and the United States." Rogers said he would discuss the matter with Saigon's leaders during a trip to South Vietnam scheduled to start May 12.

The South Vietnamese Foreign Ministry said May 9 that Saigon was prepared to discuss, in private or at the plenary sessions, 3 of the NLF's 10 points: the exchange of captives, the restoration of the DMZ's neutrality and the application of the 1962 agreements on Laos. The ministry noted that the NLF's 10 points contained many elements of the front's previously announced 5-point program and North Vietnam's 4-point plan. The ministry expressed disappointment at the NLF's "refusing the principle of mutual withdrawal of external forces and asking for a unilateral and unconditional withdrawal of allied forces."

The North Vietnamese Communist Party newspaper *Nhan Dan* asserted May 10 that the U.S. insistence on mutual troop withdrawals was a reactionary policy that could only lead to what it called further U.S. setbacks. *Nhan Dan* upheld the NLF proposal that the question of Vietnamese forces in South Vietnam should be resolved "by the Vietnamese parties among themselves." At the Apr. 30 meeting in Paris, Tran Buu Kiem had said that "on the basis" of the NLF's 5-point plan, the front was prepared for "discussions to make the conference move forward." The points were: (1) abolition of South Vietnam's "disguised colonial regime" established by the U.S.; (2) free general elections to select a National Assembly that would draw up a new constitution; (3) establishment of a coalition government representing all political factions; (4) reunification of Vietnam through negotiations between North and South; (5) a Vietnamese foreign policy based on "peace and neutrality."

Abridged text of the NLF's 10-point proposal:

. . . Proceeding from a desire to reach a political solution with a view to ending the United States imperialists' war of aggression in South Vietnam and helping restore peace in Vietnam, . . .

On the basis of the political program and the 5-point position of the South Vietnam National Liberation Front, which keeps with the 4-point stand of the government of the Democratic Republic of North Vietnam.

The South Vietnam National Liberation Front sets forth the principles and main content of an overall solution to the South Vietnam problem to help restore peace in Vietnam as follows:

(1) To respect the Vietnamese people's fundamental national rights, *i.e.* independence, sovereignty, unity and territorial integrity, as recognized by the 1954 Geneva agreements on Vietnam.

(2) The United States government must withdraw from South Vietnam all United States troops, military personnel, arms and war materiel of the other foreign countries of the United States camp without posing any condition whatsoever; liquidate all United States military bases in South Vietnam; renounce all encroachments on the sovereignty, territory and security of South Vietnam and the Democratic Republic of Vietnam.

(3) The Vietnamese people's right to fight for the defense of their fatherland is the sacred, inalienable right to self-defense of all peoples. The question of the Vietnamese armed forces in South Vietnam shall be resolved by the Vietnamese parties among themselves.

(4) The people of South Vietnam shall settle themselves their own affairs without foreign interference. They shall decide themselves the political regime of South Vietnam through free and democratic general elections: a constituent assembly will be set up, a constitution worked out and a coalition government of South Vietnam installed, reflecting national concord and the broad union of all social strata.

(5) During the period intervening between the restoration of peace and the holding of general elections, neither party shall impose its political regime on the people of South Vietnam. The political forces representing the various social strata and political tendencies in South Vietnam that stand for peace, independence and neutrality—including those persons who, for political reasons, have to live abroad—will enter into talks to set up a provisional coalition government based on the principle of equality, democracy and mutual respect with a view to achieving a peaceful, independent, democratic and neutral South Vietnam.

The provisional coalition government is to have the following tasks: (A) To implement the agreement to be concluded on the withdrawal of the troops of the United States and the other foreign countries of the American camp. (B) To achieve national concord, and a broad union of all social strata, political forces, nationalities, religious communities and all persons, no matter what their political beliefs and their past may be, provided they stand for peace, independence and neutrality. (C) To achieve broad democratic freedoms—freedom of speech, freedom of the press, freedom of assembly, freedom of belief, freedom to form political parties and organizations, freedom to demonstrate, etc.; to set free those persons jailed on political grounds; to prohibit all acts of terror, reprisal and discrimination against people having collaborated with either side, and who are now in the country or abroad, as provided for by the 1954 Geneva agreements on Vietnam. (D) To heal the war wounds, restore and develop the economy, to restore the normal life of the people and to improve the living conditions of the laboring people. (E) To hold free and democratic general elections in the whole of South Vietnam with a view to achieving the South Vietnam people's right to self-determination, in accordance with the content of point 4 mentioned above.

(6) South Vietnam will carry out a foreign policy of peace and neutrality:

To carry out a policy of good neighborly relations with the Kingdom of Cambodia on the basis of respect for her independence, sovereignty, neutrality and territorial integrity within her present borders; to carry out a policy of good neighborly relations with the Kingdom of Laos on the basis of respect for the 1962 Geneva agreements on Laos.

To establish diplomatic, economic and cultural relations with all countries, irrespective of political and social regime, including the United States, in accordance with the 5 principles of peaceful co-existence: mutual respect for independence, sovereignty and territorial integrity, nonaggression, noninterference in internal affairs, equality and mutual benefit, peaceful co-existence, to accept economic and technical aid with no political conditions attached from any country.

(7) The reunification of Vietnam will be achieved step by step, by peaceful means, through discussions and agreement between the 2 zones, without foreign interference. Pending the peaceful reunification of Vietnam, the 2 zones shall re-establish normal relations in all fields on the basis of mutual respect. The military demarcation line between the 2 zones at the 17th Parallel, as provided for by the 1954 Geneva agreements, is only of a provisional character and does not constitute in any way a political or territorial boundary. The 2 zones shall reach agreement on the status of the demilitarized zone and work out modalities for movements across the provisional military demarcation line.

(8) As provided for in the 1954 Geneva agreements on Vietnam, the 2 zones ... shall undertake to refrain from joining any military alliance with foreign countries, not allow any foreign country to maintain military bases, troops and military personnel on their respective soil, and not recognize the protection of any country or military alliance or bloc.

(9) To resolve the aftermath of the war: (A) The parties will negotiate the release of soldiers captured in war. (B) The United States government must bear full responsibility for the losses and devastations it has caused to the Vietnamese people in both zones.

(10) The parties shall reach agreement on an international supervision about the withdrawal from South Vietnam of the troops, military personnel, arms and war materiel of the United States and the other foreign countries of the American camp. ...

Tran Buu Kiem said May 14 that the front's program "forms a whole" and that negotiations should be conducted on the basis of the principles and contents of the plan. Speaking at a luncheon in Paris, Kiem said he opposed only partial acceptance of the front's plan. He singled out U.S. State Secy. Rogers' May 9 statement that some of the points were "clearly unacceptable" as "showing a negative attitude." Nguyen Trieu Dan, spokesman

for the South Vietnamese delegation, which also had expressed
hope that some of the points could be discussed separately, said
that Kiem's statements "will make progress in the talks more
difficult." In his speech, Kiem said the NLF would support the
overthrow of the Saigon government and "its replacement by
a cabinet of peace." As to the composition of a future coalition
government in Saigon, Kiem made clear that the NLF "expects
to deal on a basis of equality with the other political formations."

Pham Dang Lam, head of the South Vietnamese delegation,
had declared May 12 that the NLF was "not a political party"
but an armed, subversive group aimed at overthrowing a legal
government. As a result, he said, the front "has to be dissolved
and to become a political party." Lam had said May 11 that Saigon opposed the NLF political program because it sought to
"impose a provisional coalition government and a definitive coalition government even after the elections, regardless of the results
of these elections." Saigon, however, was prepared for "serious
discussions" on the NLF's 10-point program as well as Pres.
Thieu's 6-point plan, Lam said.

The U.S. published its plan May 14. Pres. Nixon proposed an
8-point formula that included provisions for mutual withdrawal
of "the major portions" of U.S., allied and North Vietnamese
troops from South Vietnam and internationally supervised elections to insure "each significant group in South Vietnam a real
opportunity to participate in the political life of the nation." The
President's plan was advanced in a nationally televised speech,
his first full-length report to the American people on the war in
Vietnam. It was in direct response to the 10-point NLF plan.
Nixon said his proposals were "not offered on a take-it-or-leave-
it basis." "We are willing to talk about anybody's program—
Hanoi's 4 points, the NLF's 10 points, provided, it can be consistent with the very basic principles I have set forth here tonight,"
he said.

On the matter of troop withdrawals, Nixon dropped ex-Pres.
Johnson's demand that Hanoi acknowledge the presence of its
forces in South Vietnam. "If North Vietnam wants to insist that
it has no forces in South Vietnam," he said, "we will no longer
debate the point—provided that its forces cease to be there, and
that we have reliable assurances that they will not return." Arguing
against unilateral American withdrawal from Vietnam, Nixon said
such a move would "not survive the damage that would be done

to other nations' confidence in our reliability." Furthermore, he said, "if Hanoi were to succeed in taking over South Vietnam by force—even after the power of the United States has been engaged, it would greatly strengthen those [Communist] leaders who scorn negotiation, who advocate aggression and who minimize the risk of confrontation with the United States." "Almost without exception, the leaders of non-Communist Asia have told me that they would consider one-sided American withdrawal from Vietnam to be a threat to the security of their own nations," Nixon asserted. For the U.S. to abandon South Vietnam, he warned, "would risk a massacre that would shock and dismay everyone who values human life." It also "would threaten our long-term hopes for peace in the world." Nixon insisted that in addition to pulling out of South Vietnam, North Vietnamese soldiers must quit neighboring Cambodia and Laos "on a specified time-table." Cambodia and Laos must be included, he said, "to insure that these countries would not be used as bases for a renewed war."

Nixon reiterated the previously stated U.S. position that "we seek no bases in Vietnam; we seek no military ties; we are willing to agree to neutrality for South Vietnam if that is what the South Vietnamese people freely choose." The U.S., the President said, was "prepared to accept any government in South Vietnam that results from the free choice of the South Vietnamese themselves. We have no intention of imposing any form of government upon the people of South Vietnam, nor will we be a party to such coercion."

Nixon noted reports from Hanoi that "indicated that the enemy has given up hope for a military victory in South Vietnam but is counting on a collapse of American will in the United States." "There could be no greater error in judgment," he declared. "We can have honest debate about whether we should have entered the war in Vietnam," Nixon said. "We can have honest debate about how the war has been conducted. But the urgent question today is what to do now that we are there. . . . We have ruled out attempting to impose a purely military solution on the battlefield. We have also ruled out either a one-sided withdrawal from Vietnam, or the acceptance in Paris of terms that would amount to a disguised American defeat." In an appeal to the American people for support of his plan, the President said it "can lead to a peace we can live with and a peace we can be proud of." He added: "In my campaign for the Presidency, I pledged to end this war in a way that would increase our chances to win true and lasting peace. . . . I am determined to keep that pledge. If I fail to do so, I expect the American people to hold me accountable for that failure."

Henry Cabot Lodge was recalled to Washington from Paris May 15 to receive new instructions from Nixon. Following a joint meeting with Nixon, the cabinet and the National Security Council, Lodge described the President's plan as "a basis for real, solid, meat-and-potatoes discussion about the real matters of substance" at issue in the war. "If there is a desire on the other side to have solid negotiations, why, this provides the opportunity," he said. Lodge dismissed initial negative reaction by the NLF saying that "I don't think we take those statements of that kind at face value."

Text of Nixon's 8 "specific measures" for a Vietnam settlement, proposed "on the basis of full consultation" with South Vietnamese Pres. Nguyen Van Thieu:

As soon as agreement can be reached, all non-South Vietnamese forces would begin withdrawals from South Vietnam. Over a period of 12 months, by agreed-upon stages, the major portions of all U.S., allied and other non-South Vietnamese forces would be withdrawn.

At the end of this 12-month period the remaining United States, allied and other non-South Vietnamese forces would move into designated base areas and would not engage in combat operations.

The remaining U.S. and allied forces would complete their withdrawal as the remaining North Vietnamese forces were withdrawn and returned to North Vietnam.

An international supervisory body, acceptable to both sides, would be created for the purpose of verifying withdrawal, and for any other purpose agreed upon between the 2 sides.

This international body would begin operating in accordance with an agreed timetable and would participate in arranging supervised cease-fire in Vietnam.

As soon as possible after the international body was functioning, elections would be held under agreed procedures and under the supervision of the international body.

Arrangements would be made for the release of prisoners of war on both sides at the earliest possible time.

All parties would agree to observe the Geneva accords of 1954 regarding South Vietnam and Cambodia and the Laos accords of 1962.

Nixon's speech was praised and supported by Congressional leaders of both parties but did not still the voices of the doves. Senate Democratic leader Mike Mansfield (Mont.), a critic of the Johnson Administration on Vietnam, said May 14 that he was

"impressed" with the "flexibility" of the Nixon plan. Chairman
J.W. Fulbright (D., Ark.) of the Senate Foreign Relations Committee characterized the speech as "conciliatory on the whole."
Although "I would go further," he said in a TV interview after
the speech, "I don't fault the President for not going further"
since it was his "first effort." 2 other doves praised the speech
May 14: Sen. Jacob K. Javits (R., N.Y.), who had criticized
Nixon's Vietnam policy May 9 as "sterile," called his plan "a
real step on the road to peace"; Sen. Charles Percy (R., Ill.)
described it as "the basis for a future negotiated settlement." But
Sen. Frank Church (D., Ida.) May 15 called Nixon's speech a
"bitter disappointment" because it showed that the new Administration's plan for ending the war was "the same as the Johnson
plan." In the House May 15, 8 Democrats, 6 of them from New
York, introduced legislation calling for a cease-fire and the unconditional withdrawal of 100,000 U.S. troops.

In a speech to the National War College May 19, Fulbright
urged a revision of the U.S. foreign policy of "chronic warfare
and intervention." Advocating a withdrawal from Vietnam even
if it led to less than a standoff with the Communists, Fulbright
cited a 10-to-one disparity between U.S. military expenditures
and spending for health, education, welfare and housing. Sen.
Stuart Symington (D., Mo.) said in a speech in Kansas City May
19 that the U.S. was "overcommitted" politically, militarily and
economically and "cannot continue its efforts to be the policeman
of the world."

The initial Soviet reaction to Nixon's plan, as expressed May
15 by the government newspaper *Izvestia*, was negative. *Izvestia*
said the proposals "boiled down to another attempt to justify
United States aggression against the Vietnamese people." Just
hours before Nixon delivered his speech, *Izvestia* had charged that
the President was following the same policy on Vietnam as his
predecessor, ex-Pres. Johnson. The "world and American public
opinion earlier had hoped that the aggression in Vietnam was the
policy of the former Administration, only inherited by the new
Administration," *Izvestia* said. "But months have passed and the
policy remains the same. All that has changed are the words used
to describe it." The Soviet journal praised the NLF's 10-point
plan as placing the question of terminating the conflict "on a
realistic track."

South Vietnamese Pres. Nguyen Van Thieu praised Nixon's

proposal May 15, saying that Nixon "has shown sincere goodwill to go forward to serious and useful talks with the Communist side to bring peace to Vietnam." Thieu said his government believed that the Nixon plan was in agreement with the Saigon government's basic principles for a solution. Thieu said May 17 that he would seek a meeting with Nixon "because I feel it is necessary to set up a common policy at this juncture in the situation."

Lodge formally presented the U.S. plan May 16 at the 17th plenary session of the Paris talks. Lodge said after the meeting that the Communist delegations had given "every indication" they would consider the newly-stated U.S. position. Lodge said that in future Paris meetings, he expected to "comment upon each individual issue" in the NLF's plan "just as we hope you will address the elements of our position." He emphasized that "peace can be achieved by a formal negotiated settlement or it could be achieved by an informal understanding, providing that the understanding is clear and that there are adequate assurances that it would be observed."

Tran Buu Kiem and Xuan Thuy, heads of the NLF and North Vietnamese delegations, respectively, criticized some aspects of Nixon's proposal but did not seem to reject it outright. The NLF and the North Vietnamese government had taken issue May 15 with Nixon's call for mutual troop withdrawals from South Vietnam. An NLF statement said: "Faced by the just and reasonable character of the National Liberation Front's 10-point over-all solution and by a favorable response of world opinion to this solution, Pres. Nixon seeks to give an appearance of goodwill in his speech of May 14. In fact, the United States still clings to its old unjust and unreasonable formula for a mutual withdrawal of troops, now submitted in a new form that places the aggressor and the resisting victims of aggression on the same footing—a proposal that we have repeatedly rejected."

A North Vietnam broadcast called it "completely unrealistic to talk of mutual withdrawal of aggressor troops and defender troops. The plan of the Nixon Administration is not to end the war but to replace the war of aggression fought by U.S. troops into a war of aggression fought by the puppet army of the United States."

The differences in the U.S. and Communist stands were pointed up May 20 by Xuan Thuy. Speaking at a Paris luncheon, Thuy warned that U.S. support of Pres. Thieu would prevent "any progress" at the talks. He charged that Nixon, in advancing his 8-point formula, had failed to mention "the fundamental, most important points such as sovereignty, independence, unity and territorial integrity of South Vietnam." Nixon also had ignored the question of who would organize the first elections in South Vietnam, Thuy said. If Nixon continued to support the Thieu regime, Thuy said, it meant that Nixon "wants the elections to be organized by it. This will never be accepted by the National Liberation Front."

At the 18th plenary session Lodge said May 22 that similarities in Nixon's and the NLF's plans could provide the basis for substantive discussions and negotiations. But Nguyen Thanh Le, spokesman for the North Vietnamese delegation, asserted after the meeting that the "respective positions" of the U.S. and the Communists were "as different as day and night."

Lodge said that the issues on which both sides appeared to be in agreement were reunification of North and South Vietnam, restoration of the DMZ, prisoners of war and observance of the Geneva accords guaranteeing the neutrality of Cambodia and Laos. On the matter of prisoners, Lodge appealed to the Communists "in human terms instead of the language of diplomacy" to identify the captives it held. He said he found the Communists' reaction to Nixon's plan obscure.

Harold Kaplan, spokesman for the U.S. delegation, said after the meeting that "the heart of the issue" remained the matter of mutual troop withdrawals from South Vietnam. He said if there was to be serious negotiations North Vietnam must be prepared to take its forces out of the South.

VIETNAMIZATION

Preliminaries

The Nixon policy of withdrawing U.S. ground forces from Vietnam and replacing them in their combat role with ARVN (Army of the Republic of Vietnam) troops, which came to be known as the "Vietnamization policy," unfolded slowly during 1969.

The reversal of Pres. Johnson's "Americanization" of the war had actually begun before Nixon assumed office, and the question of troop withdrawals had been involved in the background discussion during the early months of the Nixon Administration. The emergence of the new policy, however, was suggested by Defense Secy. Melvin R. Laird, in testimony before the Senate Armed Services Committee Mar. 19. He said the Administration was not planning any U.S. troop pullout "at the present time." But Laird drew a distinction between preparing the South Vietnamese to defend themselves after outside troops were withdrawn and readying the South Vietnamese to replace U.S. forces in combat. Attributing the former goal to the Johnson Administration, Laird said he was changing the objective to the latter, to prepare the South Vietnamese for replacement duty and to "work toward a situation in which United States forces can in fact be withdrawn in substantial numbers." He requested $156 million to accelerate this process.

Appearing Mar. 21 before the Disarmament Subcommittee of the Senate Foreign Relations Committee, Laird stressed the effort to modernize the South Vietnamese army and "reduce the involvement" of the U.S. in Vietnam. "I have heard this before," Sen. J.W. Fulbright (D., Ark.) told him. "It is an old broken record going back to [ex-Defense Secy. Robert S.] McNamara." "You've got to do something radical to change this war or we're going down the drain," Fulbright warned. "Soon it will be Nixon's war, and then there will be little chance to bring it to an end. It it time to de-escalate and settle it."

According to Administration sources in Washington Mar. 11, Laird was considering the withdrawal of 40,000 to 50,000 U.S. combat and support troops from Vietnam in 1969. In an interview broadcast Apr. 30 by National Educational Television, State Undersecy. Elliot L. Richardson said that the Nixon Administration "looks forward" to the time when the South Vietnamese capability "will be great enough to justify withdrawals." "As progress is made" in "Vietnamization" of the war, he said, "one might expect some withdrawals."

Rumors and suggestions of the new policy continued through March and April. The pressures on the U.S. arising from the effort in Vietnam were further manifested in additional cuts in the fiscal 1970 defense budget, which were announced by Laird Apr. 1 as responses to the "extremely difficult and dangerous economic and fiscal situation." Laird disclosed his plans in testimony before the House Armed Services Committee. To attain a $613 million reduction planned in defense spending, several Vietnam war programs were scaled down. B-52 bomber raids in South Vietnam were to be decreased by more than 10%—from a level of 1,800 a month to 1,600 a month; Laird admitted that this was contrary to a "strong recommendation" from Gen. Creighton W. Abrams, commander of the U.S. forces in Vietnam, to maintain the current level. Ground, air and ship munitions were cut; ground munitions were reduced to a level (75,000 tons a month) actually below that of the anticipated use (87,000 to 92,000 tons a month), and this would force the military to dip into stockpiles. 18 ships were to be deactivated. Some of them were involved in the war effort, but, according to Laird, only in the "low priority forces" category.

In a Gallup Poll conducted Mar. 28-31 (reported Apr. 9), 44% of 1,502 adults questioned, or 3 persons out of every 5 who expressed opinions, approved of the way Nixon was handling the situation in Vietnam. 30% of those interviewed reserved judgment and gave no opinion, and 26% of those interviewed disapproved of the President's handling of the Vietnam situation; many of those who disapproved preferred dramatic alternatives ranging from immediate withdrawal to all-out escalation.

In his speech on Vietnam policy May 14, Nixon hinted that he would order a partial withdrawal of U.S. combat troops from South Vietnam before an agreement with the Communists on a total withdrawal and regardless of developments at the Paris talks. The President said that Gen. Creighton W. Abrams had reported to him May 12 that the training of Saigon's forces was reaching a point where they would soon "be able to take over some of the fighting fronts now being manned by the Americans."

The U.S. had presented to South Vietnam Apr. 19 a squadron of 20 A-37 jet bombers in one of a series of moves publicized as de-Americanizing the war. The planes, handed over to the Saigon regime in a ceremony at Nhatrang, made up the first of 3 squadrons South Vietnam was scheduled to receive in 1969. In accepting the jets, Pres. Nguyen Van Thieu said that "with increased aid from the United States and her other allies, South Vietnam is determined to gradually take over all the burdens of the war." Answering charges that South Vietnam was permitting its allies to bear the brunt of the fighting, Thieu said government casualty figures in 1968 and in the first 3 months of 1969 were higher than those of the U.S. and other allies.

The issue of troop withdrawals re-emerged in Senate debate. Sen. George D. Aiken (R., Vt.) proposed in a Senate speech May 1 that the U.S. start immediately to remove its forces from Vietnam. A similar appeal for withdrawal of "a substantial number" of U.S. troops from Vietnam was made by Senate Republican whip Hugh Scott (Pa.) in a speech in Pittsburgh May 2. Aiken was a long-time "dove," but Scott generally had supported the U.S. policy.

Aiken, senior Republican member of the Senate Foreign Relations Committee, said the U.S. "would do well to advise the South Vietnamese government immediately of our intentions and then start an orderly withdrawal of our military personnel, turning that country and that war back to its rightful owners. It may take some time to complete this operation, but it should be started without delay." The South Vietnamese "now appear to be strong enough to stand on their own feet," and "there is little danger that South Vietnam could be taken from the outside," Aiken said. "Common sense should tell us that we have now accomplished our purpose as far as South Vietnam is concerned."

Scott called for "a bold move to flush out the intentions of the other side" by "the withdrawal of a substantial number of American troops from Vietnam." He made the proposal in a speech before the University of Pittsburgh Alumni Association (the speech was also released in Washington). It was time "to prod the North Vietnamese out of the sea of propaganda and onto the high ground of real bargaining sessions," he said. "A measured withdrawal" of U.S. forces "would provide that kind of test" of Hanoi's intentions.

During an ensuing floor discussion, Aiken's speech was indorsed by Senate Democratic leader Mike Mansfield (Mont.), Democratic whip Edward M. Kennedy (Mass.) and Republican Sens. Jacob K. Javits (N.Y.) and Charles H. Percy (Ill).

(A scaling down of the fighting in Vietnam was advocated May 24 by Averell Harriman, who called for the immediate withdrawal of 50,000 U.S. troops. The former chief U.S. negotiator at the Paris peace talks said he was "convinced there will not be progress in the political field until there is reduction of violence." "We cannot expect the Viet Cong to stop their attacks as long as we are exerting maximum military pressure on them" he said. "If we take some steps to reduce the violence, if we take the lead, I'm satisfied that they will follow.")

Allied Conferences, Nixon & Thieu at Midway

In advance of what obviously was a major policy move, State Secy. William P. Rogers visited South Vietnam May 14-18 for high-level consultations. On arriving in Saigon May 14, Rogers said that Pres. Nixon had directed him to explore in depth with Pres. Nguyen Van Thieu "how we can most effectively move forward from the present position further in the direction of peace." Rogers assured the South Vietnamese that the U.S. supported their unconditional right to determine their own political future. He explained that the term unconditional meant that "the decision must not be imposed, in whole or part, by outside forces; it must be made by a process which permits the people of South Vietnam their own free choice. If the other side were willing to accept this principle, then the prospects of peace would be greatly improved."

Rogers conferred May 15 with Foreign Min. Tran Chanh Thanh and Prime Min. Tran Van Huong and met with Pres. Thieu May 16. A U.S. statement on the Rogers-Thieu talks said that both men had agreed that the political future of South Vietnam, including possible elections, was open to direct negotiation between the Saigon government and the National Liberation Front. Rogers and Thieu also were said to have discussed replacing some U.S. troops with South Vietnamese, allied negotiating strategy in Paris, the current military situation and a possible summit meeting between Thieu and Nixon. Also attending the talks were Vice Pres. Nguyen Cao Ky, Amb. Ellsworth Bunker and Gen. Creighton W. Abrams.

Rogers toured the Mekong delta May 17 and visited Hué May 18. In Hué he placed a wreath at the mass graves of civilians who had been slain by the Viet Cong in 1968. He left Saigon May 19 to attend a meeting of the Southeast Asia Treaty Organization (SEATO) in Bangkok, Thailand.

Seato's 14th annual Ministerial Council meeting, held in Bangkok May 20-21, was followed by a conference May 22 of the 7 allied nations fighting in South Vietnam. No concrete decisions were announced at the SEATO conference. But a communiqué May 21 reaffirmed the need for SEATO to maintain peace and security in Southeast Asia. It urged a concerted drive to make SEATO's "role more effective and more responsive to the new Communist tactics being employed to undermine the stability and orderly progress of free societies." The communiqué charged that Communist aggression remained a threat to peace in Southeast Asia and "must not be allowed to succeed." It expressed "grave" concern over the presence of North Vietnamese troops in Laos. (The countries fully respresented at the conference were the U.S., Britain, Australia, New Zealand, Thailand and the Philippines.)

In a speech at the SEATO conference's opening session May 20, Rogers reaffirmed American intentions to come to the aid of any SEATO member under attack even if the organization declined to act. Rogers vowed that when the U.S. forces were "no longer needed in South Vietnam, we shall not abandon in peace what we have fought for in war—the peaceful evolution of Southeast Asia."

A communiqué issued May 22 by the foreign ministers of the 7 allied nations fighting in South Vietnam declared that North Vietnamese forces must be withdrawn from Laos and Cambodia, as well as from South Vietnam, as part of a general peace settlement. The statement was signed by foreign ministers of the U.S., South Vietnam, Thailand, South Korea, Australia, New Zealand and the Philippines.

The White House announced May 20 that Nixon would meet Nguyen Van Thieu on Midway Island June 8. The statement said: Nixon and Thieu "had desired to hold such a meeting as soon as possible to establish personal contact and discuss together the conduct of the war in Vietnam and the search for a peaceful solution." Rogers' recent visit to Saigon and "the discussions he held there paved the way for the meeting."

After conferring with Thieu for 5 hours on Midway June 8, Nixon announced that 25,000 U.S. troops would be withdrawn from South Vietnam by Aug. 31. During their conference, Nixon and Thieu reviewed political, economic and military developments in Vietnam and the general situation in Southeast Asia. A joint communiqué issued after the talks largely reiterated previously expressed U.S. and South Vietnamese views on the war. Nixon termed the troop withdrawal plan a "significant step forward" toward a lasting peace. He said he would announce plans for a further U.S. troop pullback "as decisions are made." He said the withdrawal had been recommended by Thieu and Gen. Creighton W. Abrams. Seeking to allay fears that the removal of American troops would harm the allied war effort, Nixon said: "I want to emphasize 2 fundamental principles: No actions will be taken which threaten the safety of our troops and the troops of our allies, and 2d, no action will be taken which endangers the attainment of our objective, the right of self-determination for the people of South Vietnam."

Thieu said the announcement was "good news for the American people that Vietnamese forces replace United States combat forces." He said it was "the constant duty of the Vietnamese people to take over more responsibility and to alleviate the burden of the United States people to support us and defend freedom in Vietnam." Thieu denied he had come to Midway "to dissipate or discuss" reported differences between Washington and Saigon on current peace efforts. "We have had close consultation before, and we have a very close understanding," Thieu said.

Among the major points of the Nixon-Thieu statement:

● The South Vietnamese people should be allowed to decide their political future "without interference of terror." Nixon and Thieu "rejected Communist attempts to predetermine the outcome of future elections before they are held." They opposed "any attempt to impose upon the Republic of Vietnam any . . . form of government, such as coalition, without regard to the will of the people of South Vietnam."

● It would be appropriate to offer guarantees and safeguards for free elections. Provisions for international supervision could be written into any future political settlement.

● Progress was being made to modernize and improve the Vietnamese armed forces. The replacement of American soldiers by Vietnamese troops "should be carried out in consonance with the security situation prevailing at the moment."

● Allied proposals in Paris for a settlement "represent a reasonable basis for peace." Although the National Liberation Front's (NLF) 10-point plan "contained certain unacceptable provisions," other aspects of the plan were similar to the views expressed by Washington and Saigon. Thieu "reiterated his willingness to talk directly to the NLF about moves relating to a peaceful settlement."

● Nixon and Thieu repeated their call for the mutual withdrawal from South Vietnam of all non-South Vietnamese forces, "agreeing that withdrawals could commence simultaneously and proceed expeditiously on a basis of a mutually acceptable timetable." Foreign forces should also be pulled out of Laos and Cambodia.

● Thieu renewed his pledge to uphold "the principle of social and political justice" in South Vietnam and noted his government's adoption of "the policy of national reconciliation."

● Nixon promised to assist South Vietnam in expanding its economy and balancing its budget.

Administration leaders accompanying Nixon to the Midway meeting included State Secy. Rogers, Defense Secy. Laird, Presidential aide Henry Kissinger, Gen. Earle G. Wheeler, chairman of the Joint Chiefs of Staff, Gen. Abrams, Amb. Ellsworth Bunker and Henry Cabot Lodge, chief U.S. negotiator at the Paris talks.

Thieu's staff consisted of Foreign Min. Tran Chanh Thanh, Defense Min. Nguyen Van Vy, Gen. Cao Van Vien, chairman of the Joint General Staff, and Bui Diem, Saigon's ambassador to Washington.

On returning to Washington June 9, Laird expressed the hope that if the South Vietnamese continued to assume more of the burden of fighting, further U.S. troop withdrawals could be made in August and at "regular intervals thereafter." Laird said the 25,000 U.S. soldiers to be taken out of South Vietnam would be largely combat units of the Army and Marine Corps. Most of the units were to be returned to the continental U.S., but some were to be redeployed to Hawaii and Okinawa, he said. No Air Force or Navy elements were involved in the initial cutback, Laird explained, because, as support forces, they were required to supply and support the South Vietnamese units that were to replace the American forces in the combat zones. Laird said that as a result of the Midway conference, "we return closer to peace, and we have a program moving forward to change the role of the United States in Vietnam and Southeast Asia." The decisions reached at Midway, he said, "should be a signal to North Vietnam that the United States is going to maintain its objective, the right of self-determination for the people of South Vietnam."

In a televised news conference in Saigon June 9, Thieu warned South Vietnamese newspapers against describing the planned U.S. troop withdrawal with "detrimental" phrases that might undermine the morale of the army and the nation. He particularly cited the term "withdrawal," as applied to the planned departure of 25,000 American troops: "This is replacement, not withdrawal. 'Withdrawal' is a defeatist and misleading term." Thieu reiterated his opposition to a coalition government. "I solemnly declare that there will be no coalition government, no peace cabinet, no transitional government. . . . I cannot sacrifice the lives of 17 million Vietnamese people . . . ," he declared. Thieu said he would be willing to discuss with the Communists the holding of elections. Asked whether the constitution could be amended to permit national balloting before 1971, Thieu said this matter was open for negotiation with the Communists. Thieu said Nixon had not discussed elections with him at Midway because Nixon "did not want to interfere in the political decisions of the South

Vietnamese people."

Nixon's announcement of the troop withdrawal was hailed by Senate Republican leader Everett Dirksen (Ill.) June 9 as "the first tangible, specific, immediate step to de-Americanize" the war. House Republican leader Gerald Ford (Mich.) had expressed hope June 8 that more U.S. withdrawals would follow "as we move toward our objective of a withdrawal of all foreign troops from South Vietnam."

Sen. George McGovern (D., S.D.) June 8, however, labeled the withdrawal plan as "tokenism" that "doesn't fundamentally change the character of our involvement." Sen. Eugene McCarthy (D., Minn.) said June 8 that he did not see "any significant indication of any program to try and resolve or end the war." Sen. J. W. Fulbright (D., Ark.), who had expressed concern June 6 that the Midway conference might result in Nixon's "adopting him [Thieu] as our boy," said June 9 that he found in the announcement "nothing that gives me hope that we are moving toward a negotiated settlement." Sen. Albert Gore (D., Tenn.) June 10 objected to "piecemeal withdrawal" as a plan for "prolonging the war." Sen. Edward M. Kennedy (D., Mass.), muting his comment because "it's too early to make any broad categorization," expressed hope that the troop withdrawal "would signify a change in American policy" that "would reflect itself in a reduction in the violence."

The National Liberation Front and North Vietnamese delegations in Paris June 9 assailed the Midway communiqué. An NLF spokesman held that the refusal of Nixon and Thieu to accept a coalition government for South Vietnam was "an obstacle to progress" in the Paris negotiations. A North Vietnamese spokesman asserted that Nixon's decision to disengage 25,000 American troops was a "preposterous farce," "a grain of sand thrown in the ocean." The spokesman said: "Refusing to withdraw immediately and completely the American troops without posing any conditions, the Nixon Administration declares that it will proceed only with the redeployment of American forces by the repatriation of 25,000 soldiers among the 540,000 now in Vietnam." The "Midway farce," the Hanoi official asserted, showed the "obstinancy" with which the U.S. pursued the course of "aggression and of neo-colonialism." The Soviet government newspaper *Izvestia* June 9 compared the Midway conference with "the mountain laboring to give birth to a mouse." Scorning the planned withdrawal of 25,000

American troops, the newspaper said that "in place of constructive steps is a hopeless propaganda stunt with the goal of raising a racket around 'an important contribution to peace,' and instead of a search for a political decision there is a clumsy maneuver to camouflage the unwillingness of Washington to take the decision that the world is waiting for." The Soviet press agency Tass said that the Midway communique proved that the Nixon Administration was "not abandoning the principles that became bankrupt a long time ago." It called the troop reduction "only a drop in the sea as compared to what still remains."

Nixon said June 10 that his Midway conference with Thieu had "opened wide the door to peace." He invited North Vietnam to "walk with us through that door." The first step toward peace, he said, could come from a troop withdrawal or "serious negotiations in Paris, or both." "If they fail to act in one direction or another," he said, "they must bear the responsibility for blocking the road to peace and not walking through that door we have opened." Nixon made these remarks at a White House ceremony welcoming him home from Midway. He told those assembled—Administration officials, Congress members and federal workers—that the conference had a 3-fold meaning: (1) It "brought home the message" that the South Vietnamese were ready to "take over a substantial portion" of combat in the war; (2) it showed that Thieu "completely approves and supports" Nixon's 8-point peace program; (3) it signified that "we finally have reached the point where we can begin to bring Americans home from Vietnam." The President stressed that the planned U.S. troop withdrawals did not mean "that the war is over." "There are negotiations still to be undertaken," he said. "There is fighting still to be borne. . . . "

Troop Removals Begin

The *N.Y. Times* reported June 17 that the Nixon Administration planned to withdraw 45,000 to 75,000 more U.S. troops from South Vietnam in 2 stages, in August and in October. The pullout would be in addition to the removal of the 25,000 announced on Midway June 8. The additional disengagement would depend on whether ARVN forces operated more aggressively and whether Communist forces attempted successfully to launch new military drives, the Times reported. The proposed new withdrawals were said to involve 2 combat divisions, the 10,000 Army reserve troops remaining in South Vietnam and various support and service elements. The *Times* said that if North Vietnam refused to agree to a mutual foreign troop withdrawal from South Vietnam, the U.S. would remove 340,000 American soldiers from the country over the next 3 years, while "indefinitely" retaining a force of 200,000 men to bolster South Vietnamese troops against Communist attack.

(The Defense Deparment disclosed June 17 that of the 25,000 American men to be taken out of South Vietnam in the initial pullback, about 16,000 of them, soldiers and Marines, were scheduled to be redeployed to Hawaii, Okinawa and Japan. About 8,000 Army men, including about 2,000 active duty reservists and National Guardsmen, would be returned to the U.S. About 1,000 Navy men would be reassigned in the Pacific and the U.S. The principal combat units to be reassigned were identified as the 9th Marine Regimental Landing Team [8,000 men], to be sent to Okinawa; the First Brigade of the 9th Infantry Division and the division's headquarters [7,400 men], to Hawaii; the 2d Brigade of the 9th Division [6,000 men] and 1,200 reservists, to the U.S.)

Nixon June 19 expressed hope that his Administration could "beat" a proposed timetable for withdrawal of 100,000 combat troops from Vietnam in 1969 and an additional 100,000 to 150,000 by the end of 1970. The President's views were made known at a televised news conference. The timetable for a withdrawal had been proposed by ex-Defence Secy. Clark M. Clifford June 18 in an article in the quarterly *Foreign Affairs*.

Presidential aides stressed June 20 that Nixon's statements were expressions of "hope" rather than firm commitment. Nixon's remarks had been applauded quickly by several Senate "doves." Sen. Edward Kennedy June 20 interpreted the remarks as "a definite commitment that ought to be carried out." Sen. J.W. Fulbright said June 20: "I certainly hope he can do it. If he means it, I will certainly applaud him." Senate Democratic leader Mike Mansfield said June 20 that he hoped "this schedule can be met." But Mansfield June 21 characterized the President's remarks as "overreaction" to Clifford's article.

Clifford had called for a total pullout of U.S. ground combat forces, coupled with continued U.S. logistic and air support for South Vietnamese armed forces. He said this would pose "a painful dilemma" for the enemy—that of either accepting "a prolonged and substantial presence of American air and logistical personnel" or agreeing to a mutual withdrawal of all external forces. Clifford suggested that U.S. field commanders be given new orders "to discontinue efforts to apply maximum military pressure on the enemy and to seek instead to reduce the level of combat." As for the South Vietnamese government, Clifford said the Administration should make it clear that (1) a proposed initial withdrawal of 100,000 troops would be "the beginning of a process" leading to withdrawal of all U.S. ground combat forces, and (2) "American objectives do not demand the perpetuation in power of any one group of South Vietnamese." If the later were made clear to Saigon, Clifford said, it would put pressure on the South Vietnamese regime to open itself to "individuals representative of other nationalist elements in South Vietnamese society."

Nixon, commenting on the Clifford proposal said at his news conference: "I would hope that we could beat Mr. Clifford's timetable, just as I think we've done a little better than he did when he was in charge of our national defense." He expressed hope "that we will not be in Vietnam as long as" Clifford had suggested "we will have to be there." "We have started to withdraw forces," Nixon said." "We will withdraw more. Another decision will be made in August." Referring to Clifford's call for new orders to field commanders, Nixon said his orders were "to conduct this war with a minimum of American casualties." U.S. casualties, he said, were in direct ratio to the level of enemy attacks.

As for the Paris negotiations, Nixon said: "There is no substantial evidence . . . to report" but "we hope within the next 2 to 3 months to see some progress in substantive discussions." Pres. Nguyen Van Thieu "will be making an offer of his own with regard to a political settlement," and "under those circumstances there is no question about our standing with Pres. Thieu. . . . We are not going to accede to the demands of the enemy that we have to dispose of Pres. Thieu before they will talk." The U.S. was not "wedded" to the Thieu regime, but Thieu was "the elected president of Vietnam" and was working with the U.S. "to bring this war to a conclusion."

The first contingent of departing U.S. troops, 814 men from the 3d Battalion of the 60th Regiment, 9th Infantry Division, left Vietnam July 8. They were flown to McChord Air Force

Base in Tacoma, Wash.

(Australian Prime Min. John G. Gorton had said July 6 that Australia might withdraw its entire 8,000-man force from South Vietnam if there was a "great and continuing" withdrawal of U.S. troops. Gorton said it would not be a question of a reduction, which he termed "scarcely tenable," but rather a complete withdrawal.)

Withdrawal Debated, Truce Urged

Sen. Jacob K. Javits (R., N.Y.) proposed June 29 that the Nixon Administration devise a timetable for the withdrawal of all U.S. combat forces from Vietnam by the end of 1970. Javits, in a TV appearance, said: "I believe that the time has come for an orderly reorganization of the Vietnam war to substitute the total combat responsibility carried by the U.S. now with the Vietnamese." He said the U.S. might continue to provide logistical support, but "they [the South Vietnamese] would be fighting this war."

Vice Pres. Spiro T. Agnew said July 1 that it was a "tragedy that, in some cases, sincere opposition" to the Administration's Vietnam policy was "undermining our negotiations for peace and prolonging the war." "The Viet Cong remains intransigent," he said, "because of the slender hope that the voices of dissent at home will force us to alter—perhaps even abdicate—our policy of proving that confrontation with the United States is costly." Addressing the Midwestern Governors' Conference in Wichita, Kan., Agnew called in a "myth" that "there is an easy way out of Vietnam through unilateral withdrawal." He said: "Our diplomatic credibility is as much at stake as the independence of South Vietnam." "Our progress and success depend on the staying power of the American people."

Agnew's remarks were deplored in the Senate July 2 by Sens. J.W. Fulbright, chairman of the Foreign Relations Committee, and George McGovern. Fulbright said Agnew's speech "reflects further what is becoming more apparent every day—the similarity if not the identity of the present Administration's view of the war with the past Administration." (Fulbright told the Senate July 23 that "one reason no progress has been made in the Paris peace talks is because there has been no progress in the U.S. mind whether to stay" in Vietnam or get out.) McGovern said "it increasingly appears that ... we are following the same strategy that has produced our earlier years of grief." McGovern revealed in his speech that he had met privately in Paris May 22 with the chief North Vietnamese and Viet Cong negotiators. He said he had emerged from the all-day session convinced that fruitful peace negotiations could not begin unless the U.S. (1) agreed to "unconditional withdrawal" of all its troops or indicated "some assurance we are moving in that direction," and (2) discontinued its "unqualified embrace" of the Thieu-Ky regime in Saigon. It was his impression, he said, that the other side might accept a provisional government that included military elements of the Thieu-Ky regime but not one enabling that regime "to hold on to the ballot box." In a *Christian Science Monitor* interview July 3, McGovern said it was time to push for a "breakthrough toward peace" by experimenting with a 30-day cease-fire. He said July 6 that the U.S. should take advantage of the current lull in Vietnam fighting to "go into a *de facto* cease-fire."

A call for a "standstill cease-fire" by all sides in Vietnam—advocated by the National Committee for a political Settlement in Vietnam—was indorsed June 15 by Cyrus R. Vance, a former U.S. representative at the Paris talks.

Sen. John Stennis (D., Miss.), chairman of the Senate Armed Services Committee and long-time advocate of military victory in Vietnam, said July 6 that the U.S. might have to "draw a line" in Vietnam, possibly around Saigon, and protect that area "and all those who want to come behind" the line. "We cannot continue this indefinitely," he said, "fighting over the terrain of that entire country." Drawing a line, he said, might be a way to attain "possible ultimate termination" of the pattern of recurrent battles without "substantive gain."

Defense Secy. Laird said July 15 that he thought "we've certainly turned the corner" toward peace in Vietnam. He gave their assessment in response to questions before the Senate Foreign Relations Committee. Laird told the committee that while there had been no change in the current orders of U.S. field commanders in Vietnam to maintain maximum pressure on the enemy, "the whole matter is under review." He said orders had been given by Pres. Nixon "to make the reduction of American casualties" a primary objective of the U.S. commander in Vietnam. He added: "I anticipate other changes"; the effort to shift more of the combat burden to Vietnamese forces was proceeding while U.S.

forces were being reduced.

Senate Democratic leader Mike Mansfield, addressing a party dinner June 26, had said Senate Democrats would "uphold the President's hand" in his effort to end the war, "but we cannot and will not acquiesce in the indefinite absence of peace." Mansfield said July 18 that he thought the U.S. should get out of South Vietnam and Thailand "lock, stock and barrel."

In the House July 22, Rep. Paul Findley (R., Ill.) called on fellow Republicans "to reinforce the President's decision to disengage and to broaden public support for it." "What the President needs," he said, "even more than a response from Hanoi, is a response from the American body politic and especially from Republicans in Congress" so he could "proceed forthrightly and confidently with disengagement."

An attempt to express unified support for Pres. Nixon's Vietnam policies took place in the Senate July 22. The move was made by 7 Republicans and one Democrat, many of them critics of the war. The effort was organized by Sen. Charles H. Percy (R., Ill.), who urged North Vietnam to respond to U.S. troop withdrawals. "There is nothing to be gained from prolonging the conflict," he said. He cautioned the enemy that the American people backed Nixon's opposition to a unilateral American withdrawal. Sen. George D. Aiken (R., Vt.) urged the enemy "to state frankly whether they actually desire peace and will cooperate with us so that our future policy may be guided accordingly." Senators joining them were Claiborne Pell (D., R.I.), John Sherman Cooper (R., Ky.), Jacob K. Javits (R., N.Y.), Charles E. Goodell (R., N.Y.), George Murphy (R., Calif.) and James B. Pearson (R., Kan.).

Nixon's 'Asia Doctrine'

Pres. Nixon left Washington at the end of July for a global tour that included visits to the Phillipines, Indonesia, Thailand, India, Pakistan, Rumania and Britain, and he made an unannounced visit to Vietnam. In the course of the Asian part of the tour, the President enunciated what was in effect a reformulation of American policy in Asia.

Nixon outlined his Asian policy during an informal news conference (with no direct quotation permitted) July 25 on Guam, a stopover point on his way to Manila. As reported, Nixon said:

The U.S. would not become involved in more wars like that in Vietnam; it would reduce its military commitments throughout Asia; it would keep its treaty commitments and watch Asian developments. He indicated that while U.S. military assistance to Asia would be reduced, new forms of economic aid to the region were being considered. The President opposed military involvements (such as the Vietnam war) that tended to generate emotional and economic discord at home. As for the problem of military defense, except for the threat of a major power involving nuclear weapons, the Asian nations themselves would have to deal with internal subversion or external aggression, Nixon said. Nixon reportedly expressed doubt that non-Communist Asian nations would soon be able to form collective security arrangements, but he was optimistic about signs of economic progress in these nations and the apparent decline in their vulnerability to Communist ideology. The President said he might order a reduction of military operations in Vietnam if this would further negotiations to end the war.

Nixon publicly restated his Asian policy in a speech made on his arrival in Manila July 26. He said that "if peace is to come from Asia—and I emphasize this point—the United States will play its part and provide its fair share," "But," he continued, "peace in Asia cannot come from the United States. It must come from Asia. The people of Asia, the governments of Asia, they are the ones who must lead the way to peace in Asia." The crux of Nixon's message to Philippine leaders, according to Presidential aides, was that the responsibility for Asian security must be borne primarily by Asians themselves. While the U.S. realized the importance of Asia and was determined to honor its treaty commitments, it would shun future wars of the Vietnam type and reduce to Asian military commitments.

In an extemporaneous speech shortly after his arrival July 28 in Bangkok, where he and Mrs. Nixon were greeted by King Phumiphol Aduldet and Queen Sirikit, Nixon spoke of the U.S. "obligations" to Thailand under SEATO (Southeast Asia Treaty Organization) and said the U.S. "will stand proudly with Thailand against those who might threaten it from abroad or from within." The statement seemed in conflict with his statement on Asian policy July 25, which stressed that defense problems would be handled primarily by Asian nations themselves. But his Bangkok remark was generally interpreted as public reassurance to an ally deeply involved in Vietnam. White House Press Secy. Ronald L. Ziegler noted later July 28 that "Thailand has not asked for any troops and the President is not talking about sending troops here." An "additional [Presidential] statement" also was released later, although it had been prepared before the extemporaneous remarks. It said the U.S. determination to honor its commitments was "fully consistent with our conviction that the nations of Asia can and must increasingly shoulder the responsibility for achieving peace and progress in the area." "If domination by the aggressor can destroy the freedom of a nation," it said, "too much dependence on a protector can erode its dignity."

Nixon and his national security adviser, Henry A. Kissinger, conferred July 29 with Premier Thanom Kittikachorn and Foreign Min. Thanat Khoman. Presidential aides later issued a statement saying that Thai leaders had authorized announcement of complete agreement with Nixon's view that they and other threatened Asian countries must combat subversion with their own forces and had not requested commitment of U.S. ground forces to a counter-insurgency effort.

During a 5½-hour visit to South Vietnam July 30, Nixon conferred with Pres. Nguyen Van Thieu and visited American troops of the First Infantry Division at Dian, about 12 miles south of Saigon. After his meeting with Thieu, Nixon said that "we have gone as far now as we can or should go in opening the door to peace, and now it is time for the other side to respond." In his remarks to the troops, Nixon described the war as "one of America's finest hours." He told GIs they were doing their job and assured them that "we are going to try to do ours to see that you didn't fight in vain." While the war was "the most difficult any army has ever fought" and it was "the first time in our history when we have had a lack of understanding of why we are here, what the war is all about," he said, "what happens in Vietnam, how this war is ended, may well determine what happens to peace and freedom in the world."

En route to India, Nixon told newsmen July 31 that he had made the trip to Vietnam to demonstrate solidarity with the Thieu government. Saigon, he said, was not going to become Ho Chi Minh City, South Vietnam's governmental institutions were strong and Thieu was a capable and excellent political leader— one of the 4 or 5 best in the world.

Senate Democratic leader Mike Mansfield July 28 had expressed support for Nixon's Asian policy, as outlined at his Guam news conference. "He is not advocating isolationism," Mansfield said in a Senate speech, "nor is he advocating the abandonment of Asia." He added: "His intent, I believe, is to avoid future Vietnams but, at the same time, to render what assistance is feasible and possible to the nations of Asia."

Statements on the Vietnam policy also were delivered in the Senate July 28 by Sens. Jacob K. Javits (R., N.Y.) and Thomas F. Eagleton (D., Mo.). Javits supported Nixon's "basic, substantive changes in Vietnam policy" and urged "a definite timetable for the withdrawal of all U.S. combat troops by the end of 1970." Eagleton urged a move toward an immediate cease-fire and, if necessary, a "major, unilateral de-escalation."

Sen. George McGovern said in the Senate Aug. 1 that Nixon possibly had been afflicted by "a new strain of Asian virus" that was responsible for his comments that: The Apollo 11 feat (man's first step on the moon) was surpassed only by the creation of the universe; the Vietnam war represented "our finest hour"; the U.S. would go to war on behalf of Thailand; and Nguyen Van Thieu was a great statesman.

FIGHTING CONTINUES

In South Vietnam, sharp fighting continued through April, following the end of the Viet Cong spring offensive, as U.S. forces tried to clear the field of enemy troops.

U.S. Helicopters Used Widely, Losses Heavy

At least 76 U.S. helicopters were lost between Apr. 1 and May 5, U.S. military officials reported May 5. 50 of the aircraft were shot down by enemy ground fire, and 26 were destroyed in rocket, mortar and ground attacks, in collisions with other helicopters or in other mishaps. 17 of them were shot down between Apr. 22 and 29. In the worst helicopter disaster of the war, a big U.S. 'copter crashed and burned 75 miles north of Saigon May 6. 2 American crewmen and 32 South Vietnamese soldiers were killed. The crash was attributed to mechanical failure. 3 'copter collisions claimed the lives of 36 allied military personnel: 8 Americans and 8 South Vietnamese Apr. 23 in a landing zone 9 miles south of the demilitarized zone; 12 U.S. Marines May 2; 8 American crewmen May 4 at a point 18 miles northeast of Saigon.

A U.S. helicopter gunship accidentally killed 5 government militiamen and a U.S. military adviser Apr. 23 during a sweep in the Central Highlands, 30 miles north of Banmethout.

In one of the bloodiest battles of the war, U.S. infantrymen and aircraft killed 213 enemy troops Apr. 26 about 45 miles northwest of Saigon, near the Cambodian border. American losses were described as unusually light for the severity of the action —one man killed and one wounded. The action occurred during a Communist attack on a U.S. base deliberately set up to attract enemy fire. The attackers, numbering about 400 men, suffered the heavy losses when they attempted to storm the position's barbed wire perimeter after pounding it with mortars and rockets.

U.S. B-52s carried out one of the heaviest raids of the war in South Vietnam Apr. 24, dropping almost 3,000 tons of bombs on suspected enemy concentrations along the Cambodian frontier 70 miles northwest of Saigon. About 100 planes from bases in Thailand and Guam centered the strike on an area regarded as the Communists' main supply and concentration point directly threatening Saigon. The B-52s struck the same area Apr. 25 as well as other suspected Communist strongpoints west of Kontum in the Central Highlands.

The U.S. command reported Apr. 26 that American planes and artillery that day had attacked North Vietnamese gun positions in Cambodia on the South Vietnamese border. The attack followed a Communist assault on a U.S. artillery base on the frontier. About 400 North Vietnamese were repulsed with a loss of 157 killed. U.S. infantrymen were reported to have repulsed a North Vietnamese attack in the same area Apr. 27, killing about 100 of the enemy. U.S. losses totaled 10 killed in the 90-minute clash 8 miles from the Cambodian frontier.

Troops at another U.S. artillery base 12 miles from the Cambodian border—Camp Carolyn—drove off an attack by about 800 North Vietnamese Apr. 28 after 6 hours of hand-to-hand fighting, air strikes and artillery barrages. Enemy losses totaled 101 killed and 33 captured. 9 Americans were killed and 62 wounded. The attackers succeeded in penetrating the base's barbed wire defenses at 2 points and held 3 of the perimeter bunkers and one of the gun positions for nearly 2 hours.

U.S. Marines killed 129 North Vietnamese May 9 in an area 18 miles southwest of Danang. The clashes erupted after the enemy force was spotted by a Marine observer. The fighting continued sporadically for 12 hours as the Americans pursued the fleeing North Vietnamese. U.S. losses totaled 6 killed and 12 wounded.

North Vietnamese and Viet Cong forces launched widespread rocket attacks against allied military and civilian targets throughout South Vietnam May 11-12. The 159 shellings, accompanied by about half a dozen ground assaults, were described as the largest since the Tet offensive in 1968. Sources in Paris speculated that the assault was partly intended to show that the Viet Cong's just proposed 10-point peace proposal was not a sign of military weakness. A U.S. command spokesman said May 13 that it was still too early to determine whether the attacks were the start of a threatened summer offensive.

A captured Viet Cong document, made public by allied officials May 9, had hinted that such a drive would start at the end of May, possibly May 19 to celebrate the 79th birthday of Ho Chi Minh. The document said the attack would be "aimed at forcing the Americans to adopt a policy 'in our direction.' " "We should attack the enemy to drive him into a deadlock and compel him to adopt a settlement for the war in our favor," the statement said. The Viet Cong paper said that the post-Tet offensive had forced Pres. Nixon "to adopt a clearer policy for Vietnam." But it conceded that the drive had failed in several respects. The front acknowledged that the offensive was "not very successful in the cities and suburban areas" and that "there was not a single mass destruction of enemy forces."

The May 11-12 Communist attacks were followed May 13 by 14 more assaults, including one in which 5 rockets hit the Tansonnhut airport in Saigon. In the previous 2 days, the enemy had fired from 10 to 300 shells in 70 of the attacks and fewer than 10 in the others. In addition to military targets, 7 provincial capitals and 21 district towns came under fire. 12 terror attacks against civilians in Saigon resulted in the killing of 8 persons and the wounding of 34, the allied command reported. 6 other civilians had been killed and 41 wounded in Bentre in one of 9 terror attacks in the Mekong delta. Initial reports said that 500 North Vietnamese had been killed in the May 11-12 ground fighting. In one of the battles, American forces killed 102 North Vietnamese southwest of Pleiku in the Central Highlands.

Battle of Apbia (Hamburger Hill)

U.S. and South Vietnamese forces captured Apbia Mountain in the Ashau Valley May 20 in one of the bloodiest battles of the war. But 8 days later they abandoned the mountain.

A total of 597 North Vietnamese were reported killed in the original fighting for the 3,000-foot peak. U.S. casualties were at least 50 killed and about 270 wounded. The battle was part of a 2,800-man allied sweep of the Ashau Valley that had started May 10.

Apbia Mountain, about one mile east of the Laotian border, had come under heavy allied air strikes, artillery barrages and 10 infantry assaults since May 10. The Communist stronghold was captured in the 11th attack, when 1,000 troops of the U.S. 101st Airborne Division and 400 South Vietnamese fought their way to the summit, encountering only rear-guard resistance from North Vietnamese entrenched in tunnels and bunkers. The bulk of the enemy force, estimated at 900 men, had been withdrawn during the night, leaving behind 250 men. The enemy troops that abandoned the mountain were pursued by the allied soldiers toward the Laotian frontier. U.S. soldiers killed 11 more North Vietnamese in scattered clashes around the mountain May 22.

In the first 9 days of fighting for the peak, U.S. troops had reached the top 3 times only to be thrown back by small-arms fire and rocket-propelled grenades.

The allied operation in the Ashau Valley had been disclosed May 15. The purpose of the drive was to cut off the North Vietnamese in the valley and to stop infiltration from Laos menacing Hué to the northeast and the U.S. base at Danang to the southeast. U.S. paratroopers, pushing northeast, had found the Communist force not in the Valley but on Apbia Mountain, referred to as "Hamburger Hill" by U.S. troops. The heavy fighting in the Ashau Valley and elsewhere was reflected in the high casualty figures for May 11-17 released by the U.S. high command May 22. U.S. forces suffered 430 fatalities, their highest weekly death toll since the week ended Mar. 1. 527 South Vietnamese and 5,686 North Vietnamese and Viet Cong were slain May 11-17. In the same period, 2,185 Americans and 1,643 government soldiers were wounded.

Danang was shelled by Communist rockets May 14. A government spokesman reported 22 South Vietnamese civilians killed and 21 wounded in the attack. U.S. troops killed at least 100 Viet Cong and North Vietnamese soldiers May 16 in 4 separate battles in the areas of Saigon, Bencat, Ankhe and Danang. U.S. losses were one killed and 3 wounded, all in a Central Highlands battle 6 miles northeast of Ankhe. The Americans attacked enemy bunkers and later found the bodies of 30 Communist soldiers. A force of more than 1,500 Viet Cong and North Vietnamese troops May 18 attacked a U.S. artillery base and a South Vietnamese army camp about half a mile apart near Xuanloc, 38 miles east of Saigon. The enemy was diven off after 5 hours of intense fighting. 14 U.S. soldiers were killed and 39 wounded. The bodies of 24 North Vietnamese were found around the artillery base. Saigon claimed that its forces had killed 54 North Vietnamese in the assault on the government camp. Government losses were put at 4 killed and 14 wounded. The government camp, defended by about 2,400 troops, was hit by more than 200 rockets and mortar shells before it came under assault by 1,200 enemy troops, a South Vietnamese army spokesman said. At the same time, about 400 North Vietnamese soldiers were attacking the U.S. artillery base, and some penetrated the outer defenses of the base with explosive charges. All were killed or driven back.

The U.S. command May 23 reported 15 U.S. planes and 27 helicopters lost over South Vietnam May 11-17. The aircraft were shot down, destroyed on the ground or lost to other causes. Since Jan. 1, 1961, the U.S. had lost 2,713 planes and 2,675 helicopters in Vietnam at a cost of approximately $5.6 billion.

The U.S.' initiation of the operation and the high casualties suffered by American forces in the Apbia battle and elsewhere prompted fresh Congressional criticism of the conduct of the war.

Sen. Edward M. Kennedy denounced the U.S. fight for Apbia as "senseless and irresponsible." In a Senate speech May 20, Kennedy called for "a new order to the field cutting back these offensive operations." "Pres. Nixon has told us, without question," Kennedy said, "that we seek no military victory, that we seek only peace. How then can we justify sending our boys against a hill a dozen times or more, until soldiers themselves question the madness of the action?" The level of U.S. field operations, he said, "runs opposite to our stated intentions and goals in Paris."

An immediate rebuttal to Kennedy's speech was given by Senate Republican whip Hugh Scott, who told the Senate he would not try to "2d-guess" battlefield tactics. "If our military are told to contend for a hill, it is part of the strategy which is essential to maintaining the military posture while we talk for peace." Kennedy's remarks were denounced again in the Senate May 26 by Sens. Margaret Chase Smith (R., Me.), John G. Tower (R., Tex.) and Harry Byrd Jr. (D., Va.).

In a report from Saigon May 21, a military spokesman defended the Apbia battle as neccessary to cut the enemy's infiltration route and prevent an assault on Hué. "We are not fighting for terrain as such," he said. "We are going after the enemy." This view was supported in Washington May 21 by Lt. Gen. Lewis W. Walt, Marine Corps assistant commandant, who called the mountain a primary strategic site and said the enemy could not mount an assault on Hué "without holding that hill."

In Phubai, South Vietnam May 22, Maj. Gen. Melvin Zais, commander of the 101st Airborne Division (involved in the Apbia fight), defended the struggle as a "tremendous victory." He said he knew "for sure" Kennedy "wasn't here" when he denounced the battle. Zais said his orders were "to destroy the enemy forces" in the Ashau Valley; he did not have any orders to reduce casualties by avoiding difficult battles. "We found the enemy" on Apbia, "and that is where we fought him." The mountain's "only tactical significance" was the fact that enemy troops "were on it. The hill itself had no tactical significance." There was good military truth" in going into the Ashau Valley, he said, and "not one iota of truth in the allegation that it was military egotism." Zais' remarks were cited at a White House news briefing May 23 by Press Secy. Ronald Ziegler, who indicated that the fight for Apbia was in response to enemy activity and was not a change "in our tactics or military strategy." U.S. combat "initiatives" had "not increased" the previous week, he said, and "our studies confirm that casualty rates are largely the result of enemy-initiated actions."

Senate Democratic Leader Mike Mensfield disagreed May 24 with Ziegler's assessment. He said: "We are not just holding the line when we continue search and destroy missions, when we send B-52s over Cambodia. . . . The more we increase our military pressure in Vietnam the less pressure there will be in Paris for a peaceful settlement of the war."

Defense Secy. Melvin Laird said May 25 that a policy of keeping "maximum military pressure on the enemy consistent with the lowest possible casualties" had been set by both Presidents Nixon and Johnson. Laird told a luncheon group May 22 that the enemy had coordinated its 10-point peace proposal in Paris with "a significantly higher level" of attacks against military and civilian targets in Vietnam.

White House sources were made available to newsmen by the President May 26 to buttress contentions that there had been no intensification of large or small ground operations by the Nixon Administration and that the level of casualties depended on enemy, not U.S., initiatives.

Kennedy returned to his theme in addressing the New Democratic Coalition in Washington May 24. Deploring the "cruelty and savagery of the past week," he said: "It would have been immoral if we remained silent" about "an unjustified war, an immoral war." "We do have a responsibility in demilitarizing that war and bringing our boys home." The war "contaminates our atmosphere. . . . It separates our young." Another speaker, Sen. George S. McGovern, commended Kennedy "for raising his voice . . . eloquently . . . in protest against a truly senseless slaughter."

Troops of the 101st Airborne Division were reported to have abandoned Apbia Mountain May 28. A division spokesman said the Americans "have completed their search of the mountain and now are continuing their reconnaissance-in-force mission throughout the Ashau Valley." Another U.S. officer had commented that "we feel we've gotten everything out of this mountain that we're going to get "

The divisional report of the withdrawal from the mountain was contradicted by a U.S. command statement issued in Saigon later May 28. The command statement denied any implication that American soldiers had quit Apbia. " . . . We still have a sizable force on the mountain, and they still have tactical control of the top," the command said. A U.S. Defense Department spokesman in Washington was quoted as saying that "U.S. forces are still in position in substantial numbers on Hill 937 [Apbia], and the helopad there is still in use." The abandonment of Apbia was confirmed, however, by a newsman who flew over the peak May 29. He said the nearest unit of the 101st Division was more than a half mile away.

Nearly 3 weeks later U.S. intelligence sources reported June 17 that North Vietnamese troops had reoccupied Apbia Mountain. An estimated 1,000 North Vietnamese were back on the peak.

Maj. Gen. John M. Wright Jr., commander of the 101st Airborne Division, said he was "prepared to commit everything that it takes, up to an entire division" if it became necessary to resume the battle for the mountain. Wright said June 19, however, that "to the best of my knowledge there were no enemy troops on the peak of Apbia Mountain but ... they remained on the surrounding hills and ridgelines." "We have every reason to believe that the entire hill mass ... is part of a North Vietnamese base area," Wright said.

Fighting Elsewhere

The U.S. command disclosed May 26 the launching of 2 U.S. offensives earlier in the month in the northern provinces of South Vietnam. The report said 142 North Vietnamese had been killed in the 2 operations thus far. The first drive had begun May 8 about 18 miles east of the Laotian border and 10 miles south of the demilitarized zone. About 1,000 U.S. 3d Marine Division troops were reported to have killed 29 North Vietnamese in the initial stages of the offensive. Most of the enemy casualties were accounted for in the 2d U.S. push, launched May 16 in a coastal area 45 miles south of Danang. Troops of the U.S. 101st Airborne Division were reported to have killed 113 North Vietnamese. U.S. casualties totaled 26 killed and 102 wounded. This drive was aimed at relieving pressure on the key provincial capital of Tamky, scene of sharp fighting in recent weeks.

Saigon reported May 24 that government forces had suffered substantial losses in 2 heavy battles fought the previous day north and east of Saigon. In the first engagement, 20 South Vietnamese troops were killed and 40 wounded in a clash with an estimated 450-man enemy force east of the capital. In the day-long fight 40 enemy troops were slain, the government said. The Saigon report said that 23 government soldiers were killed and 40 wounded in the other battle about 95 miles southwest of Saigon. Viet Cong losses totaled 35 killed.

Allied-Communist clashes continued despite 2 separate truces honoring Buddha's birthday. U.S. and South Vietnamese forces observed a 24-hour cease-fire from 6 a.m. May 30 to 6 a.m. May 31. A Viet Cong-proclaimed truce started at 7 a.m. May 29 and expired at 7 a.m. May 31. The U.S. command reported June 1 that the Communists had initiated 158 incidents during the allied truce. Of these, 85 were considered significant and resulted in the death of 13 Americans and the wounding of 62 others. Enemy losses were put at 80 killed.

U.S. officials June 17 disclosed the launching of a combined U.S.-South Vietnamese search-and-destroy operation June 8 in the Ashau Valley, 28 miles southwest of Hué. 21 Americans were reported killed and 130 wounded in the offensive thus far. The drive had started the day another operation in the Ashau Valley, including the fight for Apbia, ended with the reported loss of 113 Americans killed and 627 wounded. In the action in the Ashau Valley, North Vietnamese forces twice attacked the Third Brigade headquarters of the 101st Airborne Division atop a 2,000-foot peak just east of Apbia Mountain June 14 and 15. In the first assault, 40 to 50 enemy soldiers managed to break through the base's defenses but were repelled with a loss of 31 men killed. American losses totaled 18 killed and 47 wounded. In the 2d attack, June 15, 51 North Vietnamese were slain in another futile attempt to storm the division's headquarters.

Sporadic but sharp fighting continued in other parts of South Vietnam earlier in June. *Among major developments:*

● 5 civilians were killed and 32 were wounded by 2 Communist attacks in Saigon June 2 and 5. In the first incident, a Viet Cong rocket crashed into a densely populated area of the capital, killing 2 South Vietnamese and wounding 25. The 3 other Vietnamese civilians were killed June 5 when explosives were detonated in the downtown section.

● U.S. military authorities reported 399 Communist troops killed in a series of battles with U.S. and South Vietnamese forces along the Cambodian border in Tayninh and Binhlong provinces June 6-8. The fighting was marked by Communist attempts to overrun a U.S. artillery support base 5 miles from the Cambodian frontier.

● Communist forces shelled Danang and nearby U.S. military positions June 7 while terrorists raced through the city hurling grenades and explosive charges at buildings. 5 persons were killed, including 4 U.S. airmen at the Danang air base, and 37 were wounded by a barrage of nearly 40 rockets and mortar shells. One of the shells struck and sank a South Vietnamese tanker in the Danang River.

● U.S. B-52s carried out 10 air strikes against Communist targets in the Central Highlands and northwest of Saigon June 10. In 7 of the missions flown northwest of Saigon, the B-52s "pounded base camps, enemy activity, bunker complexes and weapons positions," the U.S. command reported.

● 2 U.S. bases south of Danang came under heavy Viet Cong and North Vietnamese assault June 11. 14 U.S. soldiers were killed and 32 wounded in one attack against an infantry base at Tamky, 35 miles south of Danang. About 30 Viet Cong broke through the base's defense perimeter and fought the defenders hand-to-hand. 27 Viet Cong were killed. In the 2d assault, about 500 North Vietnamese attempted to storm a U.S. Marine camp at Anhoa, 22 miles south of Danang, but were thrown back in a 3-hour fight in which U.S. planes and artillery came to the aid of the beleaguered Marines. U.S. losses totaled 2 dead and 28 wounded. The bodies of 35 North Vietnamese were found on the battle-field.

● Communist rockets June 13 struck Danang and a U.S. Navy hospital on its outskirts. Several shells struck homes around a Navy pier in Danang, killing 10 civilians and wounding 12. The Bienhoa air base, 15 miles north of Saigon, also was struck by enemy rockets June 13. 10 South Vietnamese soldiers were killed and 13 wounded.

● Troops of the Thai Black Panther Division June 16 repelled 500 Viet Cong soldiers who 3 times assaulted their base 20 miles east of Saigon. The defenders, aided by supporting fire of U.S. jets, helicopters and artillery, killed 212 of the attackers. Thai losses totaled 6 killed and 7 wounded.

● The North Vietnamese news agency reported June 20 that the U.S. had flown 400 "manned and unmanned" missions and raids over North Vietnam June 1-15. The agency said that "300 blast bombs, 50 time bombs and 19,600 steel pellet bombs" had beed dropped.

North Vietnamese Defense Min. Vo Nguyen Giap said June 21 that since the beginning of the Vietnam war North Vietnam had been attacked 100,000 times by U.S. artillery, aircraft and naval vessels. Giap claimed that one million tons of bombs had been dropped on North Vietnam and that the U.S. had used every weapon available to it except the nuclear bomb.

Siege of Benhet

The U.S. Special Forces camp at Benhet was besieged June 23 by North Vietnamese forces using artillery and mortars. The camp, 288 miles northeast of Saigon and 6 miles from the junction of the Cambodian, Laotian and South Vietnamese borders in the Central Highlands, had been under daily artillery bombardment since early May. A U.S. military spokesman said Benhet had been surrounded by an estimated 2,000-man force and had been completely cut off. The base was defended by 250 U.S. soldiers and 750 South Vietnamese *montagnard* irregulars.

Under heavy artillery and mortar fire, a supply convoy, led by a column of tanks and armored cars, reached Benhet June 24. Despite allied counter-artillery fire, air strikes and pressure from government troops in the area, the North Vietnamese continued their bombardment. A U.S. colonel said June 26 that if the enemy wanted to take Benhet they could probably do so, but only with severe loss of life. A U.S. military spokesman said June 26 that 100 U.S. servicemen had been killed or wounded at Benhet since June 1. It was also reported that 180 South Vietnamese troops were airlifted into Benhet June 26. A total of 445 artillery shells fell on Benhet June 27, more than double any previous day's total, but the U.S. command reported no fatalities. 40 tons of supplies had been airlifted into the camp the 2 previous days. According to the *Washington Post* June 28, the U.S. command in Saigon considered the Benhet campaign a test of the ability of South Vietnamese forces against the North Vietnamese and Viet Cong. An additional 1,500-man South Vietnamese force began new sweeps around Benhet June 28. U.S. units remained in an advisory role and supplied only air and artillery support.

Col. Nguyen Bao Lien, commander of the Benhet base, said at a news conference June 30 that he had used the camp as "bait" to draw the enemy into a trap. He said: "I wanted to get them [the enemy] into a single 'kill zone' where I could concentrate massive artillery and airpower. This plan has been a military secret until now, but since the operation is almost over I can disclose the truth." U.S. advisers at Benhet expressed skepticism at Lien's statement.

Allied commanders at Benhet said July 2 that the Benhet siege had ended. According to intelligence reports, the attacking force had moved west toward mountain sanctuaries in Cambodia and Laos. During the Benhet campaign, which actually had begun in early May, an estimated 3,600 enemy soldiers were killed, most of them North Vietnamese. Allied deaths were estimated at 350. Reversing their position July 5, allied military officials in Saigon said the Benhet battle had been a major victory. Previously, the allied command had described the battle as simply another engagement in the Central Highlands.

(The U.S. military command in Saigon had said July 3 that it had conducted bombing raids in Cambodia to defend Benhet. According to the London *Times* July 4, this was the first time the U.S. had admitted bombing enemy troops in Cambodia. The admission came one day after State Secy. Rogers had announced that the U.S. and Cambodia had resumed diplomatic relations.)

In sporadic fighting during this period, these developments took place :
● The U.S. military command reported increased fighting below the demilitarized zone (DMZ) June 17-21. An estimated 250 enemy troops were reported killed during the 5-day period, while 30 U.S. sevicemen were reported killed and 71 wounded. No South Vietnamese casualties were reported.
● A force of 10,000 enemy troops was reported to have been sent to surround the provincial capital of Anloc, 60 miles north of Saigon. U.S. air and ground

forces moved in June 23 to meet the threat of an attack.

● The U.S. command in Saigon June 20 claimed that 403 enemy soldiers had been killed during a drive June 19-20 against the provincial capital Tayninh, 50 miles northwest of Saigon and 12 miles from the Cambodian border. Another 72 enemy troops were reported killed during an unsuccessful attack on a U.S. artillery camp 15 miles north of Tayninh. U.S. casualties were listed as 20 killed and 50 wounded, while South Vietnamese casualties were 14 killed and more than 20 wounded. The fighting around Tayninh continued through the 3d week of June.

● U.S. Marines of the 9th Regiment repulsed a North Vietnamese attack on their camp a mile south of the abandoned Khesanh base June 24. The marines claimed 29 enemy soldiers were killed and their own losses were 3 dead and 13 wounded.

(The U.S. Navy June 25 transferred 64 river patrol gunboats to the South Vietnamese navy. The boats were valued at $18.2 million. The transaction reportedly represented the largest single transfer of U.S. equipment to the Saigon government. Since June 1968, the U.S. had transferred 167 vessels, most of them heavily armed, 50-to-60 foot patrol and assault boats, to South Vietnam. The 64 vessels raised the total number of boats in the South Vietnamese navy to more than 600. Gen. Creighton W. Abrams, commander of U.S. forces in Vietnam, signed over the vessels to Gen. Cao Van Vien, chief of staff of South Vietnamese forces, in a ceremony on the Saigon River water-front.)

Summer Lull

State Secy. William P. Rogers reported July 2 that Communist infiltration and combat activities in South Vietnam had decreased since mid-June. At his 3d Washington news conference, Rogers said it was "too early" to determine the significance of the reduced enemy activities. He said that the lull could affect U.S. troop withdrawals and that "if we find the other side is not fighting as they have been, then we will have to review our military planning."

After Rogers' news confereuce, Defense Department officials said enemy forces had mounted only about 25 ambushes and attacks in Vietnam during the past week, the lowest level since late April. In March and May, the officials said, enemy attacks had reached nearly 200 a week. They also reported that about 10,000 North Vietnamese soldiers had infiltrated into South Vietnam during June. But, according to the officials, Hanoi had been placing fewer soldiers at the North Vietnamese end of the infiltration trails in the last 2 or 3 months. No statistics were given. U.S. sources in Saigon had reported June 28 that North Vietnamese infiltration into South Vietnam in January-May was 40% lower than in the corresponding period of 1968. According to the U.S. figures, North Vietnamese were infiltrating at a rate of 10,000 a month in 1969, compared with 17,000 a month in 1968.

The U.S. military command in Saigon reported July 3 that 3 North Vietnamese regiments (about 7,500 men) had withdrawn across the demilitarized zone (DMZ) during the past 3 weeks. The units were identified as the 27th, 36th and 138th Regiments. A U.S. spokesman said "there is no military reason behind the pulback. It could be an answer to our own withdrawal of 25,000 men, or even a response to our proposal in Paris for the neutralization of the DMZ. But at this point it is impossible to tell."

Maj. Gen. Ormond Simpson, commander of the First Marine Division, based in Danang, said at a news conference July 4 that fighting in the northern provinces of South Vietnam was at its lowest level in 8 months. He added that, for the first time in 17 months, the only enemy troops his soldiers had encountered south of Danang were Viet Cong. The U.S. military command reported July 4 and 5 that Communist mortar and rocket attacks had continued during the 2 days, but only a few of these were considered significant. Intelligence reports also showed that incidents against South Vietnamese military units and civilians had decreased markedly. The fighting, however, picked up July 6 as the Communists shelled 43 targets during the night; 21 of the attacks were considered significant. Casualties and damage was reported minor. More than 500 U.S. air strikes, an average number, were flown July 6. There was another lull in the ground fighting July 7.

The U.S. military command in Saigon reported July 10 that U.S. casualties during the week ended July 5 had been at the lowest level since the 2d week of January, when 151 men had been killed. The U.S. reported 153 soldiers killed in action, 772 men wounded and requiring hospitalization. The week earlier, 241 soldiers had been killed. The decrease in casualties was attributed to the combat lull. 247 South Vietnamese soldiers were killed and 586 wounded during the week ended July 5; this was the lowest South Vietnamese toll in 2 months. The U.S. reported 2,331 enemy deaths, compared with 3,333 during the week ended June 28.

Despite the lull, sporadic but sharp fighting continued throughout South Vietnam. 5 rockets were fired into the Saigon riverfront district July 8, touching off a large blaze. This was the 2d rocket attack in the district in 3 days. 50 miles south of Danang, a Viet Cong ambush July 8 killed 9 U.S. servicemen and wounded 7 others.

Gen. Earle G. Wheeler, chairman of the Joint Chiefs of Staff, visited South Vietnam July 16-20 on a fact-finding mission for Pres. Nixon. Wheeler specifically sought to determine whether there was any political significance to the lull in Communist battle activity. Wheeler said he saw none when he gave a preliminary assessment in Saigon on concluding his tour July 20. Wheeler explained: "The enemy's level of combat has always been on a cyclic basis. In other words, he has in the past launched offensives and thereafter withdrawn into sanctuaries in Laos and Cambodia and the remote areas of the country, and then come back again after he's had a chance to refit, replace his troops and retrain them. Therefore, I would be unable to allege any political motivation to the present low level of combat." Wheeler took issue with a report that North Vietnam had withdrawn 3 divisions from near the DMZ. The North Vietnamese, he said, "habitually have followed a cyclic pattern" of withdrawal. Therefore, no orders had been issued "changing the operational directives" of U.S. troops in the DMZ area, Wheeler said. Wheeler conceded that the Communist infiltration rate into South Vietnam had dropped, but he said "it has been cyclic in the past, and I would ... say that I'll have to wait another few months before I know exactly what the enemy is up to." He returned to Washington July 22 and described the situation in South Vietnam as "good." He said the program to improve South Vietnam's forces so they can assume greater combat responsibility "is on schedule—as a matter of fact, ahead of schedule in some areas."

The U.S. command reported July 24 that 182 American soldiers had been killed July 13-19, compared with 148 the previous week. South Vietnamese headquarters reported that 295 government troops had been killed in the same weekly period, a decline of 16% over the previous week. Allied headquarters reported that Communist combat deaths had dropped to 2,203 July 13-19 from 2,369 the previous week.

Among military actions between July 17 and 28:

● The outskirts of Saigon were hit by 4 to 6 Communist rockets July 17,

killing 2 Vietnamese civilians and wounding 2 others.
● U.S. troops killed 27 Communist troops in a 4-hour battle 6 miles northeast of Tayninh July 18. There were no American casualties.
● The 9th Infantry Division base at Dongtam, about 40 miles south of Saigon, was hit by 20 Communist rockets July 19. 6 American soldiers and 3 Vietnamese civilians were wounded. The base was among 33 allied positions and towns struck by rockets and mortars in 24 hours.
● The U.S. command announced July 19 that U.S. Marines July 16 had concluded a 2-month sweep against an enemy force in Quangtri Province, south of the demilitarized zone. Losses totaled 697 North Vietnamese and 131 Americans killed.
● 27 enemy rocket and mortar assaults on allied bases and towns occurred July 20. U.S. losses were 3 killed and 13 wounded. The Bienhoa air base, 15 miles north of Saigon, was among the targets hit.
● U.S. and government troops killed 212 Communist soldiers in scattered actions July 25-27.
● In the biggest battle since the lull began, U.S. troops July 28 killed 53 enemy soldiers in day-long fighting 25 miles north of Saigon. Losses suffered by the 2d Brigade of the 25th Infantry Division totaled 3 dead and 14 wounded. More than 1,000 U.S. troops, supported by tanks and armored personnel carriers, surrounded a suspected Viet Cong stronghold, known as the Citadel, following reports that the Communists had massed there to replenish their supplies. The Americans fought their way through hedgerows and bunkers before overwhelming the Viet Cong force. The enemy was identified as elements of 2 battalions of the 268th Viet Cong Regiment.

In a further reduction of American combat commitment, troops of the First Brigade of the 9th Infantry Division July 23 turned over a fire support base at Cailay in the Mekong delta to South Vietnam's 7th Division.

Fall Offensive

The battlefield lull was punctuated by a sharp outbreak of Communist-initiated attacks at the beginning of August. The most intense assault since May 11 was mounted Aug. 12 with rocket, mortar and infantry attacks on 150 allied cities, towns and bases. The heaviest attacks were centered on Anloc, a provincial capital 60 miles north of Saigon; Quanloi, northeast of Anloc; Tayninh, northwest of Saigon; and Locninh, 70 miles north. Heavy assaults also were directed at U.S. military positions in the Danang and Hué areas in the north.

Allied military sources reported Aug. 13 that 1,450 North Vietnamese and Viet Cong had been killed in the previous 24 hours' fighting, while 90 U.S. and 107 government troops were slain. American wounded totaled 500 and South Vietnamese 371. U.S. officers reported that about 2,000 North Vietnamese troops

had attacked in the Anloc-Tayninh-Locninh area, where they suffered their heaviest casualties, 400 men killed. Some North Vietnamese managed to fight their way into Locninh, Anloc and
Quanloi but were driven out. Communist commandos fought their
way into the U.S. First Marine Division's headquarters at Danang
but were driven out with 11 men killed and 4 captured. 2 Marines
were killed. U.S. Marines fought off another attack 22 miles south
of Danang, killing 40 North Vietnamese. U.S. losses totaled 5
killed and 23 wounded.

The North Vietnamese attacks eased overnight. 19 shellings
were reported Aug. 13, only 8 of them causing casualties or damage.
Communist troops were said to be withdrawing into Cambodia
in some areas north of Saigon in the face of attacks by U.S. fighter-
bombers.

A spokesman for Gen. Creighton W. Abrams, U.S. commander, said the Communist assaults were "probably the start of
their fall offensive." U.S. military officials in Saigon had disclosed Aug. 11 that intelligence reports based on captured enemy
documents and interrogation of prisoners indicated "that the
enemy is preparing for a fall campaign to be conducted during
August and September."

Among actions reported earlier in August:

● A Communist explosive charge damaged a bridge 40 miles southeast of
Saigon Aug. 3. The blast wrecked nearly half of the 210-foot span and blocked
traffic on Highway 15, one of South Vietnam's busiest roads.

● U.S. troops fired 3 artillery barrages into the demilitarized zone Aug. 5,
silencing 2 Communist rocket positions and touching off explosions and fires.
The American shelling was in response to Communist rocket assaults against
allied positions just south of the DMZ.

● 2 Americans were killed and 99 wounded in a Viet Cong commando assault
on the U.S. convalescent hospital at Camranh Bay Aug. 7. 53 of those injured
were patients. Before withdrawing without suffering casualties, the Communist
raiders, reportedly numbering 6 men, destroyed 10 wards and damaged 3
others and blew up the hospital's water tower and an officers' barracks. The
attack coincided with a 15-round Communist rocket barrage at the nearby
Camranh air base.

● Communist-planted bombs later Aug. 7 blasted a South Vietnamese air
force school in Saigon, killing at least 8 persons and wounding 62. The injured
included 4 U.S. soldiers. 3 subsequent blasts in the area wrecked houses, stores
and cars.

● The U.S. command reported Aug. 8 that in the previous 24 hours 174 Communist and 14 U.S. and 17 government soldiers had been killed in significant
actions ranging from the DMZ to the Saigon area. In addition, 164 Americans
and 51 South Vietnamese were wounded. This was the largest 24-hour casualty
toll since June 18, U.S. spokesmen said. The heaviest Communist death toll,

102 men, was inflicted in fighting with U.S. Marines just below the DMZ. U.S. losses were listed as 8 killed and 23 wounded.

● In fiercer fighting along the DMZ Aug. 10, North Vietnamese attacked 2 U.S. Marine bases 1,500 yards apart. The attackers, using grenades and dynamite bombs, killed 17 Marines and wounded 83. 17 Communist bodies were found inside the perimeter of one Marine camp partly overrun by the raiders. The engagement produced the heaviest U.S. Marine loss for one day since Feb. 25, when 36 Marines had been slain in the same outposts.

● About 50 U.S. B-52 bombers Aug. 9 raided North Vietnamese troop concentrations 65-75 miles north of Saigon, along the Cambodian border. After being forced from cover, the North Vietnamese, numbering about 100 men, came under ground attack by U.S. infantry. 64 of the enemy were killed and 6 were captured.

2 weeks prior to the outbreak of the latest heavy fighting, U.S. combat deaths in a single week (the July 20-26 period) had dropped to 110, the lowest weekly toll since Jan. 1 and the 4th lowest in 2 years. The Communist death toll of 1,963 was the lowest for the enemy since Jan. 1, allied officials reported.

By mid-August, allied military officials were reported to have concluded that the widespread attacks launched by Communist forces Aug. 11 actually were the start of a new enemy offensive. Allied authorities estimated that nearly 4,000 Communist soldiers had been killed and 251 captured Aug. 11-19. About 200 U.S. troops were killed in the week's upsurge of fighting. Casualties suffered by South Vietnam totaled more than 300 killed and more than 1,200 wounded. In the Aug. 3-9 period, 96 Americans had been killed. This was the lowest weekly U.S. death toll since Aug. 12, 1967. A total of 225 South Vietnamese government and 2,214 Communist troops had been slain Aug. 3-9.

The forces that had launched attacks against allied positions Aug. 11 came under heavy counterassaults by U.S. and South Vietnamese troops. The heaviest of the fighting raged north of Saigon along the Cambodian border and just south of Danang. U.S. troops Aug. 13 killed 79 soldiers near the Cambodian frontier, where enemy forces were reportedly poised for new assaults against allied bases and towns. U.S. troops killed 96 more Aug. 14-15 in frustrating attempts to storm U.S. camps in Haunghia, Tayninh and Binhlong Provinces along the Cambodian border. Communist gunners shot down an American helicopter in the Aug. 14 fighting. All 7 men aboard were killed.

American troops sweeping an area 20-30 miles south of Danang Aug. 17 came on a force of 1,200 North Vietnamese troops ready to attack a refugee camp at Hiepduc. Savage fighting raged in the sector through Aug. 20 during which 218 enemy troops and 16 Americans were killed. U.S. wounded totaled 66. 2 companies of the American Division's 169th Light Infantry Brigade had been reinforced by 600 troops after sustaining 40% casualties in the fighting Aug. 19. The 2 U.S. companies suffered the heavy losses while breaking out of a North Vietnamese encirclement.

U.S. troops killed at least 650 North Vietnamese in a fierce battle in the Queson Valley 30 miles south of Danang Aug. 17-26. More than 60 Americans were listed as slain in the fighting. The clash broke out when 1,200 troops of the U.S. Americal Division and South Vietnamese soldiers Aug. 17 found about 1,000 North Vietnamese entrenched in a complex of bunkers and tunnels. The battle assumed its greatest intensity Aug. 20 when the allied force stepped up its drive in an effort to reach the wreckage of a U.S. command helicopter shot down by ground fire Aug. 19. U.S. infantrymen fought their way to the stricken 'copter Aug. 25 and reported that all 8 men aboard were dead. Among the victims were Lt. Col. Eli P. Howard Jr., 41, commander of the division's 3d Battalion, 196th Light Infantry Brigade. AP photographer Horst Faas reported that some of the American soldiers had questioned whether reaching the helicopter was worth the heavy battle losses. But staff officers said that the drive for the helicopter was only part of the overall operation. The fighting to get to the aircraft had reached its climax Aug. 23 when U.S. soldiers captured a knoll, known as Hill 102, about 1,000 yards from the wreckage. 4 companies of the Americal Division, about 250 men, occupied the hill against light resistance. The knoll had been a major obstacle to the American advance. North Vietnamese machinegun emplacements there had inflicted serious losses and damage on U.S. troops and helicopters. U.S. units had attempted earlier to outflank the hill but had to withdraw under heavy fire.

During the fighting in the Queson Valley, an American infantry company had first defied an order to go into combat Aug. 24 and then changed its mind. The company's commander, Lt. Eugene Shurtz Jr., 26, was relieved of his post Aug. 25. Shurtz, commander of Company A of the 196th Light Infantry Brigade, was transferred to another assignment with the division. Neither he nor his men were disciplined. Company A had been ordered to move down Nuilon Mountain to recover the bodies of the 8 Americans killed in the helicopter downed Aug. 19. The unit had

attempted to make the push during the 5 previous days but was
thrown back with heavy losses. Shurtz phoned Lt. Col. Robert C.
Bacon, battalion commander, that his men refused to carry out
the mission because they "simply had enough—they are broken."
Bacon dispatched his executive officer and a sergeant to Company
A to "give them a pep talk." The sergeant, Okey Blankenship,
confirmed that the men were exhausted and that they complained
they were being pushed too hard. But Blankenship sharply ad-
monished the men for refusing to obey orders and finally persuaded them to move out of their position; they followed him down
the slope of the mountain. Bacon said Aug. 27 that the incident
"was certainly a contributing factor" in relieving Shurtz of his
command, but it "was not solely based on that." Bacon explained
that he had been dissatisfied "with the progress the company was
making" and felt that Shurtz did not have "the experience to
handle the job." Shurtz said Aug. 29 that only 5 men of Company A had refused to go into combat. The 5, he said, had
"desired to see the inspector general rather than move with the
company," but the "remainder of the company was ready to go."
Some members of the unit interviewed in the field Aug. 29 denied
Shurtz' statement. They conceded that 5 soldiers at first had
balked but "the whole company definitely was behind the refusal."

Fighting in the Danang area flared up again Aug. 25-26. U.S.
troops Aug. 25 killed 138 North Vietnamese in day-long clashes
in the vicinity of U.S. artillery posts atop small hills. American
losses totaled 12 killed and 97 wounded. During the Aug. 26 fighting, the North Vietnamese shot down a U.S. Marine helicopter,
but all 6 Americans aboard escaped injury.

U.S. troops had killed 48 Communist troops Aug. 24 in a 7-
hour battle near Cuchi, 28 miles northwest of Saigon. The battle
broke out when an American patrol spotted about 60 men dug in
near the headquarters of the U.S. 25th Infantry Division. The
U.S. command reported an additional 130 enemy slain in 3 other
clashes 30 miles northwest of the capital. The U.S. Army hospital
at Camranh Bay was shelled Aug. 24 for the 2d time in less than
a month. 5 mortar shells wounded 19 patients.

U.S. B-52s Aug. 25 dropped bombs on "enemy activity, base
camps, bunkers, supply and staging areas" near the Cambodian
border, 80 miles north of Saigon, the U.S. command reported.
The 5-mission raid was concentrated within 10 miles of the district

capital of Lochninh, where Communist forces had launched their fall offensive. The B-52 strike was aimed at blunting an expected round of enemy attacks in the same area.

Infiltration From North Declines

Despite the increase in fighting during this period, both the State and Defense Departments, in separate statements Aug. 27, reported a sharp drop in North Vietnamese infiltration into South Vietnam, but each agency gave different interpretations of its meaning. The State Department regarded the development as significant, while the Pentagon was more cautious in its assessment:

● The State Department said that "North Vietnamese infiltration" currently was "lower than the North Vietnamese casualty figures in the South." This suggested, the statement said, that the North Vietnamese were "not replacing all of their casualties and that there may be a net reduction in enemy field forces which occur as the result of attrition in the North Vietnamese component of these forces." Although the department said it considered "these facts significant," it insisted that U.S. policy remained "mutual troop withdrawal of all non-South Vietnamese forces" from South Vietnam.

● The Defense Department conceded that infiltration "is down considerably compared with last year's average," indicating that "it is possible that the enemy has suffered some decline in total troop strength." But even at the "current average rate of infiltration," the enemy was "substantially replacing his losses," the department estimated. The Pentagon said the reduction of North Vietnamese reinforcement into the South was possibly motivated by these factors: The primary infiltration routes in Laos during the spring were "difficult and wet," thus reducing the number of men entering South Vietnam; because of an abatement in combat, there was less need for the enemy to send more troops to the South; "the enemy has sufficient main force troops in South Vietnam and in nearby sanctuaries which he can deploy within the country to launch selected attacks . . . without immediately increasing his infiltration rate."

● Citing specific figures, the Defense Department said Aug. 28 that North Vietnam had sent 10,000 troops into the South Jan. 1-June 30, 1969, compared with 200,000 during the like period in 1968. "This indicates to both us and the State Department that the enemy has suffered a decline in total troop strength in South Vietnam," the statement said. According to the Pentagon, 119,000 enemy troops had been killed during the first half of 1968, and their combat death toll for that year was 181,000. This compared with 93,653 killed between Jan. 1 and June 30, 1969, plus an additional 10,237 killed in July, the department said. (As of Jan. 30, the Pentagon had estimated, there were 240,000 enemy troops in the South: 100,000 to 140,000 North Vietnamese regulars and 65,000 Viet Cong administrative and logistical forces.)

State Department spokesman Robert McCloskey denied Aug. 28 that there was "anything materially or substantially different in the statements issued" by the 2 departments. "Defense is the repository for this kind of information, and I would let Defense speak for the government on this matter," he said.

White House Press Secy. Ronald L. Ziegler said at the Western White House in San Clemente, Calif. Aug. 28 that there was no difference between the State and Defense Departments' interpretations of the drop in North Vietnamese infiltration. He said Pres. Nixon would take into consideration the decrease in this movement plus "the high points of the enemy activity on Aug. 11 and 12" before making a decision on withdrawing more American troops from South Vietnam.

U.S. chief negotiator Henry Cabot Lodge confirmed at the Paris talks Aug. 28 that Nixon had deferred action on a further troop pullout "until we can further evaluate" the Communists' "recent military activity, in particular the recent wave of attacks, and examine potential activity in the future." Denying Communist charges that the U.S. was intensifying combat activity, Lodge reaffirmed that the U.S. had reduced "for over a month now" the rate of B-52 attacks. (750 American soldiers had left South Vietnam July 30 and another 2,850 departed Aug. 1. Their removal brought to 10,250 the number of Americans who had left since the withdrawals had started July 8.)

Ho Chi Minh Dies

Ho Chi Minh, the president and leader of North Vietnam, died Sept. 3 at the age of 79. The country's leadership was placed in the hands of a collective group of the Vietnam Workers Party, North Vietnam's Communist party.

Ho's death was reported Sept. 4 by Hanoi radio, which announced that he had died "after a grave and sudden heart attack." A Hanoi broadcast Sept. 2 had disclosed that the North Vietnamese leader had been gravely ill for serveral weeks and that his condition was deteriorating. A state funeral attended by world Communist leaders and other foreign dignitaries was held in Hanoi Sept. 9. A period of national mourning began Sept. 4 and lasted until Sept. 11.

The Sept. 4 broadcast called on "the entire party, the entire army and the entire people to: . . . strengthen our unity; contribute . . . to the great task of defeating the United States aggressors; liberate South Vietnam; realize the noble aspirations and wishes of Pres. Ho by building and achieving a peaceful, unified, independent, democratic and prosperous Vietnam." The statement was signed by the Central Committee of the Vietnam Workers Party, the Standing Committee of the legislative National Assembly, the State Council of the Democratic Republic of Vietnam and the Presidium of the Central Committee of the Fatherland Front of Vietnam.

The formation of a collective leadership to succeed Ho was announced in an editorial published by the Communist party newspaper *Nhan Dan* and broadcast by Hanoi radio Sept. 6.

It was disclosed later that power was delegated to these 4 men: Le Duan, first secretary of the Communist party; Truong Chin, member of the Communist party's Politburo and chairman of the National Assembly; Gen. Vo Nguyen Giap, defense minister; and Premier Pham Van Dong.

The *Nhan Dan* editorial called on the people to rally behind the "collective" of Ho's "closest comrades-in-arms and most outstanding disciples." The editorial said North Vietnam would press Ho's goals of continuing the war until "there is not a single aggressor in our country." Quoting Ho's previous demands, the statement said that the Vietnamese people "firmly demand the withdrawal of all U.S. and satellite troops, not the withdrawal of only 25,000 or 250,000 but a total, complete, unconditional withdrawal."

The North Vietnamese news agency reported Sept. 9 that Vice Pres. Ton Duc Thang, 81, was serving as acting president. The agency made the disclosure in announcing that Thang had greeted the arrival of Cambodian Chief of State Norodom Sihanouk in his capacity as acting president. (The North Vietnamese National Assembly Sept. 24 elected Thang as president and chose Nguyen Luong Bang as vice president. Real authority, however, remained in the hands of the 4-member leadership that had taken control Sept. 6. A cabinet shift was reported Dec. 9 to have been approved by the Standing Committee of the National Assembly. The changes included: establishment of a Ministry for Food & Food Products, merging the former General Department for Food and agencies of the Food Processing Industries; division of the Ministry of Heavy Industries into 3 agencies—a Ministry for Electricity & Coal, a Ministry for Mechanical Constructions & Metallurgy and a General Department for Chemical Products; and formation of a Ministry for Economic Affairs, combining the former Ministries of Agriculture, Industry and Finance & Trade.)

The funeral services for Ho were held Sept. 9 in Hanoi's Badinh Square and were attended by 250,000 persons. A will composed by Ho May 10 and read by Le Duan expressed regret over the split in the world Communist movement. But Ho said: "I am sure that the fraternal parties and countries will unite again." The statement called on the North Vietnamese Communist party to preserve unity and "remain worthy of its role as the leader and a very loyal servant of the people." It said "total victory" in the war was "an absolute certainty. The U.S. imperialists will have to pull out. Our fatherland will be reunified. Our compatriots in the North and South will be reunited under the same roof."

After reading Ho's message, Duan delivered a eulogy in which he stressed the themes expressed in Ho's will. The 30-minute rites concluded with a mass oath-taking by the 250,000 mourners pledging to carry on the mission undertaken by Ho.

(In South Vietnam, the Viet Cong's clandestine Liberation Radio reported Sept. 9 that a secret commemoration service for Ho had been held at an undisclosed spot in the South the previous day and was attended by 1,000 persons, including 23 delegations of the National Liberation Front. The ceremony was presided over by Huynh Tan Phat, head of the Provisional Revolutionary Government.)

Foreign leaders attending the Hanoi rites included Soviet Premier Aleksei N. Kosygin, Chinese Communist Vice Premier Li Hsien-nien, Cambodian Chief of State Norodom Sihanouk and Pathet Lao leader Prince Souphanouvong of Laos. The other foreign representatives included North Korean National Assembly Pres. Choi Yong Kun, Indian Foreign Min. Dinesh Singh and delegations from France, Italy, Rumania, Hungary, Mongolia, Albania and Indonesia. A Chinese delegation, headed by premier Chou En-lai, had landed in Hanoi Sept. 4, but he and the group returned to Peking the following morning, avoiding a possible face-to-face meeting with Premier Kosygin, who arrived in the North Vietnamese capital Sept. 6. A new Chinese delegation led by Vice Premier Li flew to Hanoi Sept. 8. Peking did not explain its reason for changing the delegations. During his brief stay in Hanoi, Chou had conferred with Communist Secy. Gen. Le Duan and members of the Politburo. He assured the North Vietnamese leadership of continued support in the war. Kosygin also met with

Hanoi's leaders.

A National Liberation Front statement on Ho's death Sept. 7 pledged to "persistently carry on and step up the current war of resistance, fight on resolutely till the complete withdrawal of American troops and till the total collapse of the puppet army and administration."

The Viet Cong announced Sept. 4 that its forces would observe a ceasefire in South Vietnam Sept. 8-11 to mark Ho's death. The North Vietnamese forces followed suit. The scale of fighting at the start of the truce was reduced somewhat although the U.S. and South Vietnamese did not accept or reject the Viet Cong proposal outright. South Vietnamese Pres. Nguyen Van Thieu at first had strenuously opposed any allied halt in fighting, while U.S. military commanders also displayed reluctance. A series of meetings by U.S. and South Vietnamese officials were held to avert an allied split and to coordinate a joint response to the Communist proposal. Following a meeting Sept. 6 between U.S. Deputy Amb. Samuel D. Berger and Premier Tran Thien Khiem, both governments indicated that the Viet Cong truce would be ignored publicly but accepted privately. In an apparent reversal, the South Vietnamese government Sept. 7 flatly rejected the truce, charging that "the Communists have never respected truces, even those proposed by themselves." The Defense Ministry said, "We will continue offensive operations." A U.S. military spokesman, indicating American acceptance of the ceasefire, said prior to Saigon's announcement that "in the past the United States command's actions have been the same as the Republic of Vietnam's during proposed ceasefires. I have no indication that there will be any difference this time." A compromise position drawn up Sept. 8, following a meeting of Berger, Thieu and Gen. Creighton W. Abrams, commander of U.S. forces, stated that allied military activity would be contingent on the level of enemy activity. The statement said: The Viet Cong proposal "must be viewed in the light of the savage attacks against civilians in Danang and other aggressive actions which had followed the announcement. . . . Consequently, it is not our intention to talk about ceasefires at this time. The scale of our military operations in the past has been influenced by the scale of enemy military operations. During this period the scope of our military operations will likewise be influenced by the nature of enemy military operations."

U.S. military authorities reported Sept. 8 that the Viet Cong had attacked a U.S. Marine defensive position 19 miles south of Danang a half hour before the start of the truce and that the fighting continued 15 minutes beyond the deadline. One U.S. Marine was killed.

A South Vietnamese military spokesman announced Sept. 9 that government troops had increased their offensive operations by about 15% despite an acknowledged drop by at least 30% in enemy activity during the first 36 hours of the truce. U.S. forces had reduced their ground operations considerably during that period and had grounded nearly all their bombers. Only about 10 U.S. air strikes had been reported in the previous 24 hours.

Fighting Resumes

Full-scale fighting resumed Sept. 11 following the expiration of the 3-day truce marking Ho Chi Minh's death. U.S. B-52 bomber raids over the South, suspended for 36 hours, resumed Sept. 13.

The halt in B-52 raids had been announced in Saigon Sept. 11 as "a gesture of deescalation, a political move," and was confirmed and explained in greater detail Sept. 12 by White House Press Secy. Ronald Ziegler. Ziegler said: Pres. Nixon had ordered the bombing halt "to determine whether this ceasefire period had political significance beyond the death of Ho." At first the raids had been resumed for 12 hours, on the expiration of the ceasefire, but at about half the normal level. The flights were stopped entirely after this 12-hour period "to determine again the intent on the part of the other side in terms of the level of activity and give them every benefit of the doubt as to the beginning of the level of military activity." But in view of the resumption of enemy military activity 13 hours before the end of the truce and its continuation after the ceasefire expiration, the U.S. was forced to furnish its troops with air support and so the B-52 raids were resumed. Ziegler emphasized that the purpose of the B-52 raid stoppage was only to determine Communist intentions and was not a major peace overture. Contrary to the Saigon report of Sept. 11, Ziegler insisted that the raid halt was "not an action which was intended to signal the other side or to get a response from the other side directly to that action." Ziegler refused to say whether the U.S. had informed the Communists in advance of the plan to suspend the B-52 activity.

The American decision to resume ground action on the expiration of the ceasefire had been announced by Ziegler Sept. 10 (Sept. 11 Saigon time). Ziegler said the move was in accord with the joint U.S.-South Vietnamese statement of Sept. 8, which had said the allies would reduce their activities to match those of the Communists for the truce period only. Ziegler denied that Washington and Saigon had disagreed on a common approach to the ceasefire. There was at no time "a point of misunderstanding between the United States and Saigon nor at any point was there in any way a deterioration of relationships between Saigon and the United States," he said. Asked about reports that government soldiers had stepped up their military activity while the U.S. and Communists had scaled down theirs, Ziegler said Pres. Nixon "understands the action they [Saigon] took." A statement issued by the State Department Sept. 10 also said there was "no split between the 2 governments on the matter of the ceasefire" either before or after the Sept. 8 joint declaration.

Among military developments just prior to the truce: U.S. military authorities had reported Sept. 6 that 935 North Vietnamese had been killed by U.S. troops in the fighting in the Hiepduc Valley 30 miles south of Danang since the outbreak of the battle Aug. 17. The U.S. command had reported Sept. 4 that U.S. and South Vietnamese troops had clashed in Cambodia after a U.S. Army helicopter had been attacked and had crashed one mile inside Cambodian territory. The report said that the helicopter, carrying South Vietnamese troops, had crash-landed after being fired on by the Viet Cong in South Vietnam, about 55 miles west of Saigon. A South Vietnamese died in the burning wreckage of the 'copter.

Communist forces struck more than 30 allied installations with mortar and rocket fire as the 3-day truce formally ended at 1 a.m. Sept. 11. 12 of the attacks caused damage or casualties. Both sides also stepped up ground action. In one of the most serious encounters, 4 U.S. soldiers were killed when an American landing zone about 40 miles south of Danang came under attack. 28 Communist troops were reported killed in the skirmish. Targets struck in B-52 raids, resumed Sept. 13, included enemy positions 28 miles northeast of Saigon in the Xuanloc area and near Phucat on the coast, 285 miles northeast of the capital. South Vietnam reported Sept. 13 that government militia that day had killed 51 Viet Cong in a battle with enemy forces who had kidnaped 13 children from a hamlet in northern Quangngai Province. 8 of the children were said to have been released. The government reported Sept. 13 that a Communist force that day had leveled 80% of the refugee village of Dienban in northern Quangnam Province. Enemy shelling had wounded 18 civilians and set fire to 70 houses.

U.S. military authorities reported Sept. 14 that 3 or 4 North Vietnamese battalions had infiltrated into the Mekong delta from Cambodia in the 4 weeks since the last U.S. troops had left the region as part of the American withdrawal from Vietnam. The infiltration of a Communist unit into the delta had first been observed in May. It had been identified as the 273d Regiment of the Viet Cong 9th Division. The elements of the North Vietnamese forces in the delta had been indentified as battalions of the 18th Regiment of the First Army. At least 2 of these battalions were believed to be hiding in caves in western Chaudoc Province. The U.S. command had completed its pullout from the Mekong delta Sept. 1 as it turned over the 19th Infantry Division headquarters at Dongtam to the South Vietnamese army. 2 of the division's 3 brigades of about 10,000 men were among the first of the Americans withdrawn from South Vietnam between July 8 and the end of August. The 3d brigade was shifted to Longan Province south of Saigon.

(In a further move aimed at Vietnamizing the war, the U.S.' Blackhorse Army Base, 38 miles northeast of Saigon, was turned over to South Vietnamese army control Oct. 24. The base, headquarters of the U.S. Army's 11th Armored Cavalry, was to be used by South Vietnam's 18th Division as an infantry regiment base and a training center.)

The U.S. command reported Sept. 15 that for the first time in the war a regular North Vietnamese unit had launched an attack in the Mekong delta. The 18B Regiment, numbering about 2,000 men, had attacked a government training center 6 miles north of Triton but was thrown back with a loss of 83 men killed, the command said. 4 government soldiers were killed and 19 wounded in 7 hours of fighting. U.S. helicopters Sept. 16 accidentally killed 7 civilians and wounded 17 near the Mekong delta provincial capital of Baclieu, 120 miles southwest of Saigon. The victims were fired on while fleeing from an area where government troops were searching for a Viet Cong unit. The 'copters had received permission from the South Vietnamese commanders to open fire, the U.S. command said. In a similar mishap, U.S. helicopters killed 14 civilians and wounded 5 and 2 militiamen Sept. 22 while firing on what were described as "suspected enemy soldiers" 25 miles west of Tamky, capital of northern Quangtin Province. A military spokesman said the aircraft had opened fire on persons dressed in black and green clothes, similar to those worn by the Viet Cong.

2 civilians and 3 militiamen were slain Sept. 16 when about 200 Viet Cong charged into the village of Mailinh near Quangngai city, about 340 miles north of Saigon. The attackers tossed grenades into houses and shot at villagers as they fled for cover. The grenades and mortar shells destroyed 170 homes.

U.S. B-52s carried out 22 bombing missions against bases and supply dumps along the Cambodian border Sept. 17-19. B-52s Sept. 21 bombed enemy positions near the demilitarized zone in the heaviest raids in more than 4 months, the U.S. command reported. 35 planes were said to have dropped more than 1,000 tons of bombs on North Vietnamese concentrations north of the Rockpile, the U.S. Marine base near the DMZ. The B-52 raids followed a North Vietnamese assault Sept. 17 against 2 U.S. Marine outposts just below the DMZ in which 23 Americans were killed and 24 wounded. In the attack against one of the positions, several North Vietnamese soldiers managed to breach the camp perimeter of the 3d Regiment of the 3d Marine Division. The siege was finally broken by artillery and air strikes. 23 North Vietnamese were killed in the 2 attacks.

7 U.S. helicopters were downed by ground fire in 3 separate actions. 2 were lost in the northern provinces Sept. 21, and 3 were downed by North Vietnamese gunners Sept. 22 during an air assault on Communist positions near Tamky, south of Danang. The 2 other 'copters, observation aircraft for the 82d Airborne Division, were shot down Oct. 2, 20 miles north of Saigon. One American was killed and 10 wounded in the fighting on the ground. Another U.S. aircraft, a Phantom fighter-bomber, was brought down that day 95 miles northeast of Saigon. One crewman was killed. A U.S. Phantom jet collided with a South Vietnamese civilian DC-4 airliner at Danang Sept. 24, killing all 62 Vietnamese civilians aboard the airliner and 2 persons on the ground. Both planes were coming in for a landing at the Danang airfield at the time. The U.S. jet, returning from a bombing mission, landed safely.

Conflict slackened during the following week. The U.S.

command reported Oct. 2 that 95 U.S. soldiers had been killed in South Vietnam Sept. 21-27; this was the lowest American death toll since the week of Aug. 12, 1967. The relatively small number of combat deaths reflected a lull in the fighting that continued through Oct. 6, punctuated only by shelling of South Vietnamese and American positions, largely in the Mekong delta, Oct. 5-6. Other combat deaths for the Sept. 21-27 period were 308 South Vietnamese and 2,832 Communists. A South Vietnamese spokesman said Sept. 27 that during the previous 7 days 163 civilians had been assassinated by the Communists and 338 had been wounded and 94 kidnaped.

The U.S. command reported Oct. 9 that 64 Americans had been killed in South Vietnam Sept. 28-Oct. 4; this was the lowest U.S. weekly death toll since the first week of Dec. 1966. The continued battlefield lull was marked by a similar sharp drop in South Vietnamese and Communist casualties. The allied command said 209 government troops had been killed Sept. 28-Oct. 4, compared with 308 the previous week. North Vietnamese and Viet Cong deaths totaled 1,899, a drop from the 2,382 recorded in the Sept. 21-27 period.

These were other indications of a slackening of the fighting and a de-emphasis of the U.S. combat role:

● U.S. and South Vietnamese forces were reported Oct. 9 to have withdrawn from the Ashau Valley. The last major elements of the U.S. 101st Airborne Division and the South Vietnamese First Infantry Division had pulled out in September, according to Maj. Gen. Ngo Quang Trong, the South Vietnamese commander. "We found that because of the lack of enemy activity there was no longer any need to stay there," he said.

● The U.S. command announced Oct. 9 that 5 Air Force units were being demobilized and that the transfer of 2 others to South Vietnam was being canceled.

● Government forces Oct. 10 assumed complete responsibility for the defense of Saigon as the last American combat unit in the city moved out to an area 20 miles away. The unit, the 3d Brigade of the 82nd Airborne Division, was among 35,000 U.S. troops scheduled to leave Vietnam by Dec. 15.

● 80 U.S. Navy river-patrol boats were transferred to the South Vietnamese navy in Saigon Oct. 10, bringing to 229 the number of such vessels turned over to the Vietnamese since June 1968.

● The U.S. command acknowledged Oct. 12 a sharp drop in B-52 raids. The number of these attacks had dropped by about 1/3 in the previous 9 days, and a total of 212 missions had been flown in September, compared with 271 in August. But the command said Oct. 13 that the de-escalation of B-52 attacks did not apply to the provinces bordering Cambodia—Tayninh, Binhlong and Phuoclong—where 8 strikes had been carried out in the previous 24 hours, about the daily average for the past month.

● American troop strength in South Vietnam had dropped to 505,600 men, the U.S. command announced Oct. 13. This represented the smallest number of American troops in the country since the period before the major buildup that had followed the Communist Tet offensive in Feb. 1968.

In one of the few combat actions reported, Communist gunners downed 4 U.S. helicopters Oct. 8 and 10. The first 'copter was downed 28 miles south of the demilitarized zone, and 2 crewmen were killed. 2 of the 3 other aircraft were hit Oct. 10 during ground fighting 75 miles north of Saigon, and the 3d helicopter was shot down 4 miles south of the DMZ, with 3 Marines killed and one wounded.

Ships of a Chinese fishing fleet and a Soviet trawler were attacked off the coast of South Vietnam in September and October: Peking charged Oct. 10 that Chinese fishing vessels had been fired on by U.S. planes and ships in the Gulf of Tonkin between Sept. 19 and 24 and Oct. 4. The statement claimed that in the September incident, 24 boats "flying Chinese national flags . . . were fishing . . . in the Gulf of Tonkin" when "a U.S. guided-missile cruiser and a U.S. destroyer kept following in their wake and made provocations against them" and then "wildly opened fire." U.S. planes, including helicopters, simultaneously "flew several sorties in succession over the Chinese fishing fleet . . . and even dived at them," the statement said. In the Oct. 4 incident, according to Peking, "2 U.S. military planes wildly strafed 4 other Chinese fishing vessels" in the gulf. The U.S. State Department Oct. 10 confirmed that U.S. ships and planes had been in the gulf at the times cited by China. But the department noted that U.S. ships and aircraft were "under standing instructions not to interfere with Chinese fishing vessels" there.

South Vietnamese patrol boats Oct. 17 fired on and hit a 150-ton ship, identified by Vietnamese and U.S. sources as a Soviet intelligence trawler, after it had intruded into Vietnamese territorial waters off Danang. South Vietnamese sources said the Soviet ship came under fire when it ignored government patrol boat warnings to stop. After being hit, the vessel took evasive action and headed back into the South China Sea, the sources said. U.S. Navy officials acknowledged that the trawler had come from the northernmost part of the Gulf of Tonkin, but they did not confirm that the ship had been hit. The Soviet vessel was said to have first been observed Oct. 16 and kept under surveillance as it approached the South Vietnamese coast. Pres. Thieu confirmed Oct. 18 that his navy had fired on the Soviet ship after it had been spotted 3 miles off Danang, well within South Vietnam's 12-mile coastal limit. Thieu claimed that other Soviet trawlers, positioned 3 to 5 miles off Guam, had observed U.S. B-52 bombers taking off on attack missions against targets in South Vietnam and radioed warnings to the Viet Cong to take cover.

Year-End Stalemate

Fighting intensified in late October. The number of Americans killed in combat in Vietnam Oct. 19-25 exceeded 100 for the first time in 5 weeks, the U.S. command reported Oct. 30. U.S. fatalities totaled 102. Previous weekly death totals: Oct. 12-18—U.S. 78, South Vietnam 301, Communists 1,624 (the lowest enemy death toll claimed in more than 11 months); Oct. 5-11— U.S. 82, South Vietnam 384, Communists 1,687.

Among actions reported:

● The Saigon government reported that its forces had killed 116 Communists in 2 battles in the U Minh Forest in the Mekong delta Oct. 19. 96 North Vietnamese regulars were slain in one clash, and another 20 were killed in a skirmish 20 miles to the south. Government losses in the first operation totaled 6 killed and 16 wounded, Saigon reported. Most of the enemy dead were believed to have belonged to the North Vietnamese 273D Regiment, which reportedly had crossed into South Vietnam from Cambodia in May and had been attempting to make its way into the U Minh Forest, 75 miles south of the frontier.

● The North Vietnamese Foreign Ministry charged Oct. 22 that in the past 8 days U.S. planes had attacked populated areas in the North Vietnamese provinces of Nghean, Quangbinh and Hatinh, causing loss of life and damage to property. A U.S. Defense Department spokesman in Washington denied the charge.

● In one of the biggest actions fought by U.S. soldiers in over a month, 200 Americans of the 25th Infantry Division killed 47 Communist troops Oct. 24 in a clash 28 miles north of Saigon. American losses totaled 10 killed and 12 wounded.

● U.S. B-52s carried out heavy bombing raids Oct. 31 against suspected North Vietnamese concentrations along the Cambodian border in Quangduc Province in the Central Highlands. The bombs were dropped near 2 U.S. Special Forces camps at Duclap and Buprang, 25 miles apart, and at 2 U.S. artillery bases in the vicinity that had come under heavy mortar attacks for several days. The Duclap and Buprang garrisons were manned by 11-man Special Forces teams and several hundred mercenaries. The 2 artillery bases and another one nearby were abandoned in the wake of an upsurge of Communist artillery and infantry attacks, it was reported Nov. 2. Only one of the bases was attacked by Communist ground troops, but it was not overrun, according to Allied communiqués.

● U.S. First Infantry Division troops claimed Nov. 1 that they had blown up the abandoned headquarters of a Communist regiment near Laikhe, on a major infiltration route about 40 miles north of Saigon. Officers said the base camp

of the Dongnai Regiment, a nominally Viet Cong unit whose men were 95%
North Vietnamese regulars, apparently had been evacuated the day before.
The First Infantry Division also reported that in the last 2 weeks its troops had
uncovered 6 enemy arsenals along the Song Be River, about 13 miles north of
the division's headquarters at Laikhe.
• Fighting Nov. 4 was marked by the shelling of 45 allied bases and towns,
largely in the III Corps area around Saigon, Communist ground attacks against
3 U.S. artillery fire bases near the Cambodian border north of Saigon and
heavy clashes between South and North Vietnamese troops near Duclap. In
their biggest battle in 4 months, South Vietnamese units, supported by U.S.
planes and artillery, killed at least 80 soldiers of the 24th and 66th North Vietnamese Regiments in the Duclap area, 135 miles northeast of Saigon. Government losses were 24 dead and 38 wounded in the 10-hour battle.
• A government navy-marine task force headquarters in the Mekong delta
came under attack Nov. 6 by North Vietnamese troops striking out from their
positions in the U Minh Forest. South Vietnamese headquarters said 75 North
Vietnamese and 27 government troops were killed in the 6-hour battle, 138
miles southwest of Saigon. It was the heaviest southernmost assault launched
by North Vietnamese forces in the war.
• The government amphibious base came under a 2d attack by North Vietnamese forces Nov. 8. In a day-long clash just north of the U Minh Forest,
about 15 miles away, a South Vietnamese unit was said to have killed 80 of
the enemy while its own losses totaled 8 dead and 43 wounded.
• Saigon's outer defenses came under attack Nov. 7 for the first time since
May 1968. An estimated 100 Viet Cong fired at 2 government police posts, on
the city's southern edges.

U.S. military authorities speculated Nov. 10 that the sharp
increase in North Vietnamese-Viet Cong attacks throughout the
southern part of South Vietnam Nov. 1-10 indicated the start of
a winter-spring Communist offensive and marked the end of a
7-week battle lull. In the III Corps area alone, 85 Americans had
been killed and 664 wounded—most of them in Tayninh, Binhlong
and Phuoclong Provinces along the Cambodian border. Enemy
dead there totaled more than 1,200.

Allied commanders had moved a substantial number of
troops, mostly South Vietnamese, into 3 key areas regarded as
possible major enemy targets of combat: the western regions of
Quangduc Province, where about 5,000 North Vietnamese troops
were reported to have moved into positions around U.S. Special
Forces camps at Buprang and Duclap and nearby artillery posts,
the scene of current heavy clashes; the northwestern part of
Phuoclong Province, where North Vietnamese soldiers reportedly
had moved from Cambodian sanctuaries into the Songbe-Budop
area; and the western tip of the Mekong delta in an area extending
from the U Minh Forest to near Caudoc. U.S. military officials
had said Nov. 6 that no American troops would be committed to

the fighting taking place between North and South Vietnamese forces in the Buprang-Duclap area. It was part of Washington's continuing effort to Vietnamize the war.

U.S. and South Vietnamese combat deaths increased sharply Nov. 9-22, reflecting greater Communist pressure on allied outposts in Central Highlands and in the region below the demilitarized zone. Americans slain Nov. 16-22 totaled 130, the highest weekly toll in 2 months. The wounded totaled 653. South Vietnamese losses in the same period were 567 killed and 1,421 wounded, the heaviest government casualties of the war. According to allied figures, 3,201 Viet Cong and North Vietnamese were killed, a 3-month high. Combat deaths for Nov. 9-15: U.S. 113, 16 more than the previous week; South Vietnam 479; and Communists 3,013. Since the summer, government combat fatalities had been 60% higher than U.S. deaths. American military authorities attributed this to greater progress in Vietnamizing the war, "protective reaction" tactics in which U.S. battalion-sized operations were reduced to generally small-unit and reconnaissance patrols, and concentration of enemy attacks on government positions. American combat fatalities dropped Nov. 23-29 to 70, rose to 100 in the Nov. 30-Dec. 6 period and then fell Dec. 7-13 to 66, the 2d lowest weekly toll in 1969.

The North Vietnamese increased their pressure around the U.S. Special Forces camps at Buprang, Duclap and Budrop Nov. 9-26. Buprang and Duclap were shelled Nov. 9, and heavy ground fighting raged around the 2 bases Nov. 11. In the fighting around Buprang Nov. 14, South Vietnamese fighter-bombers accidentally dropped bombs on government troops during close-quarters fighting with the North Vietnamese. At least 20 government troops were killed and 56 wounded. 95 North Vietnamese were reported killed in the fighting around Buprang. North Vietnamese artillery in nearby Cambodia shelled the Buprang camp Nov. 17, prompting U.S. planes to attack the Communist positions there for the 2d consecutive day. The U.S. command reiterated its view that the raid on Cambodian territory was "an inherent right of self-defense against enemy attacks." Although U.S. B-52s dropped thousands of bombs on North Vietnamese positions around Buprang and Duclap, the Communist shelling of the 2 camps continued unabated.

The North Vietnamese Foreign Ministry charged Nov. 14 that U.S. planes had "deliberately and repeatedly bombed North

Vietnamese territory Nov. 12 and 13." Hanoi radio said the planes had dropped high explosives and antipersonnel bombs on the Tuyenhoa district of Quangbinh Province, just north of the DMZ. The U.S. command in Saigon denied any knowledge of the raids.

Among other military developments:

• North Vietnamese troops Nov. 13 carried out their heaviest assault against U.S. forces in the demilitarized zone area in more than a year. More than 500 soldiers attacked a U.S. armored company's defensive position, $3^1/_2$ miles south of the DMZ, killing 17 Americans. North Vietnamese losses totaled 104 killed. The U.S. command reported 122 North Vietnamese killed in 2 days of sharp clashes 6 miles southwest of the allied outpost at Conthien near the DMZ, while American losses came to 22 dead and 53 wounded. The fighting near the buffer zone had picked up Nov. 12 when a U.S. company was fired on near Conthien.

• Nearly 20 helicopters were destroyed by a Viet Cong attack Nov. 15 on a big U.S. Army base, Camp Radcliffe, at Ankhe, 260 miles northeast of Saigon. An estimated 24 infiltrators cut through the base's defense perimeter and hurled explosives at the aircraft.

• South Vietnamese forces lost 60 killed or wounded in a clash with North Vietnamese forces in the Mekong delta Nov. 18. Enemy losses were put at 14 killed. In another clash in the delta Nov. 22, a force of 130 government troops lost 7 men. The 2 fights were the first major actions in the northern delta since the U.S. 9th Division was withdrawn in the summer. A South Vietnamese spokesman said the high government casualties were "due to bad fighting on our part." A 300-man government militia force was ambushed in the delta Nov. 28 and lost 36 men. A government counterattack in the same area 72 miles southwest of Saigon resulted in the killing of 45 enemy soldiers, according to government sources.

• North Vietnamese gunners Nov. 30 shot down 4 U.S. Army helicopters about 10 miles southeast of Songbe near the Cambodian border. 5 crewmen were killed and 4 wounded.

• U.S. planes Dec. 3 bombed North Vietnamese troops inside Cambodia where they had fled after attacking the South Vietnamese district of Tuyenbinh in the Mekong delta. The government defenders, supported by U.S. air and artillery strikes, repulsed the attackers, killing 108 North Vietnamese. 6 garrison members were killed and 27 wounded. Civilian casualties in the town of Tuyenbinh totaled 15 dead and 30 wounded. U.S. planes bombed North Vietnamese forces in Cambodia for the 2d straight day Dec. 4 after Communist mortars had shelled the district towns of Caicai and Hongngu in the delta.

• A combined force of U.S. and government troops killed 53 North Vietnamese soldiers in 2 clashes near the city of Tayninh Dec. 6. One American was killed. The clashes were a result of an allied sweep and offensive to deny the rice harvest in the province to enemy troops. North Vietnamese forces came under U.S. infantry assault in Tayninh Province Dec. 7-8, and 33 were reported killed. (Another 54 North Vietnamese were said to have been slain in the same period in other scattered clashes along the Cambodian border northwest of Saigon.)

• South Vietnamese military headquarters reported that government troops had killed 158 Communists in 8 scattered engagements initiated by the South Vietnamese Dec. 14. In one of the heaviest clashes, 45 enemy troops were slain several miles from the Cambodian border north of the U.S. Special Forces camp at Budop. 15 North Vietnamese were reported slain by government troops near Budop Dec. 16.

● Government forces came under heavy Communist attack several miles northeast of Giadouc in the Mekong delta Dec. 16, losing 17 men. The South Vietnamese had been airlifted into the area by American helicopters, but they had not requested American air strike support.

● U.S. B-52 bombers Dec. 20 raided suspected Communist concentrations in the Ashau Valley region for the first time in 2 months. The U.S. command reported that 5 planes had dropped 150 tons of explosives on targets that included base camps and supply and staging areas just northwest of the valley and 2 miles from the Laotian border. The raid followed reports of increased enemy activity.

Separate truces declared by allied and Communist forces for the Christmas and New Year's holidays in South Vietnam were marked by sporadic violations resulting in reported heavy losses to the enemy. The allies observed a suspension of fighting for 2 24-hour periods, starting at 6 p.m. Dec. 25 and at 6 p.m. Dec. 31. The Viet Cong announced a halt in combat for 2 3-day periods, starting at 1 a.m. Dec. 24 and at 1 a.m. Dec. 30. The allied forces did not observe the Viet Cong's proclaimed Christmas truce, except when it overlapped their own ceasefire.

The U.S. command charged that the enemy had committed 115 violations of the allied Christmas truce; 61 of them were described as significant. During this 24-hour period 3 Americans were reported wounded and 11 South Vietnamese killed, while reported Communist losses totaled 101 killed and 13 captured. The 24-hour New Year's truce proclaimed by the allies was shattered by 30 "significant" Communist violations, claiming the lives of 5 Americans and 40 of the enemy. Allied authorities reported that since the start of the Viet Cong's 3-day New Year's truce, battles initiated by both sides had resulted in the death of 221 enemy soldiers and 16 Americans and South Vietnamese.

In the fiercest battle in 6 weeks, American forces Dec. 27 killed 72 of 250 North Vietnamese soldiers in a day-long clash 9 miles northwest of Locninh, about 80 miles north of Saigon. Most of the enemy casualties were inflicted by U.S. air strikes. Casualties among the 350 U.S. and government troops were reported light. 7 Americans were killed Dec. 28 by an explosive charge hurled by raiders who penetrated the night defensive position of the 25th Infantry Division near Laikhe, about 25 miles northwest of Saigon. U.S. jets came to the aid of the Americans and killed 3 of the attackers before the enemy force withdrew.

Shifts in Armed Strength

The last of the 60,000 U.S. troops scheduled to be withdrawn from Vietnam by Dec. 15 left the country before the end of November. The U.S. military command, disclosing this Dec. 1, said that the number of U.S. servicemen in Vietnam had dropped as of Nov. 27 to 479,500, a figure below the 484,000 maximum set by Pres. Nixon Sept. 16 and the lowest total since Dec. 1967.

The number of South Vietnamese forces was increasing while Communist totals were declining, according to separate announcements made by Saigon authorities Dec. 10 and by U.S. officials in Washington Dec. 18.

Saigon reported that 88,000 men had been added to its armed forces during the past 6 months, raising the total to 1,090,000 men compared with 1,002,000 in June. These figures included: army, 374,000; navy, 28,000; air force, 32,000; marines, 11,000; regional forces 252,000; popular forces, 178,000; paramilitary forces, including national police, civilian irregulars and pacification units, 215,000. The U.S. Defense Department reported Dec. 18 that Communist forces in South Vietnam totaled 100,000 North Vietnamese, 100,000 guerrillas and 40,000 "main force" Viet Cong. This compared with 290,000 Communist troops in 1968. In 1968, Hanoi's troops had comprised 70% of the total enemy strength, compared with a current estimate of 40%. The department said that as of Dec. 6, 6,064 civilians had been "killed by acts of Viet Cong terrorists" in 1969. This compared with 5,389 terrorist killings of civilians in 1968, excluding the Tet offensive casualties, which were not definitive.

The Philippine army's 1,350-man noncombatant contingent withdrew from South Vietnam Dec. 12-20. The force had been in the country since Sept. 1966, working on construction and medical projects.

Australian Prime Min. John G. Gorton Dec. 16 announced tentative plans to reduce his country's 8,500-man force in South Vietnam. Implementation of the partial pullout, he said, "can only occur in the light of future military developments in Vietnam and after full consultation and agreement with the South Vietnamese and New Zealand." (Army Min. Phillip Lynch reported in Canberra May 13 that Australian casualties in Vietnam totaled

294 men killed and 1,340 wounded.)

South Korean Foreign Minister Choi Kyu Hah declared Dec. 20 that his government had "no plans at present" to reduce or withdraw its 50,000-man combat force from South Vietnam. Choi said a pullout would be considered only if the South Vietnamese army became strong enough to replace allied troops on the battlefield.

Thailand Interior Min. Gen. Praphas Charusathien said Dec. 22 that his country had no intentions of withdrawing its 12,000 combat troops from South Vietnam. His remark followed a statement by Thai Foreign Min. Thanat Khoman Dec. 21 that he would formally ask the cabinet to order the withdrawal of some of the Thai soldiers.

Laos, Cambodia & Thailand

The war in Vietnam continued to generate pressures on Laos and Cambodia throughout 1969 as the U.S. sought to deny the use of territory in these neighboring states to the North Vietnamese and the Viet Cong. By far the heavier pressure was felt in Laos, which was regarded by the U.S. as the principal avenue through which men and materiel moved (down the Ho Chi Minh Trail) from North Vietnam into South Vietnam. The situation in Laos was complicated by a civil war in which the Pathet Lao (antigovernment) side was supported not only by North Vietnamese weapons and supplies but by strong contingents of North Vietnamese troops.

While visiting Vietnam in March, U.S. Defense Secy. Melvin Laird commented Mar. 10 on a Mar. 8 *N.Y. Times* report that about 100 U.S. Marines had seized several hilltops inside Laos near the northern South Vietnamese town of Dongha during an operation against Viet Cong and North Vietnamese forces. The U.S. troops were reported to have left the Laotian positions after a week. Laird said: "Our forces and our commanders are able to take necessary action to protect the safety of American troops, and this policy has been pursued for some time in Vietnam. I do not consider that an escalation."

Laird's remarks were reported Mar. 12 to have disturbed Laotian officials. One unidentified official was quoted as saying that "in effect, Secy. Laird admitted that the iceberg does in fact protrude above water. This is a dangerous admission, which the

North Vietnamese and Pathet Lao will not fail to use in their propaganda." A Laotian government communiqué Mar. 12 said U.S. Amb. Willam Sullivan had "expressed his regrets to the prime minister [Souvanna Phouma] and assured him that his country would contiune to avoid the extension of hostilities onto Laotian territory. He also informed the prime minister that the American military authorities in Saigon have informed him that the American Marines already left Laotian territory."

Controversy over the extent of U.S. involvement in Laos and Thailand arose in the Senate Sept. 17 in the final days of a protracted debate over a military procurement authorization bill. Sen. John Sherman Cooper (R., Ky.) presented a proposal to bar the use of funds for U.S. combat support of "local forces" in Thailand or Laos. Cooper said the proposal's purpose was to "prevent, if possible, the United States from moving step by step into war in Laos or Thailand, as it did in Vietnam." The proposal was passed unanimously later Sept. 17. Cooper made his move the same day the *N.Y. Times* carried a report from Laos that important military gains made recently by Laotian government troops against the Pathet Lao, the Communist-led guerrilla force, had been effected with U.S. air and logistic support.

Cooper said Sept. 17 he thought the U.S. was "fighting there" while neither the Pentagon nor the State Department had informed Congressional committees that American troops were engaged in combat in the 2 countries. Contending that the situation revealed "a very striking similarity to the way we became involved in the war in Vietnam," Cooper called Sept. 18 for a Congressional probe. Sen. Stuart Symington (D., Mo.) disclosed Sept. 19 that his Foreign Relations subcommittee on foreign commitments had already initiated an investigation into the extent of the American military involvement in Laos. "We have been at war in Laos for years," Symington said, "and it is time the American people knew more of the facts." The use of U.S. troops in Laos and Thailand for bombing missions against Communist infiltration routes into South Vietnam was well-known. No combat role in either country against insurgent forces was acknowledged, however.

Senate Democratic leader Mike Mansfield (Mont.) warned Sept. 21, in a report to the Senate on a recent Asian trip, that American "reinvolvement" in Laos had reached "disturbing proportions." "Every effort must be made to avoid any further magnification of the American presence in Laos," he said, and "most importantly, any enlarging commitment of U.S. military forces in this remote region must be restrained." Mansfield said that "at best," the U.S. involvement in Laos was costing some American lives and hundreds of millions of dollars and, "at worst, it could lead to the full assumption of a U.S. military role in the pattern of Vietnam." The U.S. role in Laos was running "directly counter to what should be anticipated from the President's new [Asian] doctrine," he declared, adding that there was "no indication, as yet, of when or how the size of the United States presence in Asia is to be reduced in any significant degree." He suggested the circulation of a Presidential directive on the new Asian policy throughout the government, a freeze on civilian and military staffs in Southeast Asia, a firm rein on military aid, "no deepening of our direct military involvement with any Asian government" and a review of U.S. treaty commitments.

At his press conference Sept. 26, Pres. Nixon said, in response to a question on the U.S. role in Laos, that "we have been providing logistical support and some training for the neutralist [Laotian] government in order to avoid Laos falling under Communist domination. As far as American manpower in Laos is concerned, there are none there at the present time on a combat basis." As for the bombing of North Vietnam's Ho Chi Minh Trail from bases in Thailand and Vietnam, Nixon said: "Laos relates very much to Vietnam, because the Ho Chi Minh Trail runs through Laos. It is necessary, under those circumstances, that the United States take cognizance of that, and we do have aerial reconnaissance. We do have, perhaps, some other activities. I won't discuss those others activities at this time."

An intensified U.S. air offensive against the Ho Chi Minh Trail, aimed at thwarting a possible Communist buildup in South Vietnam, was reported by official sources in Saigon, according to an AP dispatch Nov. 23. The U.S. command declined to comment on the report. The AP dispatch said U.S. Navy planes from 2 carriers in the Gulf of Tonkin had been diverted from missions in South Vietnam to join U.S. Air Force jets in the air strikes and cited a 2-fold purpose of the operations: to destroy repaired road networks before the Communists could transport war matériel from North Vietnam through Laos into South Vietnam and to intercept Communist troop movements through Laos. 4 U.S. planes had been shot down and 2 pilots lost in 10 days during bombing missions against the North Vietnamese supply trails, Reuters

reported from Vientiane Nov. 21. The aircraft were believed to have
been lost in attacks on the Mugia Pass that extended from North
Vietnam to Laos, about 70 miles north of the demilitarized zone
dividing North and South Vietnam. North Vietnamese troops were
said to have attacked Laotian government troops just west of the
DMZ in an effort to clear the way for an estimated 1,000 supply
trucks on the Ho Chi Minh Trail.

    U.S. intelligence sources had reported June 29 that the Cam-
bodian port of Sihanoukville had replaced the Ho Chi Minh Trail
as the major channel for Communist supplies into South Vietnam.
However, the trail was still being used to infiltrate supplies and
troops to the northern part of South Vietnam.

    Cambodia's embroilment in the Vietnamese conflict had be-
gun in 1962 when its border regions were first entered in brief
operations by South Vietnamese forces in hot pursuit of Viet Cong
and North Vietnamese troops seeking sanctuary in Cambodian
territory. In the ensuing years, these operations, joined by American forces, mounted in intensity as the Communists made wider
use of Cambodia as a haven from allied air and ground strikes.
Prince Norodom Sihanouk, Cambodian chief of state, insisted
publicly that he was helpless to prevent the movement of Communist forces into and out of Cambodia. This period was marked
also by the intensification of a long-standing Cambodian border
dispute with South Vietnam. Cambodia and South Vietnam had
competed for the Mekong delta ricelands since the 17th century.

    The UN Secretariat received documented complaints in which
the Cambodian government charged Jan. 31 and Feb. 1, 1969
that U.S. and South Vietnamese forces had killed and wounded
civilians in Cambodian territory Dec. 14, 1968 and in 3 raids in
Nov. 1968. The Secretariat Feb. 1 issued as a Security Council
document a Cambodian letter containing photos of the bodies of
7 persons identified as slain in the Dec. 14 attacks (in which a truck
had been ambushed). It quoted 2 survivors as saying that some of
the wounded had been shot to death and that the truck was looted
by the attackers, who left in "5 United States helicopters," sum-
moned by radio by "whites speaking in loud voices." The document
listed 3 incidents in Nov. 1968 in which 16 civilians reportedly had
been killed and 29 wounded. 23 civilians, including 8 children and
5 women, were injured Nov. 6 in a helicopter gunship attack at
Preytoul in Svayrieng Province. One of the wounded later died. 3
Cambodian provincial guards were killed by allied fire Nov. 15

about 110 yards inside the Cambodian border at Bosman, in Svay-rieng Province. The most serious incident was said to have occurred Nov. 16, when 3 armed motorboats fired into the village of Bat Naleak in Kampot Province. 3 children and 9 women were slain; 7 persons were wounded. Accompanying the documents was a magazine edited by Prince Sihanouk with the same photos and editorial comment. The editorial said: "The world must be aware of the savagery of the assassins." "Why, to satisfy what principles, for what military requirements were these citizens of a neutral and peaceful country selected as victims by these murderers of the American Army?"

A Cambodian note handed to the UN Security Council Apr. 18 called on the Council to demand that the U.S. "immediately halt its military operations" on Cambodian territory. The note said that it was "particulary significant" that U.S. Defense Secy. Melvin Laird had commented, during his recent trip to South Vietnam, "that the purpose of all these frontier crossings was to ensure the security of U.S. troops, thus opening the door to invasion of any country on the mere pretext of maintaining security." (Laird had made the statement in commenting on a U.S. incursion into Laos.) In a separate note to the Security Council Apr. 18, Cambodia charged that U.S. and South Vietnamese troops had killed one Cambodian villager and wounded 2 others in 4 border incidents between Mar. 17 and 25. A Cambodian communiqué Apr. 14 claimed that allied helicopters and armored vehicles had killed 2 civilians in raids against Cambodian villages in Svayrieng Province Apr. 5.

South Vietnam called on the International Control Commission Apr. 18 to ask Cambodia to stop North Vietnam from using its territory for attacks on South Vietnam. In the note to the ICC, South Vietnam charged that North Vietnamese troops had attacked the South Vietnamese border province of Kientuong from Cambodia.

The U.S. State Department disclosed June 4 that Cambodia had filed a protest with the U.S. government charging that American and South Vietnamese planes had defoliated Cambodian crops near the South Vietnamese frontier. The missions, carried out between Apr. 18 and May 14, destroyed millions of dollars worth of crops, according to the Cambodians. The State Department said June 4 that U.S. planes "engaged in defoliation operations in the Republic of Vietnam approached no closer than 5 kilometers [3 miles] from the Cambodian border." The department said the U.S. had asked the Pnompenh government June 2 to permit American observers to enter Cambodia to investigate possible crop damage. Cambodia agreed to the request. Huot Sambath, Cambodian delegate to the UN, was reported June 4 to have charged in a letter to Secy. Gen. U Thant that U.S. and South Vietnamese planes had destroyed about 37,000 acres of Cambodian rubber plantations and hundreds of acres of fruit crops. Sambath estimated the damage at about $7.7 million. In a letter to the UN Security Council May 7, Sambath had said that Cambodian police Apr. 28 had shot down 2 U.S. helicopters over Cambodian territory and that several other U.S. helicopters had violated Cambodian airspace to rescue survivors. The Cambodian letter denounced "the disgraceful tactics" used by U.S. forces "and by certain United States newspapers which represent Cambodian posts and troops as foreign encampments in order to justify aggression and bombing against Cambodia."

The *N.Y. Times* reported May 8 that Nixon Administration sources had disclosed that in the previous week, U.S. B-52 bombers had raided several Viet Cong and North Vietnamese supply dumps in Cambodia for the first time, but Cambodia did not protest. The *Times* report said that Cambodian authorities had often provided U.S. and South Vietnamese military officials at the border with information on Viet Cong/North Vietnamese troop movements into South Vietnam from Cambodia. Prince Sihanouk said Oct. 16 that 40,000 North Vietnamese and Viet Cong troops were occupying his country in 7 provinces bordering South Vietnam. Following further U.S. air strikes on North Vietnamese positions in Cambodia in November, the Pnompenh government warned Nov. 22 that these raids jeopardized U.S.-Cambodian relations. Huot Sambath said air strikes Nov. 16-18 had killed 27 Cambodians and wounded many others. A Pnompenh communiqué Nov. 25 claimed that U.S. planes had deliberately attacked a Cambodian post at Dak Dam in Mondolkiri Province Nov. 16-17. The U.S. apologized for the strikes.)

The Cambodian Foreign Ministry announced May 9 that it had agreed to raise diplomatic relations with the National Liberation Front, the political arm of South Vietnam's Viet Cong, to the embassy level. The NLF had maintained a diplomatic mission in Pnompenh for years. A Pnompenh radio broadcast June 21 said the Viet Cong had admitted its troops were using Cambodia as a sanctuary. The Viet Cong pledged to withdraw from Cambodia at the end of the Vietnam war. The broadcast quoted Prince Sihanouk as saying that the Viet Cong had signed a pledge respecting the territorial integrity of Cambodia "once peace has been restored."

The State Department disclosed June 11 that the U.S. and Cambodia had agreed in principle to reestablish diplomatic relations, suspended since May 3, 1965. Officials said the 2 countries would resume relations on the level of charges d'affaires. The agreement followed an earlier exchange of notes between Prince Sihanouk and Pres. Nixon. In one of his previous notes the Cambodian chief of state had reversed an earlier decision to resume ties with Washington. During the earlier exchange, Nixon had declared in a message delivered to Sihanouk Apr. 16: "In conformity with the UN Charter, the U.S. recognizes and respects the sovereignty, independence, neutrality and territorial integrity of the kingdom of Cambodia within its present frontiers." In response to Nixon's note, Sihanouk later Apr. 16 thanked the President "for this gesture of justice and fairness." He reported that he was ready to resume diplomatic relations with the U.S. Sihanouk said: "We have lost much in the past 4 years through not having direct contact with the Americans. The significance of relations is that they will permit the settlement, in a certain measure," of the incidents arising from intrusions into Cambodia of U.S. and South Vietnamese troops pursuing Communist forces. The resumption of relations, Sihanouk said, would permit Pnompenh "to play a new card."

Sihanouk Apr. 30 withdrew his assent to the resuming of diplomatic relations with the U.S. because the U.S. had failed to mention its stand on the disposition of a group of offshore islands, including Dao Phu Duoc, claimed by both Cambodia and South Vietnam. The key phrase in the Apr. 16 U.S. note with which Sihanouk took issue was its recognition of Cambodia's sovereignty "within its present boundaries." The State Department had declined to specify what the U.S. regarded as Cambodia's current frontier. The U.S. delivered another note to Pnompenh May 22. In its May 22 message, the U.S. asserted that "no statements had been made by or on behalf of the U.S. government contradicting, expanding or expressing reservations" to the Apr. 16 note. Sihanouk accepted Washington's explanation and reversed his Apr. 30 decision against recognition.

(Despite the reversal of Sihanouk's decision, continued exacerbation of relations between the 2 countries forestalled an actual exchange of ambassadors. Diplomatic ties were not resumed formally until after Sihanouk's ouster in 1970.)

The U.S. and Thailand announced Sept. 30 that 6,000 U.S. airmen and soldiers would be withdrawn from Thailand by July 10, 1970. A joint announcement, issued simultaneously by Pres. Nixon in Washington and by Thai Premier Thanom Kittikachorn in Bangkok, said the Americans "will be withdrawn as expeditiously as possible [starting in a few weeks] consistent with the operational requirements related to the Vietnam conflict."

The decision to reduce the U.S. military presence in Thailand followed bilateral talks that had started in Bangkok Sept. 3 at Thailand's initiative. Foreign Min. Thanat Khoman had said Sept. 8 that his government's demands for the talks had been prompted by "a campaign of deception and misrepresentation" in the U.S. to create the impression that the 1965 U.S.-Thailand military contingency agreement was about to drag the U.S. into "a 2d Vietnam" and to undermine "in the eyes of the world the position of Thailand." The 1965 accord provided for the possible use of U.S. forces to protect Thailand against any Communist attack. Khoman said the U.S. "has indicated to us that they feel the need of hospitality of their forces here to help protect the American forces in Vietnam, and the premier [Kittikachorn] and myself have said, 'by all means.'"

The U.S. had about 49,000 men in Thailand—36,000 in the Air Force, 12,000 Army support troops and 1,000 military advisers. The movement of the U.S. troops into Thailand had started in 1965 when the big buildup of American soldiers in Vietnam had begun. U.S. Defense Secy. Melvin Laird had angered Thai officials with a statement Aug. 21 that he personally disagreed with the 1965 contingency plan and noted that the Nixon Administration had not approved it. In an effort to ease Bangkok's concern over Laird's remarks, State Secy. William P. Rogers assured Thanat Khoman Aug. 25 that the U.S. would "honor its commitment to Thailand as embodied in the SEATO Treaty."

The U.S. embassy in Bangkok announced Dec. 26 that 2,400 American military personnel had been withdrawn from Thailand since October in accordance with the agreement.

U.S. support of a Thai division fighting in Vietnam cost the U.S. about $1 billion, according to a Dec. 1 *N.Y. Times* report, which credited Congressional sources. The article said the 1965 arrangement provided for a 5-year program that began in 1966; it included equipment, logistic support, financial payment for the division, military aid to the Thai armed forces in Thailand and economic aid to the Thai government. The military arrangement reportedly covered a supply of Hawk missiles and F-5 jet fighter planes. A report from South Vietnam Dec. 2 said the Thai forces in Vietnam, which had begun ground operations in Sept. 1967 attached to the U.S. 9th Division at Camp Bearcat, totaled 11,547 troops. The camp had been turned over to the Thais and 28 U.S. liaison officers July 8. (Thai battle deaths totaled 204.)

The U.S. embassy in Bangkok Dec. 2 denied any 5-year agreement involving Thai participation in the Vietnam war and called the impression erroneous that all U.S. aid to Thailand in recent years was connected with the Thai combat unit. The State Department confirmed in Washington Dec. 2 that Thailand received an unspecified additional amount of military and economic aid in connection with the dispatch of Thai troops to Vietnam.

Pres. Nixon said at his press conference Dec. 8 that the U.S. was "subsidizing" Thai troops in Vietnam but that the amount was "far less" than the billion dollars alleged. The U.S. also was subsidizing South Korean troops in Vietnam, he noted. The public was entitled "to know everything that they possibly can with regard to any involvement of the United States abroad."

NIXON & HIS CRITICS

Nixon Seeks Support Against Dissenters

Nixon Administration moves Oct. 15-21 indicated that Pres. Nixon was seeking to enlist ranking Democratic leaders in open support of his plans for ending the Vietnam war and defusing the antiwar demonstrations shaking the country.

Ex-Vice Pres. Hubert H. Humphrey revealed Oct. 15 that he had promised Nixon that, as head of the Democratic Party, he would never say, "You are the man who lost the war." Humphrey had indorsed the Administration's Vietnam position Oct. 10 after a White House meeting with Nixon. Humphrey restated his position that he believed Nixon was on the right path toward ending the war and that he would support the President as long as he stayed on this path. Humphrey said he had told Nixon that if he took the steps needed to end the war, "he can depend on Hubert H. Humphrey to support him."

Nixon Oct. 20 received support from 2 Senate critics of the war—majority leader Mike Mansfield and J.W. Fulbright—who said they were convinced that Nixon was actively seeking to end the war. Mansfield, speaking on the Senate floor, said the President should be given recognition for reducing the level of the fighting; he expressed hope that the nation would support Nixon on this course. Mansfield said such support would encourage Nixon to take additional steps toward a "responsible settlement" of the war. Fulbright made his comments to newsmen in a discussion of U.S. military involvement in Laos. Fulbright said he believed Nixon "was trying to wind down the war in Vietnam, and I assume that his [scheduled] Nov. 3 speech will provide further evidence of his determination to liquidate the war."

Nixon had met with his major foreign policy advisers Oct. 19 at the Presidential retreat at Camp David, Md. to try to devise a formula for accelerated U.S. troop withdrawals from South Vietnam. Nixon met with State Secy. William P. Rogers, Defense Secy. Melvin Laird, Atty. Gen. John Mitchell and Henry Kissinger, Nixon's adviser on national security. According to the *Washington Post* Oct. 19, the artiwar Vietnam "moratorium" demonstrations convinced some Administration officials that Nixon could broaden popular support for his Vietnam policy if a more specific timetable for troop withdrawals was advanced.

The white House circulated on Capitol Hill Oct. 21 a 3-page "fact sheet" outlining political and military steps taken by the Nixon Administration to de-escalate and end the war. Several Congress members described the move as an effort to buy additional time to implement a settlement. Others regarded it as a move to keep critics of the Administration's Vietnam policy on the defensive. The document asserted that the Administration had succeeded in reducing the level of fighting and cutting the number of casualties by withdrawing U.S. troops and by altering battlefield strategy. The paper used figures from the Johnson Administration to illustrate "that for the first time" the Administration had made "concrete and comprehensive political proposals for settlement of the war."

Sen. George D. Aiken (Vt.), ranking Republican on the

Foreign Relations Committee, said: "Unless the unexpected happens, I expect that practically all of our ground troops will be withdrawn a year from now." Aiken emphasized that his statement was not based on information supplied by the Administration. Mansfield told newsmen Oct. 21 that as a result of the Administration's change in battlefield tactics, he believed "a ceasefire and stand-fast of sorts was in operation." Mansfield added that he believed the Administration had taken a step in the direction of a unilateral ceasefire by its decision to replace the past strategy of "maximum pressure" with one of "protective reaction" by American ground troops. Senate minority leader Hugh Scott said there had been a "growth of optimism" and expressed hope for a "speedy de-escalation of the war." Fulbright remained skeptical of the Aministration's course to end the war.

In a nationally televised speech Nov. 3, Nixon said his Administration had adopted a plan in cooperation with the South Vietnamese for the complete withdrawal of all U.S. combat ground forces "on an orderly scheduled timetable." But he refused to divulge the timetable on the ground that it would remove the enemy's incentive to negotiate. They "would simply wait until our forces had withdrawn and then move in," he said. In general, the President defended the Vietnam policy he had spelled out in his May 14 policy speech, and he renewed his appeal for national unity in support of that policy.

Nixon coupled his appeal for unity with a warning that "North Vietnam cannot defeat or humiliate the United States. Only Americans can do that." He directed a special plea to "the great silent majority of my fellow Americans" for support. "I pledged in my campaign for the Presidency to end the war in a way that we could win the peace," he said. "I have initiated a plan of action which will enable me to keep that pledge. The more support I can have from the American people, the sooner that pledge can be redeemed. For the more divided we are at home, the less likely the enemy is to negotiate in Paris."

Nixon discussed the antiwar dissent within the U.S., upholding the right of any American "to advocate that point of view." But he reiterated his intention not "to be dictated [to] by the minority who hold that point of view and who try to impose it on the nation by mounting demonstrations in the street." "If a vocal minority, however fervent its cause, prevails over reason and the will of the majority, this nation has no future as a free society," Nixon said. He addressed himself in particular to "the young people of this nation who are particularly concerned . . . about this war." He said he respected their "idealism" and shared their "concern for peace." "I want peace as much as you do," Nixon declared. He said he had "chosen a plan for peace" and believed "it will succeed."

Nixon also revealed that he had taken a secret peace initiative in a letter to the late North Vietnamese Pres. Ho Chi Minh, but he said Ho "flatly rejected" it. Nixon, who released the texts of both letters, said he had sent his letter in mid-July and received an answer Aug. 30, 3 days before Ho's death. *The following is the text, released by the White House press office Nov. 3, of Nixon's letter to Ho:*

July 15, 1969

Dear Mr. President:

I realize that it is difficult to communicate meaningfully across the gulf of 4 years of war. But precisely because of this gulf, I wanted to take this opportunity to reaffirm in all solemnity my desire to work for a just peace. I deeply believe that the war in Vietnam has gone on too long and delay in bringing it to an end can benefit no one—least of all the people of Vietnam.

My speech on May 14 laid out a proposal which I believe is fair to all parties. Other proposals have been made which attempt to give the people of South Vietnam an opportunity to choose their own future. These proposals take into account the reasonable conditions of all sides. But we stand ready to discuss other programs as well, specifically the 10-point program of the NLF.

As I have said repeatedly, there is nothing to be gained by waiting. Delay can only increase the dangers and multiply the suffering.

The time has come to move forward at the conference table toward an early resolution of this tragic war. You will find us forthcoming and open-minded in a common effort to bring the blessings of peace to the brave people of Vietnam. Let history record that at this critical juncture, both sides turned their face toward peace rather than toward conflict and war.

Sincerely,

RICHARD NIXON

Following is the reply, which was received in Paris Aug. 30:

Hanoi, Aug. 25, 1969

Mr. President,

I have the honor to acknowledge receipt of your letter.

The war of aggression of the United States against our people, violating our fundamental national rights, still continues in South Vietnam. The United States continues to intensify military operations, the B-52 bombings and the use of toxic chemical products multiply the crimes against the Vietnamese people. The longer the war goes on, the more it accumulates the mourning and burdens of the American people. I am extremely indignant at the losses and destructions caused by the American troops to our people and our country. I am also deeply touched at the rising toll of death of young Americans who have fallen in Vietnam by reason of the policy of American governing circles.

Our Vietnamese people are deeply devoted to peace, a real peace with independence and real freedom. They are determined to fight to the end, without fearing the sacrifices and difficulties in order to defend their country and their sacred national rights. The over-all solution in 10 points of the National Liberation Front of South Vietnam and of the provisional revolutionary government of the Republic of South Vietnam is a logical and reasonable basis for the settlement of the Vietnamese problem. It has earned the sympathy and support of the peoples of the world.

In your letter you have expressed the desire to act for a just peace. For this the United States must cease the war of aggression and withdraw their troops from South Vietnam, respect the right of the population of the South and of the Vietnamese nation to dispose of themselves, without foreign influence. This is the correct manner of solving the Vietnamese problem in conformity with the national rights of the Vietnamese people, the interests of the United States and the hopes for peace of the peoples of the world. This is the path that will allow the United States to get out of the war with honor.

With goodwill on both sides we might arrive at common efforts in view of finding a correct solution of the Vietnamese problem.

Sincerely,
Ho Chi Minh

In his address, Nixon reviewed the original involvement of the U.S. in Vietnam, his assessment of the situation when he became President, his Administration's changes in negotiating and military tactics, the formulation of the new "Nixon Doctrine" for Asian policy and the new policy for "Vietnamization" of the Vietnam fighting:

● In January after assuming office, Nixon said, he had concluded that a precipitate U.S. withdrawal from Vietnam "would be a disaster" for South Vietnam, the U.S. and "the cause of peace." It would lead to Communist massacres in Vietnam and to "a collapse of confidence in American leadership" throughout the world. The latter situation in turn would "spark violence wherever our commitments help maintain the peace—in the Middle East, in Berlin, eventually even in the Western Hemisphere."

● Instead of a precipitate withdrawal, therefore, Nixon said he had "initiated a pursuit for peace on many fronts." But the Administration's diplomatic efforts were rebuffed. In Paris, "Hanoi has refused even to discuss our proposals." 2 private offers "for a rapid, comprehensive settlement" drew nothing but replies which "called in effect for our surrender before negotiations." In addition, his Administration had asked the Soviet Union for diplomatic assistance "on a number of occasions," and similar bids had been made to other governments having diplomatic relations with North Vietnam. "None of these intiatives have to date produced results," Nixon said.

● 11 secret or private sessions in Paris between the U.S. and North Vietnam were also fruitless, as were "other significant initiatives which must remain secret to keep open some channels of communications." "No progress whatever has been made except agreement on the shape of the bargaining table," and it was clear that "the obstacle is the other side's absolute refusal to show the least willingness to join us in seeking a just peace."

● Nixon then turned to "another plan to bring peace—a plan which will bring the war to an end regardless of what happens on the negotiating front." His Nixon Doctrine for Asian policy was part of this, as was the "Vietnamization" plan to strengthen the South Vietnamese "so that they could defend themselves when we left." "In July, on my visit to Vietnam, I changed Gen. [Creighton] Abrams' orders so that they were consistent with the objectives of our new policies." Since then, U.S. air operations had been reduced by over 20%, by Dec. 15 more than 60,000 U.S. combat troops were to have been withdrawn, the South Vietnamese "have continued to gain in strength," enemy infiltration was less and U.S. casualties had declined in the past 2 months to the lowest point in 3 years.

● Nixon revealed his plan for the complete withdrawal of all U.S. combat ground forces "and their replacement by South Vietnamese forces on an orderly scheduled timetable." The withdrawal "will be made from strength and not from weakness. As South Vietnamese forces become stronger, the rate of American withdrawal can become greater." The rate of withdrawal would depend on the status of the Paris talks, the level of enemy activity and the progress in Vietnamization. Progress on the latter 2 fronts "has been greater than we anticipated"; "as a result, our timetable for withdrawal is more optimistic now than when we made our first estimates in June." But "if the level of enemy activity significantly increases, we might have to adjust our timetable accordingly." "If I conclude that increased enemy action jeopardizes our remaining forces in Vietnam, I shall not hesitate to take strong and effective measures to deal with that situation."

There were only 2 choices "open to us if we want to end this war," Nixon declared in his Nov. 3 address: "I can order an immediate precipitate withdrawal of all Americans from Vietnam without regard to the effects of that action. Or we can persist in our search for a just peace through a negotiated settlement, if possible, or through continued implementation of our plan for Vietnamization, if necessary. . . . I have chosen this 2d course. It is not the easy way. It is the right way. It is a plan which will end the war and serve the cause of peace, not just in Vietnam but in the Pacific and the world."

Nixon called newsmen into his office Nov. 4 to exhibit stacks of telegrams as evidence of an outpouring of support from "the great silent majority" of Americans. The telegrams numbered in the "high thousands," he said, and their dominant tone was that "we silent Americans are behind you." This demonstration of support can have more effect on ending the war sooner than anything else," Nixon declared. Referring to the diplomatic effort to end the war, Nixon said: "The train will move on that track at a much faster pace in direct relation to the support of the people in the United States." (A White House source told newsmen Nov. 4 that the President believed he could get the U.S. out of Vietnam honorably "if the people stick with him 4 to 6 months." "If Hanoi believes that American public opinion will stick with the President," the source said, "Hanoi will be more inclined to negotiate seriously.")

A resolution sponsored by 50 Democratic and 50 Republican members was introduced in the House Nov. 4 to support the President "in his efforts to negotiate a just peace in Vietnam." In the Senate, Nixon's Vietnam position was supported by, among others, Sen. Robert P. Griffin (Mich.), the assistant Republican leader, and John G. Tower (R., Tex.). The resolution was approved by 21-8 vote of the House Foreign Affair's Committee Nov. 6.

Nixon's speech was criticized Nov. 4 by Sen. J.W. Fulbright, who said Nixon had "taken fully as his own the Johnson war, based on a fundamental error." The error, he said, was an assumption that the war was being waged against an international Communist conspiracy. If the assumption were accepted, Fulbright said, "there is no justification for winding down the war." He said he favored "educational" hearings by his committee to "develop the real facts about the war" for the "great silent majority" cited by Nixon.

Senate Democratic leader Mike Mansfield (Mont.) said Nov. 4 that while "the President spoke sincerely for peace," he had given "no specifics" and "I am afraid the issue of Vietnam will remain as divisive as ever in the life of the nation." Assistant Senate Democratic leader Edward M. Kennedy said that "there now must be doubt whether there is in existence any plan to extricate America from this war in the best interest of America, for it is no plan to say that what we do depends upon what Hanoi does." Sen. Albert Gore (D., Tenn.) said, "A one-sided withdrawal" of U.S. troops "on an uncertain but long-drawn-out incremental basis" meant that U.S. policy was "tied to maintenance of the Thieu-Ky regime in power [in Saigon]." Senate leaders Mansfield and Hugh Scott (R., Pa.) Nov. 7 introduced a resolution encouraging the President to end the war by negotiations and "a mutual ceasefire." The resolution was immediately supported by 40 Senators, including 26 Republicans. Bipartisan support for the resolution was achieved when Mansfield persuaded Scott to include the ceasefire provision so that the action would not be a simple blanket indorsement of the President's policy.

The speech tended to harden the position of leaders of the antiwar protest movement. Among their comments Nov. 3:

Sam Brown, spokesman for the Vietnam Moratorium Committee—
"It is clear that the word has not gotten through to the President,
and we've just got to work harder." *Stewart Meacham* of the
American Friends Service Committee and co-chairman of the New
Mobilization Committee to End the War in Vietnam—"I said . . .
if we had bad speeches from Nixon and good weather, we'd have
lots of people for the demonstration [planned for Nov. 13-15].
Well, we've had the bad speech. . . ." *Charles Palmer*, president
of the National Student Association—"It rededicated me to work
against the war, and I think it will rededicate others."

Hanoi radio Nov. 4 broadcast North Vietnam's denunciation
of President Nixon's speech and called on the U.S. to withdraw
all troops unconditionally from Vietnam and cut its ties with the
Saigon government. The broadcast said that Nixon "in reality is
still trying to maintain the presence of U.S. forces in South Vietnam for a long time in order to pursue the war of aggression"
The same charge of prolongation of the war was also sounded in
Paris by the delegation representing North Vietnam.

South Vietnamese Pres. Nguyen Van Thieu Nov. 4 praised
Nixon's speech as "one of the most important and greatest" made
by a U.S. President. He said the Nixon policy outlined in the
speech was "the right policy" and he was in complete agreement
with it. South Vietnamese Vice Pres. Nguyen Cao Ky had asserted
Nov. 2 that Nixon's speech "will be aimed at the U.S. people and
will contain nothing new." Ky said that "next year I believe
some 180,000 American troops can be replaced by the South Vietnamese armed forces."

At the Nov. 6 session of the Paris talks, North Vietnam's
chief delegate, Xuan Thuy, charged that Nixon's disclosure of
secret U.S.-North Vietnamese talks and an exchange of letters
between Nixon and Ho Chi Minh was "a perfidious trick" and a
"betrayal of a promise." "The American representatives do not
keep their promises even for little things," Thuy continued. "That
is why we have said the United States speaks in one sense and
acts in a completely different sense. It speaks much of peace, but
in reality it pursues war." (Nguyen Thanh Le, North Vietnam's
press spokesman in Paris, said after the meeting that Henry Cabot
Lodge and Thuy had agreed Mar. 8 to hold secret meetings and
that Lodge had said then that "nothing should be said of the
nature of the contents" of that meeting nor of the manner "in
which we explain our positions.")

Nixon visited Congress Nov. 13 to thank the members who supported his policy for "a just peace in Vietnam." The President's action—separate appearances before each body the same day—was considered unprecedented. Nixon's strongest appeal before each body was for bipartisan unity on issues involving U.S. security. He told the House his purpose in coming was to "express appreciation to the members ... on both sides of this aisle for the support of a just peace in Vietnam." He specifically cited a resolution backing his Nov. 3 speech on Vietnam, which was signed by 300 members (181 Republicans and 119 Democrats) and sent to the U.S. negotiators in Paris. Nixon said the war was "difficult" and "controversial," but he would "continue to act with the majority of Americans supporting a just peace." "I believe that we will achieve a just peace in Vietnam," he said. "I believe—I cannot tell you the time, the date, but I do know this, that when that peace comes that it will come because of the support that we have received. ..." Nixon delivered a similar message before the Senate. He expressed gratitude that 60 Senators had signed letters to the U.S. negotiator Henry Cabot Lodge in support of his Vietnam position. While his Administration had "been subjected to some sharp criticism" by some Senators, Nixon said, he understood it and recognized it "as being one of the strengths of our system." He appealed to the Senate "not for your 100% support" but "for your understanding and support when you think we are right and for your constructive criticism when you think we are wrong."

Administration sources Nov. 16 released a personal message in which Israeli Premier Golda Meir called Nixon's Vietnam speech "meaningful." She said it contained "much that encourages and strengthens freedom-loving small nations."

Agnew Attacks News Media

Vice Pres. Spiro T. Agnew assailed the 3 national TV networks Nov. 13 for their news coverage and specifically for what he described as the hostility of the network commentators to Pres. Nixon's Nov. 3 speech on Vietnam. He suggested public pressure for "responsible news presentations." Agnew said that TV's immense power over public opinion was in the hands of "a small and unelected elite" of network producers, commentators and newsmen; that these men were often biased and, "to a man," reflected the "geographical and intellectual confines of Washington, D.C. or New York City." He also said "the views of the majority of this fraternity do not—and I repeat not—represent the views of America."

Agnew's attack was delivered before the Midwest Regional Republican Committee in Des Moines, Ia. It was carried live by all 3 networks, whose presidents defended their networks in statements the same day. Julian Goodman of the National Broadcasting Co. (NBC) said Agnew's "attack on television news is an appeal to prejudice" and use of high office "to criticize the way a government-licensed news medium covers the activities of government itself." Dr. Frank Stanton of Columbia Broadcasting System (CBS) called it an "unprecedented attempt by the Vice President of the United States to intimidate a news medium which depends for its existence upon government licenses." Whatever the deficiencies of CBS's newsmen, he said, "they are minor compared to those of a press which would be subservient to the executive power of government." Leonard H. Goldenson of American Broadcasting Companies (ABC) said ABC news was "fair and objective" and his network would "continue to report the news accurately and fully, confident in the ultimate judgment of the American public."

Concerning the President's Nov. 3 speech, Agnew said it had been "subjected to instant analysis and querulous criticism . . . by a small band of network commentators and self-appointed analysts, the majority of whom expressed in one way or another their hostility to what he [Nixon] had to say." Agnew said that the people had the right to "form their own opinions about a Presidential address" without having it "characterized through the prejudices of hostile critics" before it "can even be digested." Agnew cited in particular an instance in which W. Averell Harriman was "trotted out" and then presented "a broad range of gratuitous advice challenging and contradicting the policies outlined by the President." Agnew identified Harriman as the negotiator in Paris at a time when the U.S. "swapped some of the greatest military concessions in the history of warfare for an enemy agreement on the shape of the bargaining table." (Harriman had prefaced his remarks with a disclaimer that "I wouldn't be [so] presumptuous [as] to give a complete analysis of a very carefully thought-out speech by the President of the United States. I'm sure he wants to end this war and no one wishes him well any more than I do.")

Perhaps, Agnew said, "it is time that the networks were made more responsive to the views of the nation and more responsible to the people they serve." He stressed that he was "not asking for government censorship or any other kind of cenorship." But he asked "whether a form of censorship already exists when the news that 40 million Americans receive each night is determined by a handful of men responsible only to their corporate employers and is filtered through a handful of commentators who admit to their own set of biases." The answers to the questions he was raising, Agnew said, must come from the industry—"they are challenged to turn their critical powers on themselves, to direct their energy, their talent and their conviction toward improving the quality and objectivity of news presentation. They are challenged to structure their own civic ethics to relate their great [freedom with their great] responsibilities. . . . And the people . . . are challenged . . . to press for responsible news presentations." He suggested that the "same wall of separation [should] exist between news and comment on the nation's networks" as in newspapers.

Ex-Vice Pres. Hubert H. Humphrey Nov. 17 denounced Agnew's speech as "an obvious and calculated appeal to our people's lesser or baser instincts." Humphrey, attending the first meeting of the Democratic Policy Council (organized in September to speak for the party on national issues), suggested that the Nixon Administration was mounting a coordinated attack on the media and on antiwar demonstrators, "or it's one of the most unusual coincidences within the memory of man." The council later Nov. 17 adopted a resolution denouncing "efforts to stifle criticism of government officials by dissenting citizens and responsible newsmen." Accompanying Humphrey to his press conference Nov. 17 was Harriman, who said Agnew's comments on news coverage "smacked of a totalitarianism which I don't like at all."

Among other opposition to Agnew's speech:

Sen. Edward M. Kennedy Nov. 14—"We are now witnessing an attack designed to put American against American—an attack with the ultimate aim of dividing this country into those who support and those who do not support our President's position on Vietnam. If it is allowed to go on, this will be tragic."

National Education Television President James Day Nov. 13—Agnew's "sweeping remarks . . . both misrepresent and misinterpret the news functions ef television."

Thomas P. F. Hoving, chairman of the National Citizens Committee for Broadcasting, Nov. 13—Agnew's "disgraceful attack . . . officially leads us as a nation into an ugly era of the most fearsome suppression and intimidation."

The American Civil Liberties Union Nov. 15—Agnew had sounded a "clear and chilling threat" of censorship.

6 former government officials and the deans of 11 law schools in New York Nov. 15 issued a statement deploring "inflammatory" remarks attributed to Agnew and other high Administration officials in connection with war dissent. Among the officials were Arthur J. Goldberg, Eugene Rostow and William P. Bundy.

Supporters of Agnew's comments included:

Secy. George W. Romney of Housing and Urban Development, a luncheon speaker Nov. 14 at the Midwest Regional Republican Conference in Des Moines, who lauded Agnew as a "champion of the 'old culture' that values historic and democratic principles."

Sen. Hugh Scott (Pa.), Senate GOP leader, who said Nov. 14 that he thought "the networks deserve a thorough goosing."

GOP National Chairman Rogers C. B. Morton, who said Nov. 15 that Agnew had stated what "had to be said" and "everyone will profit from it."

White House Press Secy. Ronald L. Ziegler told newsmen Nov. 15 that Pres. Nixon had "great confidence" in Agnew, who had, the President thought, expressed himself "with great candor." Ziegler said Nixon had not discussed the speech with Agnew. Clark R. Mollenhoff, special counsel to the President, said Nov. 15 that Agnew's speech "reflected the views of the Administration." Herbert G. Klein, Nixon's director of communications, said Nov. 16 (on CBS' "Face the Nation" program) that Agnew's speech reflected a widely held view in the top levels of the Administration. Klein added: "I think you can go beyond that. All of the news media needs to re-examine itself in the format it has and its approach to problems of news, to meet the current issues of the day"; "I include the newspapers very thoroughly in this, as well as the networks—if you look at the problems you have today and you fail to continue to examine them, you do invite the government to come in. I would not like to see that happen."

Federal Communications Commission Chairman Dean Burch said Nov. 14 that Agnew's remarks were "thoughtful, provocative and deserve careful consideration by the industry and the public." Burch said he did not consider Agnew's speech intimidating. "Had the Vice President suggested that the government censor these networks, that would have been another thing entirely," he said. What Agnew did say, Burch suggested, was that the networks should "examine themselves to see whether they were doing a good job. In other words, 'Physician, heal thyself.'" Burch also acknowledged through a spokesman, that he had requested (by telephone

Nov. 5) transcripts from the networks of their commentaries after Nixon's Nov. 3 Vietnam speech.

But Nicholas Johnson, an FCC commissioner, said Nov. 17 that Agnew's speech "has frightened network executives and newsmen in ways that may cause serious and permanent harm to independent journalism and free speech in America." While it was true "that a handful of men control what the American people see through their television screens," he said, the answer was "not to transfer this power from a handful of men in New York to a handful of men in the White House." Nixon held his 8th formal news conference, his 3d in the past 6 months, at the White House Dec. 8. It was televised during "prime" evening program time. Vietnam was the major topic. Others included the news media and Nixon's evaluation of his own treatment by the press. *Nixon said:*

On Vietnam—There were signs the war was cooling off. Enemy infiltration and U.S. casualties were down, and if this continued, "we can see that the Vietnam war will come to a conclusion regardless of what happens at the bargaining table." And it will come to a conclusion as a result of the plan that we have instituted ... for replacing American troops with Vietnamese forces." "We have a plan for the reduction of American forces in Vietnam, for removing all combat forces from Vietnam regardless of what happens in negotiations. ... Developments since my Nov. 3 speech have been on schedule." Recent infiltration figures "seem to have been inflated," and now the infiltration was not considered significant enough to change the troop withdrawal plans. Concerning infiltration, the casualty rate and Vietnamization, there was "more progress on all fronts than we had anticipated." "We can go forward with our troop withdrawal program, and ... any action that the enemy takes, either against us or the South Vietnamese, can be contained within that program." "There will be a troop cut with a replacement by South Vietnamese later this month."

On the possibility that Administration attempts to gain support for Nixon's Vietnam policy might alienate part of the public and bring about polarization: "One of the problems of leadership is to take a position. ... Sometimes it is necessary to draw the line clearly, not to have enmity against those who disagree, but to make it clear that there can be no compromise where such great issues as self-determination and freedom and a just peace are involved." As for the possible failure of the Administration "to reach" the young people: "You reach the young people more by talking to them as adults than talking to them as young people. I like to treat them as adults."

On Agnew at the media—Agnew "rendered a public service in talking in a very dignified and courageous way about a problem that many Americans are concerned about ... the coverage by news media ... of public figures." Agnew "advocated that there should be free expression" and "recognized—as I do— that there should be opinion." Perhaps his point "should be well taken" that TV "might well follow the practice of newspapers of separating news from opinion." "Perhaps the networks disagreed with the criticism, but I would suggest that they should be just as dignified and just as reasonable in answering the criticisms as he was in making them." Nixon thought the news media had "been fair" to his Administration. He had "no complaints," especially about "the extent of the coverage."

'Just Peace' Resolution Approved

The House Dec. 2 adopted by 333-55 vote the resolution backing Nixon's "efforts to negotiate a just peace."

Many Congressmen who voted against the measure protested that the House was being turned into a "rubber stamp" for the President's policies in Vietnam. House leaders of both parties differed on whether the resolution also constituted an indorsement of the Administration's overall handling of the war. Speaker John McCormack (D., Mass.) told newsmen that the resolution, which he had helped bring to the floor for a vote, was "confined" to an indorsement of Nixon's pledge for free elections in Vietnam. But House Republican leader Gerald R. Ford (Mich.) termed the measure "an indorsement of the efforts of the Administration."

The resolution was limited to a statement indorsing the President's "efforts to negotiate a just peace," and support for Nixon's Nov. 3 statement that the people of Vietnam were entitled to choose their officials in free, supervised, nationwide elections.

The resolution passed easily after the House Democratic leadership backed the measure. Democrats reportedly did so because of fears that the White House could turn Democratic dissent on the war into political capital. The only threat to the resolution came Dec. 1 when Democrats and a bipartisan coalition of doves moved to open the resolution to amendments. The attempt was thwarted by a 225-132 vote that limited consideration to the resolution that was reported out Nov. 13 by the House Foreign Affairs Committee.

Text of the resolution, which had been introduced in the House by its author, Rep. James C. Wright Jr. (D., Tex.), Nov. 4:

Resolved, that the House of Representatives affirms its support for the President in his efforts to negotiate a just peace in Vietnam, expresses the earnest hope of the people of the United States for such a peace, calls attention to the numerous peaceful overtures which the United States has made in good faith toward the government of North Vietnam, requests the President to continue to press the government of North Vietnam to abide by the Geneva Convention of 1949 in the treatment of prisoners of war, approves and supports the principles enunciated by the President that the people of South Vietnam are entitled to choose their own government by means of free elections open to all

South Vietnamese and supervised by an impartial international body, and that the United States is willing to abide by the results of such elections, and supports the President in his call upon the government of North Vietnam to announce its willingness to honor such elections and to abide by such results and to allow the issues in controversy to be peacefully resolved in order that the war may be ended and peace may be restored at last in Southeast Asia.

Dispute Continues, New Withdrawal

In a Senate speech Dec. 8, Sen. Charles McC. Mathias Jr. (R., Md.) proposed the repeal of the 4 "cold war resolutions," including the 1964 Gulf of Tonkin Resolution. The others: the 1955 Quemoy-Matsu-Formosa Resolution, the 1957 Mideast Resolution and the 1962 Cuban Resolution. Mathias also proposed a Congressional declaration in support of the Administration's "disengagement" from Vietnam—its efforts to attain a political solution of the war and its plans for an accelerated withdrawal of U.S. forces. He proposed calling on all groups in South Vietnam to enter into discussions to produce "a new broadly based government." "No plan for American military withdrawal will end the war unless the present South Vietnam government adopts a plan for its own political withdrawal," Mathias said. Mathias' proposals drew praise from Senate Democratic leader Mike Mansfield and Republican leader Hugh Scott. The Administration's opposition to the repeal of the Tonkin Resolution was made known by the State Department Dec. 17.

Sen. J.W. Fulbright Dec. 10 criticized the Administration's Vietnam policy and urged a new initiative at the Paris talks. Speaking at Washington University in St. Louis, Fulbright said the Administration's Vietnamization plan would mean "a continuing war of stalemate and attrition with a reduced number of Americans reverting to their pre-1965 'advisory' role in a semipermanent war of counter-insurgency." As for talk about avoiding a first American defeat, Fulbright called this "prideful nonsense" not in a national interest but in the interest of a national ego and a Presidential standing in history. He defined the war as "a civil conflict in which communism is, and always has been, secondary to the drive for national independence." The war was not essential to the U.S., he said, but "the early restoration of peace matters enormously because every day that this war goes on the sickness of American society worsens." Fulbright advocated pushing negotiations in Paris toward arrangements for a new interim

government in South Vietnam and for elections and for a total
U.S. troop withdrawal.

(The *N.Y. Times* reported Dec. 16 that Fulbright had made
a secret personal appeal to Ho Chi Minh June 25 to make available the names of the U.S. prisoners of war. Ho had rebuffed
the bid July 25 on the ground that the issue could only be dealt
with as part of an over-all settlement of the war. Other bids for
information on the American prisoners were reportedly made at
the State Department's request by Sens. George McGovern and
Edward M. Kennedy.)

(In Congressional testimony released by a House defense
appropriations subcommittee Dec. 1, Gen. William C. Westmoreland, Army chief of staff, had held that the war would be over if
the U.S. had continued to bomb North Vietnam. Westmoreland
did not criticize the decision to stop bombing—"most prudent
individuals would have come to the same conclusion"—and did
not advocate a resumption of the bombing.)

A 3d U.S. troop reduction in South Vietnam was announced
by Pres. Nixon in a TV report to the nation Dec. 15. He ordered
a cut of 50,000 in the troop ceiling by Apr. 15, 1970. This, Nixon
said, brought the total reduction since he took office to 115,500.

Nixon said he was taking the action despite reports of a substantial increase in enemy infiltration into Vietnam. But, he
recalled, he had "consistently said we must take risks for peace,"
and he warned Hanoi that if infiltration and enemy activity increased while the U.S. was reducing its forces, "they also will be
running a risk." The President also repeated his advice to Hanoi
that there was "nothing to be gained by delay" in the matter of
peace negotiations and "if Hanoi is willing to talk seriously, they
will find us flexible and forthcoming." The U.S. would continue
to participate in the talks and to seek a negotiated peace, despite
"the inflexible attitude" Hanoi had taken "on all issues," Nixon
said. As far as the U.S. was concerned, "anything is negotiable
except the right of the people of South Vietnam to determine
their own fate."

Nixon referred to a report he had requested on Vietnam from
Sir Robert Thompson, a British expert on Communist guerrilla
movements in Asia. In a book "published just as this Administration took office," he said, Thompson "was very pessimistic about
the conduct of the war in Vietnam." But in Thompson's report
to him Dec. 3, Nixon reported, Thompson's assessment was

"cautiously optimistic" because of what he considered improvement in the military and political situation and especially the security situation in Saigon and the rural areas. According to Thompson, "a winning position, in the sense of obtaining a just peace whether negotiated or not, and of maintaining an independent, non-Communist South Vietnam has been achieved, but we are not yet through. We are in a psychological period where the greatest need is confidence a steady application of the do-it-yourself concept where continuing U.S. support in the background will increase the confidence already shown by many South Vietnamese leaders."

Nixon expressed appreciation "to the great number" of people who had "indicated their support for our program for a just peace." Such support, he said, was underlined by the action of the House in adopting a resolution "supporting the plan for peace" that he had announced Nov. 3.

Hanoi Gets New Chinese & Soviet Aid

New aid agreements between Hanoi and China and the Soviet Union were announced during the fall of 1969.

China agreed to provide North Vietnam with an undisclosed amount of economic and military aid in 1970 under an accord signed in Peking Sept. 26. The arrangement had been negotiated in August, but the death of Ho Chi Minh had delayed the signing. The agreement was signed by Deputy Premier Le Thanh Nghi, who headed a North Vietnamese delegation, and by Chinese Deputy Premier Li Hsien-nien. An accompanying statement by Nghi thanked China for its assistance and pledged "the entire Vietnamese people to scrupulously carry out Pres. Ho Chi Minh's testament to completely defeat the United States aggressors."

(China renewed its pledge to support and aid the Viet Cong following talks in Peking Oct. 16 by Premier Chou En-lai and Nguyen Huu Tho, president of the National Liberation Front.)

Under an accord signed in Moscow Oct. 15, the Soviet Union agreed to provide North Vietnam with economic and military aid and long-term credits "necessary for strengthening its defense capacity" and restoring and developing its economy. North Vietnam was to receive food, transport equipment, cotton, fertilizers and other goods, in addition to arms and ammunition. The agreement was signed by Soviet Premier Aleksei N. Kosygin and North Vietnamese Premier Pham Van Dong.

(Swedish Foreign Min. Torsten Nilsson announced Nov. 11 that Sweden would begin a 3-year program of economic aid to North Vietnam July 1, 1970. The program would provide aid valued at to $45 million, $5 million more than originally announced. Sweden's action was a reversal of a previous decision to provide only humanitarian assistance while the war was in progress.)

PARIS NEGOTIATIONS

Government for South Vietnam at Issue

The main issue on which the talks in Paris concentrated, and on which the conference remained deadlocked, was the question of the withdrawal of foreign troops from Vietnam as a condition for negotiating a settlement to the war. An issue that became central in the discussions during the spring of 1969 was that of creating a government for South Vietnam that might be acceptable as a part of the political solution.

Xuan Thuy, head of the North Vietnamese delegation, said in Paris May 24 that there were "points of agreements" between the U.S. and National Liberation Front (NLF) positions that "could be the subject of discussions." He did not identify the points. But North Vietnamese sources were said to indicate that Hanoi and the NLF believed that 2 of Pres. Nixon's 8 peace-program points were worth exploring—early elections in South Vietnam and the future sovereignty of the country. Before leaving for Hanoi to consult with his government, Thuy said that "to permit the [Paris] conference to progress it is necessary to abandon the present administration in Saigon, that belligerent, dictatorial and corrupt administration."

Henry Cabot Lodge, chief U.S. negotiator at the Paris talks, said at the conference's 19th plenary session May 29 that a political settlement in South Vietnam would be impossible without "the full participation and agreement" of Pres. Nguyan Van Thieu's Saigon government. Lodge repeated the allied call for negotiations on 2 questions—the mutual withdrawal of all non-South Vietnamese forces from South Vietnam and a political settlement.

The North Vietnamese and NLF delegations responded that the NLF's 10-point peace plan remained the only basis for negotiations. Lodge said after the meeting that all the Communists wanted was "the unconditional withdrawal of our troops and for us to overthrow the [Saigon] government."

In remarks made during state visits to South Korea and Nationalist China May 27-June 3, Pres. Thieu expressed strong opposition to a coalition government with the NLF. Despite Thieu's apparently new hardline position on conditions for peace, U.S. officials said May 30 and 31 that there were no significant differences between Saigon and Washington.

Speaking at a news conference in Seoul following a 4-day meeting with South Korean Pres. Chung Hee Park, Thieu declared May 30 that he would "never" agree to a coalition government with the NLF. His statement followed a question on his position if such a government with the NLF became a prerequisite to a settlement of the war. Asked whether he completely ruled out any prospect for the creation of such a coalition, Thieu asserted: "Let me say again. Never. Are you satisfied?" As for the NLF's role in possible elections, Thieu said: "If the Communists are willing to lay down their weapons, abandon the Communist ideology, and abandon atrocities, they could participate in elections."

In a joint communiqué issued later May 30, Thieu and Park reaffirmed that "the imposition of any form of government, including the spurious coalition advocated by the Communist side, would be incompatible with the principle of self-determination for the Vietnamese people and therefore completely unacceptable. The so-called National Liberation Front is not recognized as a separate entity but as a creation of the Communist North Vietnam and its instrument for aggression." Thieu and Park expressed their "common resolve" to resist any Communist demand for the unilateral and unconditional withdrawal of allied forces from South Vietnam. They opposed the unilateral withdrawal of "even a part of the allied troops" unless Communist soldiers also pulled out.

Thieu flew May 30 to Taipei, where he conferred with Nationalist Chinese Pres. Chiang Kai-shek until June 3. A joint communiqué signed by the 2 leaders June 3 stated that "the existing and popularly elected and legitimate government of the Republic of Vietnam must be respected and that the absurd demand by the Communists for organization of a coalition government must be resolutely rejected."

White House Press Secy. Ronald Ziegler said May 31 that Thieu had been "totally aware of" and had approved in advance Pres. Nixon's May 14 speech outlining a peace plan that appeared to take a stand more moderate than the one since taken by Thieu. Ziegler said "there's no indication that we have that [Thieu's] support of that speech would have changed." Ziegler issued the statement at the Florida White House in Key Biscayne, where State Secy. William P. Rogers had reported to Nixon May 30-31 on his recently completed 18-day trip to South Vietnam and other Asian countries. On returning to Washington May 29, Rogers had said that people and officials he had met in South Vietnam, Thailand, Iran, India, Pakistan and Afghanistan were impressed with Nixon's 8-point peace plan for Vietnam.

The Communist representatives at the June 5 session again insisted on allied acceptance of the NLF's 10-point plan as a basis for a settlement. After the meeting, NLF spokesman Tran Hoai Nam disclosed that the front was about to engage in consultations with what he called other groups of goodwill in South Vietnam and Paris for the purpose of creating a coalition government to replace the Thieu regime. One of the South Vietnamese groups specifically mentioned by Nam was the Alliance of National Democratic & Peace Forces, supported by North Vietnam and the NLF. The North Vietnamese Communist Party newspaper *Nhan Dan* had said June 4 that a coalition government should be formed in South Vietnam with the object of organizing general elections. The elections, the newspaper said, could be held only after U.S. troops quit South Vietnam.

State Secy. Rogers declared at a Washington news conference June 5 that the U.S. was "not wedded to any government in Saigon." Rogers said that Nixon, in advancing his peace plan May 14, had made clear that "the only principle to which the Administration is wedded is that the people of South Vietnam should have the right by free choice to decide their future, so that any government which represents the will of the people in South Vietnam is acceptable to the United States." (Nixon Administration officials later explained that Rogers' statement did not mean that the U.S. was easing its commitment to the current Saigon regime. They said Rogers had meant that Washington was not bound to support the survival of the current South Vietnamese government after new national elections but that the U.S. still backed the Thieu regime under current circumstances.)

On the question of NLF participation in South Vietnamese elections, Rogers said: "We are prepared to set up an international supervisory body to make certain that the elections are fair and free"; "I certainly would not be opposed" to including the NLF in a group that would supervise the elections to guarantee the front "that their votes could be cast without coercion and counted properly." But Rogers emphasized that such arrangements were not the same as a coalition government. He said he supported Pres. Thieu's opposition to establishing a coalition government before elections or instead of them. Rogers expressed regret that the NLF had not yet responded to Thieu's invitation to direct negotiations on elections and other internal matters. He said the U.S. suspected that the NLF's goal was "to attack the the present government, cause confusion and chaos and thereby impose a governmental structure on South Vietnam that will not represent the will of the people." Rogers said: He opposed the phrase "coalition government" as used by the NLF; the term was unacceptable because "it is used to convey the thought that they [the NLF] will impose certain of their leaders on the people of South Vietnam"; "if that is what the phrase means, it would not be acceptable to anybody on our side."

Rogers reiterated previous declarations by Nixon and Thieu that if "the people want to vote for the Communists or any other system of government, and their vote is freely cast and counted [in an elections], then all parties will abide by their choice."

Provisional Rebel Regime Formed

The NLF June 10 announced the formation of a Provisional Revolutionary Government of the Republic of South Vietnam (PRG) to further challenge the Thieu regime for political control of the country. The PRG replaced the NLF delegation at the Paris peace talks June 12. A spokesman for the NLF's delegation to the talks said the decision to form the regime had been made at an All-South Vietnam Congress of People's Representatives held by 88 delegates in a "liberated area" of South Vietnam June 6-8. The purpose of the new government, the spokesman said, was "to direct the struggle of the population of South Vietnam against American aggression for national salvation."

The 2 principal groups in the new regime were the NLF and the Alliance of National Democratic & Peace Forces. The NLF spokesman said other "patriotic organizations" also were represented in the government. They included the *montagnards,* the Khmer minority, the United Buddhists of Vietnam, the Hoa Hao sect and Catholic Patriots of Vietnam.

The provisional government was headed by Huynh Tan Phat as chairman. There were 3 deputy chairmen: Dr. Phung Van Cung, Nguyen Van Kiet and Nguyen Doa. Mrs. Nguyen Thi Binh, deputy head of the NLF's Paris peace conference delegation, was appointed foreign minister. Tran Buu Kiem, head of the NLF delegation, was named minister to the chairman's office. Nguyen Huu Tho, who had been president of the presidium of the NLF's Central Committee, held the post of president of the Advisory Council. Tran Nam Trung, appointed defense minister, was regarded as the strongman in the government although he was listed as 6th in rank. Trung, about 56, was secretary general of the People's Revolutionary Party, which described itself as the "vanguard party" of the NLF. Trung controlled about 75,000 party members in South Vietnam. Phat also was an official of the People's Revolutionary Party. Phat had served as chairman of the "Saigon-Cholon-Giadinh Special Zone," as the southern branch of the Communist Party had been known until it was recognized and renamed the People's Revolutionary Party in 1962. Several high ministry posts were held by some non-Communists.

The members of the provisional government: *Chairman*—Phat; *Deputy Chairman and Interior Minister*—Cung; *Deputy Chairman and Minister of Education & Youth*—Kiet; *Deputy Chairman*—Doa; *Minister to the Chairman's Office*—Kiem; *Defense*—Trung; *Foreign Affairs* —Mrs. Binh; *Economy & Finance*—Cao Van Bon; *Information & Culture*—Luu Huu Phuoc; *Health, Social Action & Disabled Veterans* —Dr. Duong Quynh Hoa; *Justice*—Truong Nhu Tang; *Deputy Minister to the Chairman's Office*—Ung Ngoc Ky; *Deputy Ministers of Defense*—Dong Van Cong and Nguyen Chan; *Deputy Ministers of Foreign Affairs*—Le Quang Chan and Hoang Bich Son; *Deputy Minister of Economy & Finance*—Nguyen Van Trieu; *Deputy Ministers of Information & Culture*—Hoang Trong Qui and Lu Phuong; *Deputy Ministers of Education & Youth*—Prof. Le Minh Tri and Ho Huu Nhut: *Deputy Ministers for Health, Social Action & Disabled Veterans*—Dr. Ho Van Hue and Mrs. Bui Thi Nga; *Deputy Minister of Justice*—Prof. Le Van Tha; *Deputy Minister of the Interior* —Nguyen Ngoc Thuong; *President of the Advisory Council*—Nguyen Huu Tho; *Vice President of the Advisory Council*—Trinh Dinh Thao.

PRG's policy was outlined in a "12-point program of action" presented at a news conference in Paris by Tran Buu Kiem June 11. Its position appeared to be basically the same as that enunciated by the NLF in its 10-point peace program and at the Paris talks. Kiem said that under the new political arrangement, the NLF remained the "organizer and leader" of resistance to U.S. "aggression," while the provisional regime was responsible for internal and foreign policy, work that the front had been forced to assume "in the last nine years." A preamble to the PRG document pledged the provisional regime "to push forward the struggle against U.S. aggression, for national salvation, to total victory and to successfully accomplish the lofty tasks laid down by the Congress of the People's Representatives."

The statement said the purpose of the provisional government was:

(1) To lead the armed forces and the entire people, to "step up military and political struggle" against the U.S. and to force the U.S. "to withdraw totally and without conditions from South Vietnam, . . ."

(2) To abolish "the disguised colonial regime established by the United States imperialists in South Vietnam" and "to overthow the entire structure of the puppet administration" in Saigon.

(3) To "enter into consultation with the political forces representing the various social strata and political tendencies in South Vietnam that stand for peace, independence and neutrality, . . . with a view to setting up a provisional coalition government." The provisional coalition government would "organize general elections" that would lead to establishment of a permanent coalition regime.

(4) "To strengthen the resistance potential of the people in all fields, . . . [and] to consolidate and widen the liberated zone."

(5) "To achieve broad democratic freedoms, to set free all persons jailed by the United States imperialists and the puppet administration on account of their patriotic activities. . . ."

(6) "To improve the living conditions of the workers and the laboring people, to amend labor legislation and fix minimum wages, to fight against corporal punishment, wage-stoppages, and sacking of workers and laboring people."

(7) "To boost up production in order to supply the front and increase the people's potential. . . . To carry out a land policy consistent with the specific conditions of South Vietnam. . . ."

(8) "To fight against the enslaving and depraved culture and education of American brand. . . ."

(9) "To encourage" the defection to the Communist side of "the officers and men of the puppet army and police and those functionaries of the puppet administration. . . ."

(10) "To actively resolve the problems left behind by the U.S. war of aggression and the puppet regime. . . ."

(11) "To reestablish normal relations between South and North Vietnam, to guarantee freedoms of movement, or correspondence, or residence"

and to work for the reunification of the country.

(12) "To win the sympathy, support and aid of all countries and progressive people in the world, including the American people. . . . To carry out a foreign policy of peace and neutrality. . . . To establish diplomatic, economic and cultural relations with all countries, . . . including the United States. . . . "

The formation of the PRG was discounted by the U.S. State Department June 11 as "the same old wine in a new bottle." The statement said that the PRG's cabinet "does not amount to any broadening" of the NLF leadership.

Pres. Nguyen Van Thieu June 11 denounced the PRG as "a propaganda trick of the Hanoi Communists" and said that it was "not worthy of any attention." He said the formation of the PRG did not change Saigon's position at the Paris talks. The talks, Thieu insisted, "will still retain their character as a bilateral negotiation, even though some people on the other side have changed their names. In short, we will still consider these people as members of the other side, we will never consider them as an independent delegation."

At the 21st session of the Paris talks, Lawrence E. Walsh, acting chief of the U.S. delegation, said June 12 that the change of designation of the Communist delegation had no significance. Walsh said: "As far as we are concerned, the spokesmen for your side have introduced changes in name only. We place no significance on the manner in which you choose to style yourselves. Such changes in no way affect the conduct of our business at these meetings."

Pham Dong, head of the South Vietnamese delegation, said that his presence at the meeting "does not mean that the [Saigon] government recognizes the organization calling itself the Liberation Front of South Vietnam."

Mrs. Nguyen Thi Binh, PRG foreign minister, said that the PRG'S goal was "complete victory" over the U.S. and Saigon government. She called for discussions between the provisional regime and a "peace cabinet" to put an end to the conflict.

Tran Buu Kiem, minister of the presidency of the PRG Government, denied June 13 that the formation of the new regime signified greater Communist emphasis on a military solution. Kiem elaborated on the "peace cabinet" proposed by Mrs. Binh the previous day and on how it would figure in promoting a political solution. Kiem said: "If there is a peace cabinet in Saigon before the complete withdrawal of American troops, it is possible that contacts will occur between the peace cabinet and the provisional government." The representatives of the "peace cabinet" would take part in the Paris talks. Any politician would be qualified as a member of a "peace cabinet" or future coalition government "provided they stand for peace, independence and neutrality." This ruled out Pres. Nguyen Van Thieu, Vice Pres. Nguyen Cao Ky and Premier Tran Van Huong, who had "publicly stated their enmity" to these objectives.

The PRG was recognized by these 16 governments June 12-15: Algeria, Bulgaria, Communist China, Cambodia, Cuba, Czechoslovakia, East Germany, Hungary, North Korea, North Vietnam, Mongolia, Poland, Rumania, the Soviet Union, Syria and Yugoslavia. A Hanoi statement of recognition June 12 called the PRG "the legal government, the authentic representative of the South Vietnamese people." The statement said the NLF's mission in Hanoi had been granted "the status of special representative of the Republic of South Vietnam." (Cuba had announced Mar. 17 that it had extended full diplomatic recognition to the NLF. It was the first country known to have established formal relations with the NLF; this action implied recognition of the front's claim to full governmental status. The announcement was made by the Cuban embassy in Algiers where Cuban and NLF representatives had held preliminary negotiations. It said that Raul Valdes Vivo, Havana's new ambassador to the front, had presented his credentials Mar. 4 to Nguyen Huu Tho, chairman of the NLF's central committee, "somewhere in liberated South Vietnam." The Cuban Communist Party newspaper *Granma* reported Mar. 18 that Cuba had established an embassy in Viet Cong "territory" in South Vietnam. A photo of the embassy, a tent with a Cuban flag, accompanied the news story. The NLF had maintained a diplomatic mission in Havana since Dec. 1965.)

(Sweden had announced Jan. 10 that it would extend full diplomatic recognition to North Vietnam. A message conveying this decision was forwarded by Swedish Foreign Min. Torsten Nilsson to North Vietnamese Foreign Min. Nguyen Duy Trinh. In a note to Trinh, Nilsson said: "As the negotiations in Paris are now entering a stage which, it is hoped, will be decisive for the peace in Vietnam, it would appear that the time has come to establish diplomatic relations." Sweden had maintained unofficial contacts with North Vietnamese diplomats for 3 years. The U.S. State Department said Jan. 10 that Sweden's decision to recognize North Vietnam would not "help the cause of peace." Stock-

holm's action, the statement said, came at a time "when the
Hanoi regime is still continuing its efforts to overthrow by armed
force the elected constitutional government of South Vietnam."
The North Vietnamese delegation at the Paris peace talks Jan. 10
called the Swedish move "a step in right directions.")

Both Positions Unchanged

Le Duc Tho, the political leader of North Vietnam's delegation at the Paris talks, June 23 rejected any compromise with the
South Vietnamese government on the establishement of a mixed
commission of Communists and non-Communists to set up a
special election in South Vietnam. In a Paris interview with the
Washington Post (reported June 24), Tho barred international
supervision of any election, as proposed by Pres. Nixon in his 8-
point proposal. He said "such supervision would constitute interference in internal affairs." Tho also ruled out any formal or
tacit agreement to reduce the level of fighting as long as the Nixon
Administration attempted "to proceed from a position of
strength." Tho was critical of Nixon personally. He said: Nixon had
followed a policy reflecting "the most warlike military circles in
the U.S." "Mr. Nixon finds himself in a vicious circle. He wants
to withdraw U.S. forces from South Vietnam, but he fears the
puppet army and the puppet administration will collapse. . . .
What has Mr. Nixon been able to achieve in his last 5 months at
the conference table? We may say he has achieved nothing."

Tho confirmed obliquely that he had talked privately with
Henry Cabot Lodge, the chief U.S. negotiator in Paris, but he
added: "We think that private meetings do not constitute a decisive factor in settling the problem. If the U.S. is not serious and
has no good will, whatever private meetings there have been and
how many private meetings there may be, they cannot settle the
problem." Tho criticized the June 19 statement in which Nixon
had expressed hope for the withdrawal of U.S. troops. Tho said:
"Mr. Nixon also hinted at a settlement between 2 or 3 months.
His intention is to create hope among the American people. But
the fact is that no progress at all has been made in the meetings. In
fact, our positions are very far apart." (Nixon had said at his press
conference June 19: "The 2 sides are far apart. But we believe
that the time has come for a discussion of substance, and we hope
within the next 2 or 3 months to see some progress in substantive

discussions.")

Both sides repeated their previous positions at the 22d and 23d sessions of the Paris talks June 19 and 26. Lawrence Walsh, acting chief of the U.S. delegation, pressed the North Vietnamese delegation June 19 for an agreement on mutual troop withdrawals, but Col. Ha Van Lau asked the U.S. delegation whether the U.S. was prepared to withdraw all its forces from South Vietnam unconditionally. At the 23d session, the North Vietnamese and NLF delegations derided Pres. Nixon's May 14 peace proposal and his June 19 statement on the possible withdrawal of U.S. troops. Henry Cabot Lodge, chief U.S. negotiator, said after the meeting that the Communists had shown no will to negotiate. He added that there was "simply the same old insistence that we give this or that with no reciprocal action on their part."

North Vietnam and the PRG charged at the 24th session July 3 that the U.S. had intensified the war. The North Vietnamese and PRG delegations again attacked the U.S. plan to train South Vietnamese forces to replace U.S. troops, calling the plan an attempt to intensify the war.

North Vietnamese delegation chief Xuan Thuy charged July 5 that the withdrawal of 25,000 U.S. troops from Vietnam was "meaningless" when compared to the total troop level of 530,000 men. Thuy, who had returned to Paris from Hanoi earlier in the day, said he had discussed the Paris peace talks with Soviet Premier Alekesi N. Kosygin in Moscow and with Chinese Premier Chou En-lai in Peking and that both leaders had shared his opinion of the U.S. withdrawal.

Henry Cabot Lodge, chief U.S. negotiator at the Paris talks, said July 10 that a negotiated settlement of the war was impossible unless North Vienam and the PRG modified their insistence on the unilateral withdrawal of U.S. troops. Speaking at the 25th session of the conference, Lodge said that their position "is to demand capitulation by our side. This is unreasonable. We shall not capitulate." He reasserted, however, that the U.S. was willing to "negotiate and compromise" and that the Nixon Administration was willing to accept other approaches to troop withdrawal "consistent with our principles." Lodge's statement was immediately rebutted by Xuan Thuy and by Mrs. Nguyen Thi Binh, PRG foreign minister. Mrs. Binh said that progress in Paris "depends on the U.S. public opinion at large, which demands the U.S. adopt a serious attitude." Her remark was viewed by diplomats as a strong expression of her side's contention that public opinion would force the Nixon Administration to make concessions.

Elections Discussed

South Vietnamese Pres. Nguyen Van Thieu proposed July 11 that free elections be held in South Vietnam with the participation of the National Liberation Front. In a TV address, Thieu said free elections could be based on the following principles:

(1) All political parties and groups, including the National Liberation Front, which is now bearing arms against us, can participate in the elections if they renounce violence and pledge themselves to accept the results of the elections.

(2) To make sure that the elections would be conducted in all fairness, an electoral commission could be set up, in which all political parties and groups, including the NLF, . . . could be represented. . . .

(3) An international body is to be established to supervise the elections and to make sure that the elections are held under conditions fair to all.

(4) We are prepared to discuss with the other side the timetable and the modalities under which the elections will be held.

(5) There will be no reprisals or discrimination after the elections.

(6) The government of Vietnam declares that it will abide by the results of the elections, whatever these results may be. We challenge the other side to declare the same.

Thieu described his new proposal as a "comprehensive offer for the political settlement of the Vietnam conflict."

Critics said that Thieu's willingness to include the NLF in the elections could remove a major obstacle to a Vietnam settlement but that the proposal was vague on what many diplomats considered crucial questions. Thieu did not say who would control the electoral machinery, nor did he define the relationship between the proposed electoral commission and the Saigon government. Thieu did not say when the elections would be held, and he did not recommend that South Vietnam's 1967 constitution be amended to allow national elections before September 1971.

The NLF's provisional government denounced Thieu's election proposal as "perfidious trickery." A PRG (Provisional Revolutionary Government) communiqué issued in Paris July 11 said the proposal was "aimed solely at maintaining a puppet administration, which is a valet of the U.S." The PRG reiterated its call for replacing the Thieu government with a "peace committee" as the "most realistic way" of achieving "truly free and democratic elections." (Although the North Vietnamese delegation did not comment on the proposal, Le Duc Tho, Hanoi's political leader at the Paris peace talks, had rejected in advance June 23 any plan by South Vietnam for a mixed commission to set up and supervise elections.)

Pres. Nixon lauded Thieu's election proposal July 11 as "eminently fair" and said it could lead to peace if Hanoi would negotiate seriously. A statement issued by the President portrayed the election proposal as part of a carefully designed series of moves to lead toward a peaceful settlement of the conflict. The steps he cited were:

(1) The decision Oct. 30, 1968 to halt all bombing of North Vietnam and to continue the expanded Paris talks.

(2) Thieu's offer Mar. 25 to meet with the NLF and North Vietnam without preconditions.

(3) Nixon's May 14 peace plan offering mutual withdrawal of "the major portions" of U.S., allied and North Vietnamese forces from South Vietnam and internationally supervised elections.

(4) The President's Midway Island announcement June 8 on withdrawal of 25,000 U.S. troops by Aug. 31.

Nixon concluded his statement by saying: "If the other side genuinely wants peace, it now has a comprehensive set of offers which permit a fair and reasonable settlement. If it approaches us in this spirit, it will find us reasonable. Hanoi has nothing to gain by waiting."

(The South Vietnamese Foreign Ministry had said June 23 that all elections "must be held in strict obervance of the current laws and regulations." The announcement reportedly ruled out the possibility of special elections before those scheduled by the South Vietnamese constitution for 1970 and 1971. But Pres. Thieu had said June 9 that he would be willing to discuss the possibility of special elections with the Communists.)

Thieu's offer of free elections with NLF participation was formally rejected by the Communist delegations at the 26th session of the Paris talks July 17. Mrs. Nguyen Thi Binh said the PRG "categorically exposes and rejects the so-called solution of free elections as a treachery of the United States and the Saigon administration." She asserted that Thieu's condition that the Viet Cong give up violence was tantamount to asking them "to renounce the right of resistance against the United States for national salvation." Mrs. Binh charged that a statement made by South Vietnamese Foreign Min. Tran Chanh Thanh July 12 radically qualified Thieu's offer. Thanh had said that the election was barred to avowed Communists or to candidates who made Communist propaganda. Thanh also had said the South

Vietnamese army would ensure order during the elections. Mrs. Binh asserted that the latter statement made certain that Thieu's proposed international elections commission "would be in fact an executive body of the Saigon puppet administration."

The North Vietnamese delegation "denounced, condemned and rejected" Saigon's election proposal. Nguyen Thanh Le, spokesman for Hanoi's delegation, said after the meeting that the NLF's 10-point plan remained the "correct" means of reaching an agreement. An article appearing in the North Vietnamese Communist Party newspaper *Nhan Dan* July 13 had charged that the Saigon plan was aimed at "reperforming with a new decor the general elections farce staged time and time again by the U.S. and puppets." The newspaper asserted that "general elections of whatever kind staged by Thieu under Nixon's manipulation are only designed to maintain and consolidate the U.S. aggressive war machine." The North Vietnamese press agency July 19 quoted Ho Chi Minh as saying that no free elections could be held in South Vietnam as long as U.S. troops stayed in the country and the current Saigon regime remained in office. Ho insisted that free elections must be organized by a provisional government as proposed by Hanoi and the NLF.

South Vietnamese Vice Pres. Nguyen Cao Ky July 15 assailed Thieu's election offer as a "grave step backward in our national policy of anti-communism." "But still the Communists have rejected it, so I would think that there is no more reason to maintain and prolong the Paris talks," Ky said.

Thieu conceded July 17 that his proposal was "our last step backward." But he rejected Ky's suggestion that Saigon should quit the Paris talks if his offer was not accepted. Thieu's defense of his proposal was in response to the South Vietnamese Senate's action earlier July 17 condemning him for allegedly overstepping his presidential authority by making concessions to the Communists. The Senate, by 18-12 vote, approved a resolution that denounced Thieu's election plan as "contrary to the basic position of the government as enunciated by the president on Nov. 2 [1968] and Apr. 7, as well as by resolutions of both House and Senate." At a news conference July 19, Thieu again declined to say which side would head the proposed international elections commission. Thieu said the commission "only has the right to give equal opportunity to all candidates to campaign freely for office and to watch the counting of votes to assure fairness. But the election will be

held under the South Vietnamese government—that is very clear."
Asked whether the Communists would be permitted to campaign as
such in the proposed election, Thieu replied: "We are fighting for
a non-Communist South Vietnam. We can never let Communist
ideology or propaganda be made in South Vietnam. It would
be against the constitution as it is now written."

(Thieu also said that South Vietnamese troops would not be
able to replace all the U.S. combat troops in South Vietnam by the
end of 1970. He held that "the replacement rate depends on
whether the United States government helps us with enough funds
and enough equipment. We can replace many of them, but not
the totality.")

Thieu said July 21 that it would take at least 2 years to hold
elections with NLF participation. He explained that is would require 12 months to withdraw all U.S. and North Vietnamese
troops from South Vietnam, 6 months to negotiate with the NLF
the details of the proposed elections and another 6 months to
establish the international elections commission. Thieu said July 26
that his declared proposal of free elections with Viet Cong
participation had been "the final solution we can afford to offer."
Asserting that the Vietnam negotiations had reached "a turning
point," he said: "We have nothing more to say at Paris. What
remains to be discussed are details." "Now we can say to our
allies: 'If you want to abandon us, do it, because we cannot do
otherwise.' "

No progress was noted at the next 2 meetings in Paris. Pres.
Nixon's visit to Asia was denounced by the North Vietnamese delegation at the July 31 meeting. Xuan Thuy declared that the trip
proved that the U.S. "refused to withdraw from South Vietnam
and seeks to maintain the Thieu-Ky-Huong administration, a
dictatorial, warlike and corrupt administration." Henry Cabot
Lodge replied that the Communists had misinterpreted the purpose of Nixon's visit. Lodge then repeated the warning that the
President had made on his trip: the U.S. had gone as far as it
could in proposing a peaceful solution.

Following the Aug. 7 session, PRG spokesman Duong Dinh
Thao indicated that the PRG had begun discussions with groups
in and outside of Vietnam to form a coalition government as a
rival to the Thieu regime. The Viet Cong's Liberation radio had
disclosed Aug. 2 that the PRG had begun a drive to gain wider
international recognition. The broadcast said a report to this

effect had been delivered at a meeting of the PRG Council of Ministers July 22-23. It was submitted by Tran Buu Kiem, minister to PRG Pres. Huynh Tan Phat. In addition to the 16 nations previously reported to have recognized the PRG, these countries had extended recognition: Albania, Congo (Brazzaville), Egypt, Iraq, Mali, Mauritania, Sudan and Yemen.

(South Vietnamese Vice Pres. Nguyen Cao Ky predicted Sept. 13 that any attempt to form a coalition government in South Vietnam with the Communists would lead members of the armed forces to stage a coup "inside 10 days." Ky said South Vietnamese military officers were concerned about the concessions Thieu had made so far at the Paris peace talks. Thieu "cannot afford any more concessions," he said. "It is a matter of his survival." Ky said Thieu had agreed with Ky that "if we don't make a social revolution, someone else will." If Thieu "does nothing, then I will speak out and tell the people what we must do," Ky pledged.)

Philip C. Habib, sitting in for Lodge, told the Communist delegations at the Aug. 21 meeting in Paris that "there can be no negotiated settlement to the war unless you are prepared to withdraw all North Vietnamese troops and elements from South Vietnam, Laos and Cambodia back to North Vietnam."

Inconclusive Negotiations

The Paris negotiators during September and October returned to the debate over the withdrawal of troops from South Vietnam as the condition for ending the war. Both sides continued to insist on the positions with which they had entered the conference. At the 33d meeting, however, the prisoners-of-war issue surfaced briefly on the U.S.' initiative.

The 33d session, scheduled for Sept. 4, had been postponed until Sept. 13 because of Ho Chi Minh's death. At the Sept. 13 meeting, chief U.S. representative Henry Cabot Lodge renewed the American demand for humane treatment of prisoners of war as provided by the Geneva convention and for impartial inspection of prison camps in North Vietnam. North Vietnamese representative Ha Van Lau asserted that U.S. pilots in North Vietnamese prisons were "air pirates" to whom the Geneva convention did not apply. He said they were being treated humanely, and he barred outside inspection.

The North Vietnamese Red Cross said Sept. 13 that it had informed the International Red Cross at a meeting in Istanbul Sept. 6-13 that U.S. pilots held by Hanoi "will not enjoy" the protection of the Geneva convention because they had been captured while committing "crimes against humanity." The captive U.S. airmen "come under the jurisdiction of North Vietnam, an independent and sovereign state," the statement said. The North Veitnamese Red Cross insisted that the Hanoi government "has always applied a humane policy toward the captured American pilots."

Chief North Vietnamese delegate Xuan Thuy had indicated at a news conference Sept. 2 that the talks could make progress if the U.S. accelerated its troop withdrawal. Describing the pullout of 25,000 U.S. soldiers as "insignificant," Thuy said "it is evident that if withdrawals occur at the present rate, we cannot make a judgment. On the other hand, if Mr. Nixon withdraws forces in a considerable and rapid way, we will take account of it."

U.S. press spokesman Stephen J. Ledogar said after the 34th session Sept. 25 that the Communist renunciation of the latest U.S. troop withdrawal plan proved that "negotiations have reached a stage where no useful purpose is served by further flexibility and reasonableness." Ledogar's statement was in response to assertions made by Lodge after the meeting that the Communist delegations "seemed more rigid than they have been for several months. They rejected our proposals for peace in what I thought were rather harsh terms." Lodge said they had "repeated their demands for our immediate withdrawal and turning over the country to them without any indication that they are ready to negotiate."

Trinh Dinh Thao of the Provisional Revolutionary Government declared in Paris Sept. 27 that "the fallacious arguments advanced" by Pres. Nixon at his news conference the previous day "against the total and unconditional withdrawal of United States troops from South Vietnam strips even more naked the designs of the Nixon Administration to prolong the American occupation" of Vietnam. Nixon's support of South Vietnamese Pres. Thieu was an expression of "the obstinacy of the White House in maintaining a regime in South Vietnam that is warlike and rotten to the core," Thao said.

At the Oct. 2 session, Mrs. Nguyen Thi Binh of the PRG charged that women prisoners had been tortured and killed in a

South Vietnamese prison outside Saigon. Saigon press spokesman Nguyen Trieu Dan later dismissed the charges as "lies and calumnies."

North Vietnam proposed in Paris Oct. 16 that the U.S. and the PRG immediately enter into "private and direct" talks to end the war and eliminate the South Vietnamese government as a party to a settlement. Lodge made a counter-suggestion for secret talks among all 4 participants. The White House also rejected Hanoi's proposal. It issued a statement saying: "We would not meet alone with the Viet Cong," but the U.S. was prepared to convene "with all the participants together in any format." The U.S., the statement added, had no intention to "shut out" the Saigon regime from any phase of the peace talks.

In advancing the proposal, Xuan Thuy insisted that the PRG was the only legitimate representative of the people of South Vietnam. Thuy pressed Lodge for a direct answer to his proposal. Lodge reiterated his own offer and asked Thuy if he was prepared to accept it. Alluding to the previous Communist agreement to deal with the Saigon government as "one of the parties" in the 4-power talks, Lodge said: "Your position now can only mean that your policy has changed and that you are not prepared to negotiate genuinely . . . with all parties concerned."

U.S. press spokesman Stephen Ledogar said after the talks that there was "nothing new" and no "substantial change in the so-called offer," which he described as a "tactical ploy." South Vietnamese spokesman Nguyen Trieu Dan said after the meeting that North Vietnam's proposal to eliminate Saigon from private talks was "absurd." Dan, however, praised the offer to the limited extent that the Communists "now accept the principle of private talks" first advanced by Pres. Nguyen Van Thieu Mar. 25.

The Oct. 23 session was adjourned abruptly after Lodge refused to deliver a prepared speech because of what he called the Communists' "intransigence." Asserting that his action "was within the scope of my instructions," Lodge said: "You have done nothing but repeat your demands for unilateral actions on our part and engaged in vituperative language. Under these circumstances, I see no point in delivering the statement I have prepared today." Lodge then proposed that the meeting be adjourned until Oct. 30, and the other delegates agreed. Nguyen Thanh Le, spokesman for Hanoi's delegation, asserted that the U.S. government had shown "bad faith" and that its attitude toward the talks was "not serious." Mrs. Nguyen Thi Binh, PRG delegate, said Lodge's action reflected "the obstinate attitude of the United States government in pursuit of its policy of prolonging the war."

The Communist delegations Oct. 30 rejected a proposal by Lodge to hold private talks starting Nov. 4 to "break out of this sterile situation and promote serious negotiations." Lodge suggested that the principal U.S., South Vietnamese, North Vietnamese and Viet Cong representatives, accompanied by no more than 3 advisers, discuss in private any subject they wished and agree on exactly what "would be said to the press after each session." These discussions would "not mean we would entirely replace" the regular Thursday sessions, U.S. spokesman Ledogar said after the meeting. In rejecting Lodge's proposal, Xuan Thuy charged that its purpose was to "camouflage the truth" and "to fool public opinion" about Washington's refusal to end "the war of aggression" and withdraw all U.S. troops from Vietnam. Thuy stated that the U.S. instead should accept his proposal of private talks between the U.S. and the PRG, with South Vietnam excluded.

Lodge said he regretted that the Communists had "rejected our proposal . . . since the regular Thursday meetings have served only as a propaganda forum not as a peace forum." The North Vietnamese had turned down a similar U.S. proposal in May 1968 by Cyrus Vance, then deputy chief of the U.S. delegation, before the start of the U.S.-North Vietnamese discussions that led to the current 4-party conference.

State Secy. William P. Rogers said Nov. 18 that he saw "no immediate prospects" for successful negotiations with Hanoi. Although the U.S. had had "numerous diplomatic contacts" with North Vietnam before and after the death of Ho Chi Minh, Rogers said, "it would be wrong to suggest that they have indicated any success." Officials specified later that Rogers was referring to contacts through 3d parties. One of the 3d parties, the Soviet Union, was "not being helpful at the moment," Rogers said, but "it might be helpful somewhere along the line" later. Rogers made the comments after appearing at a closed session of the Senate Foreign Relations Committee. Chairman J.W. Fulbright (D., Ark.) commented after Rogers' testimony that the U.S. was on "an irreversible course of withdrawal" from Vietnam but that it could be "a very long and drawn-out" process. Another past critic of Vietnam policy, Sen. Frank Church

(D., Idaho), said he was encouraged that the "general direction of our policy is now out of Vietnam rather than in."

Lodge Leaves, Impasse Remains

The White House announced Nov. 20 that Henry Cabot Lodge had resigned as head of the U.S. delegation to the Paris talks. Lodge's deputy, Lawrence E. Walsh, who had not attended the talks since June, also relinquished his post. Both resignations were effective Dec. 8. Philip C. Habib, Lodge's chief adviser, was to become acting head of the delegation pending the appointment of a permanent successor. Nixon Administration officials said that the decision not to name an immediate replacement for Lodge was not intended to downgrade the stalemated Paris negotiations. White House Press Secy. Ronald L. Ziegler said Pres. Nixon "continues to hope peace can be achieved in Vietnam through successful negotiations."

In his letter of resignation to Nixon, Lodge said he was leaving the post because "personal matters at home require my attention." Noting that the President had "left no stone unturned" in efforts to find a peaceful solution, Lodge said it was "sad" that the Communist negotiators had "flatly refused to reciprocate in any kind of meaningful way." Nixon thanked Lodge for agreeing "to serve as an adviser so that I will continue to have the benefit of your experience and wisdom on Vietnam." Walsh attributed his resignation to the deadlocked talks. In his letter to the President, he said that "in view of the manner in which" the Paris negotiations were "now being conducted by the other side, no purpose would be served by my continuing to hold this office."

At the Nov. 20 session of the peace talks, Lodge told the Communists that Nixon would not "be pressured into departing from the course which he has set" by threats of escalating military operations. Lodge said the U.S. "will not accept your side's take-it-or-leave-it position" and "your one-sided approach to discussion of the Vietnam question has not shown good will." The Communist delegation raised the issue of the alleged slaying of Vietnamese civilians by American troops at Songmy and accused U.S. soldiers of committing similar atrocities in 1969.

Xuan Thuy charged Nov. 22 that Lodge had assumed an inflexible position at the talks by limiting U.S.-North Vietnamese private discussions to the matter of troop withdrawal. The charge was denied Nov. 24 by Lodge and the White House. Thuy, in an interview with the *N.Y. Times*, said he had told Lodge that "there had been previous bilateral conversations" between the U.S. and North Vietnam: "I said that problems concerning South Vietnam should properly be discussed" with the Provisional Revolutionary Government (PGR) "but that if the discussions were to deal with general problems we were prepared to do so." Thuy said the 2 most vital questions to be discussed were troop withdrawal and a coalition government for South Vietnam. But the Communist delegate insisted that Lodge had spurned this proposal and only wanted to discuss troop pullout, a "question that is advantageous to him."

Thuy said Nixon's policy of Vietnamizing the war and supporting the Thieu regime was another means of continuing the conflict. That is why Hanoi opposed a ceasefire in advance of an overall settlement, he said. North Vietnam wanted to put an end to all the fighting, Thuy asserted, not just between Americans and Vietnamese, but between Vietnamese and Vietnamese. Thuy refuted Nixon's statement in his speech Nov. 3 that a Ho Chi Minh letter to him was a "complete rejection" of efforts to end the war. Thuy cited the last paragraph of Ho's message, which said: "With goodwill on both sides we might arrive at common efforts in view of finding a correct solution of the Vietnamese problem."

Lodge declared Nov. 24 that Thuy's statement was "false" and accused him of "intransigence" in insisting that the U.S. withdraw unilaterally "without any indication of what the North Vietnamese would do." Lodge denied that he had refused to discuss general problems with Thuy, that he sought only to limit the private talks to the matter of military pullout, and that the U.S. "wishes to continue the war."

The White House denial of Thuy's remarks, issued by Press Secy. Ronald Ziegler, said it was untrue that the U.S. was not willing to hold private talks on "general problems" dealing with South Vietnam. American negotiators, however, were willing to discuss but not to "negotiate" the political future of South Vietnam, he said. Ziegler emphasized that the U.S. was prepared to negotiate any matter "except the right of the South Vietnamese government to determine their form of government without outside interference." Ziegler noted that there had been 11 private U.S.-North Vietnamese meetings, all arranged "at our initiative."

In reiterating his call for a resumption of private talks, Thuy

Nov. 25 rejected the distinction drawn by Washington between discussing and negotiating. Thuy denied that "every private meeting we have held has been at the request of the United States"; some had been held at Hanoi's request, he said.

Lodge declared at his final session Dec. 4 that the only concrete progress" made at the talks since their start in May 1968 was agreement on the size of the table. He said the obstacle to negotiating an end to the war was the Communists' "absolute refusal to join us in seeking a just peace."

At his press conference Dec. 8, Pres. Nixon denied that the talks in Paris were being downgraded because of the lack of a chief negotiator since Lodge's resignation. "We're simply waiting for a serious proposal," Nixon said. The chances of a negotiated settlement were "not good"; the enemy's proposals were "quite frivolous." But, as the Vietnamization program continued to work and it became apparent that it would succeed, Nixon predicted, "the pressures for the enemy then to negotiate a settlement will greatly increase, because once we are out and the South Vietnamese are there, they will have a much harder individual to negotiate with than they had when we were there."

Xuan Thuy boycotted the Dec. 11 session in protest against what his delegation insisted was the "sabotage" and "downgrading" of the talks by the U.S. failure to name a replacement for Lodge. Nguyen Thanh Le, North Vietnamese spokesman, referred to Philip Habib, acting chief of the U.S. delegation, as a representative of "unelevated rank." He said the U.S. had "deliberately lowered the level of the Paris conference and is seeking deliberately to sabotage it." Ha Van Lau, Thuy's deputy who attended the session, accused Nixon of "trying to freeze" the talks by his program of Vietnamization rather than negotiating a settlement in Paris. Mrs. Nguyen Thi Binh, PRG negotiator, reiterated a Dec. 8 proposal calling for the unconditional withdrawal of U.S. and allied forces from South Vietnam during a 6-month period in exchange for "guarantees for security during the withdrawal." State Secy. William P. Rogers, visiting the U.S. negotiating team in Paris, had dismissed the Communist offer Dec. 8 as "nothing new." Defense Secy. Melvin R. Laird, who accompanied Rogers, said that if the Paris deadlock continued, the U.S. would intensify Vietnamization, which, he said, "provides the means for the orderly disinvolvement of American troops from combat . . . without impairing our objective—the right of self-determination for the people of South Vietnam." In an interview made public Dec. 11, North Vietnamese Defense Min. Vo Nguyen Giap described Vietnamization as "drop-by-drop troop withdrawal," which, he said, was a subterfuge aimed "at camouflaging its intention to continue the war of aggression." He warned that Vietnamization "will become a tragedy not only" for South Vietnamese troops but also for the American forces. Giap charged that American military activity in Laos was threatening the security" of North Vietnam.

Allied and Communist negotiators remained deadlocked after concluding the Dec. 18 and 30 sessions, the last 2 of the Paris talks during 1969. Xuan Thuy boycotted the Dec. 18 meeting in protest against Nixon's alleged downgrading of the talks by failing to appoint Lodge's successor. Mrs. Binh denounced Nixon's plan to withdraw another 50,000 U.S. troops from South Vietnam. As long as U.S. and other allied troops "continue to commit aggression on our soil, we cannot consider the withdrawal of 50,-000 troops as an act of goodwill," she said. At the insistence of the U.S., the Dec. 25th session was canceled because of Christmas.

The prisoner-of-war issue re-emerged at the reconvened session Dec. 30. U.S. delegate Habib submitted a list of 1,406 Americans missing in action as of Dec. 24. Habib said he was submitting the roster in the hope "that your side, even at this late date, will indicate which men are prisoners and those whom you know to be dead, as a matter of humanitarian concern for their families." About 430 Americans had been confirmed as prisoners of war in North Vietnam. The Communist delegation denounced the American move as "a perfidious maneuver to camouflage the fact that the United States is pursuing the war, committing crimes against the Vietnamese people and misleading public opinion, which demands that the United States end the war and withdraw its troops." (An official of the pro-Communist Pathet Lao in Laos had said Nov. 11 that his side was holding 158 U.S. airmen as prisoners. They were said to include 51 men whose planes had been shot down over Laos in 1968 and 41 who had been captured between January and June 1969.)

U.S. DEBATE

In the aftermath of his trip to Asia, Pres. Nixon sought to implement his policy of withdrawing U.S. ground forces from combat while containing mounting domestic criticsm as his Vietnam policies.

Troop Withdrawals

The decision on a further U.S. troop withdrawal from Vietnam, scheduled for announcement in late August, had been deferred until some time after Nixon returned to Washington from his summer headquarters near San Clemente, Calif., White House Press Secy. Ronald L. Ziegler announced Aug. 23. Ziegler indicated that a major factor in deferring the decision was the increase in enemy-initiated fighting.

The level of enemy activity in the war also was related to further American withdrawals by State Secy. Willian P. Rogers. At a news conference Aug. 20, Rogers said: While the U.S. could continue its program of withdrawing troops from Vietnam whether the combat lull continued or was broken by the enemy, a "high level" of enemy attacks would make U.S. withdrawals more difficult. The enemy's infiltration was "still down, considerably down," but "war itself has grave risks," and the U.S. was "willing to take sensible risks for peace. So, in deciding what to do in terms of troop replacements for the future, the President and all of us are going to keep those considerations in mind." (Administration spokesmen increasingly used the term "troop replacements"—meaning South Vietnamese troops replacing U.S. combat troops—instead of the term "troop withdrawals.")

In discussing the summer lull in the fighting, Rogers said the U.S. "did something to lower the level of activity." The fact is," he said, "that the lull was partly because of the reaction of the United States, and the reason that the activity increased was because of the enemy's action." "We did respond, and we are prepared to [again] if the other side wants to," Rogers said, but U.S. forces were holding back. Asked about the possible consideration of "territorial accommodation," Rogers said: "If the other side wanted to negotiate a political settlement and they did have political strength in certain areas, I think that would be a factor we'd have to consider. But at the moment, I don't think it's under consideration."

The Defense Department had conceded Aug. 14, in response to critical comment from some Congressional and foreign quarters, that the number of U.S. troops in Vietnam actually had increased since Nixon took office. But the Pentagon attributed the increase to troop arrivals scheduled during the preceding Administration and said the trend was downward since Nixon's announcement in June of a planned withdrawal of 25,000 troops. The Pentagon released further figures Aug. 15 revealing that U.S. troop strength in Vietnam had reached its lowest point of 1969—532,-500—only 2 days prior to Nixon's inauguration, and rose to its highest point—542,500—a month later (Feb. 22). As of Aug. 14, the U.S. total stood at 534,200.

Nixon Sept. 16 announced his decision to withdraw about 35,000 more U.S. troops from South Vietnam. The President used troop ceiling figures 1%-2% higher than the actual number of troops because most units operated below authorized strengths. He stressed, however, that with this 2d reduction, "a minimum of 60,000 troops will have been withdrawn from Vietnam by Dec. 15." The first-stage reduction of 25,000 troops had been completed in August. Nixon called the withdrawal of 60,000 troops "a significant step." While he realized the difficulty of communicating "across the gulf of 5 years of war," he said, " . . . the time has come to end this war. Let history record that at this critical moment, both sides turned their faces toward peace rather than toward conflict and war." (The President said he had ordered a reduction of the authorized troop ceiling in Vietnam to 484,000 by Dec. 15. The ceilng had been 524,500, down from a maximum of 549,500, when the Nixon Administration took office. Actual troop strength in Vietnam, subject to daily fluctuations, was put at 508,000.)

The U.S. decision on the 2d-stage withdrawal had been prematurely disclosed in Saigon Sept. 15 by South Vietnamese Vice Pres. Nguyen Cao Ky, who had said 40,500 U.S. troops would be withdrawn by the end of November. Ky also said 150,000 to 200,000 U.S. troops were expected to be withdrawn by the end of 1970. White House Press. Secy. Ronald L. Ziegler later Sept. 15 declined to comment on Ky's figures. Ziegler stressed that it was Nixon's decision and that it had been determined prior to the high-level meeting that the President had conducted on Vietnam Sept. 12 with his ranking military and diplomatic advisers, including Gen. Creighton W. Abrams, the U.S. commander in Vietnam. Newsmen being briefed on Mr. Nixon's announcement Sept. 16 were told repeatedly that the troop withdrawals were not an automatic procedure and that the enemy had to realize there was a floor to U.S. troop strength in Vietnam below which the U.S. would not go.

Nixon, addressing the 24th regular session of the UN General Assembly Sept. 18, asked UN members for aid in the negotiations for ending the war. In an apparent reference to the Sept. 2 statement of North Vietnam's Xuan Thuy on U.S. troop withdrawals from Vietnam, Nixon reported that the U.S. was "prepared to withdraw all our forces." He called on the 126 UN members to "use your best diplomatic efforts to persuade Hanoi to move seriously into the negotiations which could end this war."

Nixon Sept. 19 announced a 50,000-man reduction in the planned draft calls for the balance of 1969. The President also warned that if Congress did not act on a draft reform bill before the end of its current session, he would take "unilateral action" to remove inequities in the draft system by executive order. Nixon said scheduled draft calls for the rest of 1969—32,000 men in November and 18,000 in December—would be "canceled." Defense Secy. Melvin R. Laird explained that the 29,000-man October draft call announced Sept. 2 would be spread over the rest of the year with calls of 10,000 in October, 10,000 in November and 9,000 in December. Laird indicated that cuts in induction rates planned for 1970 would depend on events in Vietnam.

The President and Laird emphasized that a decrease in military manpower needs and a desire to lessen draft inequities motivated the reductions. Administration officials indicated, however, that the timing and emphasis of the announcement had been determined by a desire to counteract expected antiwar protest on college campuses. In discussing Vietnam troop cuts at a Sept. 17 news conference, Laird had said that the reductions ordered Sept. 16 would have "a very significant effect upon programmed draft calls."

The foreign ministers of Australia, New Zealand, the Philippines, Thailand and South Korea announced at the U.S. Mission to the UN in New York Sept. 20 that their combined force of 70,000 combat men in South Vietnam would not be reduced despite Nixon's withdrawal decision. The 2 other participants at the meeting, State Secy. William P. Rogers and South Vietnamese

Foreign Min. Tran Van Lam, briefed the 5 Asian allies on military and political developments since their last conference May 22. U.S. officials said Rogers and Lam had been questioned about the effects of the U.S. withdrawals and their duties assumed by South Vietnamese units. Lam told newsmen after the meeting that "there is no question at this point of any troop withdrawals" by the 5 allies. The conferees, however, were said to have discussed phasing out allied forces "as the end of the war approaches."

Hanoi Sept, 21 assailed Nixon's Sept. 18 order to withdraw an additional 35,000 U.S. troops from South Vietnam as a "perfidious trick" that actually constituted a prolongation of the American "war of aggression." The Communist statement, broadcast by Hanoi radio, contended that the American troops to be removed were "an insignificant part of the half-million-odd United States troops in South Vietnam." It said that although Nixon had called for self-determination for the South Vietnamese, the U.S. had "trampled underfoot the South Vietnamese people's right to self-determination." U.S. efforts to strengthen the South Vietnamese army meant that Washington "still entertains schemes to carry out neo-colonialism and prolong the partition of Vietnam," the statement said. A statement issued by the Viet Cong's Provisional Revolutionary Government Sept. 20 had charged that Nixon's troop withdrawal order and his speech to the UN General Assembly Sept. 19 was "a perfidious piece of deception aimed at appeasing public opinion, covering up its scheme to prolong the war and prolong the U.S. military occupation of South Vietnam."

The Communist delegations at the 34th session of the Paris conference Sept. 18 had scorned the U.S. troops withdrawal plan as a "farce." Terming the withdrawals mere "driblets," the Communists said that only a quick, total and unconditional pullout of U.S. and allied forces could lead to peace.

South Vietnamese Pres. Nguyen Van Thieu had said Sept. 16 that the U.S. decision to withdraw more troops was "the measure of the progress in the strengthening" of the South Vietnamese army. He said the pullout was "in conformity" with his government's "policy to shoulder an increasing share in the struggle to defend freedom in Vietnam." But Thieu predicted Sept. 27 that it would take "years and years" to withdraw all U.S. troops from South Vietnam. Speaking at the graduation of village officials from a government training school in Vungtau, Thieu said his government had "no ambition, no pretense to replace all the U.S. troops in 1970" because "we are not so powerful yet to replace all your heavy" military equipment. But he said South Vietnamese forces were prepared to take over from U.S. troops "within a timetable to be decided between the 2 governments, provided the U.S. government furnishes us enough equipment, ... and enough time ... for recruiting and training." "The replacement of troops," he said, "is not a one-year problem, it is a problem that will take years and years." Thieu said he would submit to the Nixon Administration before the end of 1969 a list of Saigon's military requirements once he learned how many more American troops were to be withdrawn from his country. Saigon agreement to any further U.S. troop pullout was contingent on whether these requests for military materiel were met, Thieu said. Thieu said that despite some U.S.-South Vietnamese differences on approaches to ending the war, the 2 sides were in basic agreement. He warned that if the U.S. insisted that Saigon accept a coalition government with the Communists or lose American backing, he would reply, "Thank you, we will continue to fight until victory." Thieu explained that by victory he meant "no coalition with the Communists and no domination by the Communists."

In a TV interview (ABC's "Issues and Answers") taped Sept. 24 and broadcast Sept. 28, Thieu said that he could accept a 150,000-man U.S. troop cut in 1970 provided the U.S. "furnish us enough substantial aid for that." Thieu said that despite American military withdrawal, the U.S. should "stay behind and help us economically and in more sophisticated weapons, like atomic warfare that we have not." When interviewer Frank Reynolds asked whether he was referring to the acquisition of American atomic weapons, Thieu ignored the question.

South Vietnamese Vice Pres. Nguyen Cao Ky predicted Oct. 5 that the withdrawal of U.S. troops by the end of 1970 will have reached the point "when you can say the U.S. military effort will consist mainly of logistical-support functions, and that the Vietnamese will have assumed all ground-combat responsibility."

U.S. Defense Secy. Laird said Oct. 16 that he expected the U.S. to maintain several thousand military men in South Vietnam for training and advisory purposes after the fighting ended. He said the size of this "residual force" would probably be smaller than the 55,000-man contingent stationed in South Korea since 1953 and larger than the 6,000 to 7,000 U.S. advisers in

Vietnam before the U.S. escalation. 2 Administration spokesmen clarified Laird's remarks Oct. 17. White House Press Secy. Ziegler stressed Laird's own qualification that he was discussing "contingency" planning. State Department spokesmen Robert J. McCloskey cautioned that Laird's statement should not be construed to mean that the U.S. had abandoned hope for a negotiated settlement. Both spokesmen emphasized Nixon's expressed readiness to withdraw all U.S. trops from South Vietnam in a peace settlement.

Ex-Vice Pres. Hubert H. Humphrey commented in Tokyo Oct. 19 that he expected the U.S. to carry out "a systematical and accelerated" withdrawal of its forces from Vietnam. He said Oct. 22 that the U.S. had "succeeded" in its objectives in South Vietnam—to prevent the spread of Communist armed aggression and to give the South Vietnamese time for self-determination. If the South Vietnamese had not used that time, he said, "that's their problm. We have done as much for a friend as a friend can be expected to do."

Sen. Fred R. Harris (Okla.), Democratic national chairman, Oct. 19 urged a faster systematic U.S. withdrawal, with emphasis upon the word "systematic," he said, as a signal to Hanoi of the U.S. determination to achieve its objective of self-determination for the South Vietnamese.

Issues Debated

Sen. Edward M. Kennedy (D., Mass.) Sept. 18 condemned the Nixon Administration's policy in Vietnam and the South Vietnamese government of Pres. Nguyen Van Thieu, which he called "corrupt and repressive." In a Boston speech Kennedy said that despite the 1968 Presidential election and "the promises of a new President and . . . new rhetoric, the war in Vietnam is virtually unchanged." He said the Administration's troop withdrawals were "token," "more an exercise in politics and improvisation while the level of fighting and casualties continues." The refusal to compromise on the issue of a coalition government for South Vietnam, Kennedy said, was asking the enemy "to accept defeat, and we have not defeated them." "We have not been willing to consider the continued control of the Thieu regime as a negotiable question, and . . . as long as we remain unmoved on this issue there can be no peaceful solution." "It is time to say to the Saigon government," he continued, "if you will not agree to a sensible compromise—even if it endangers your personal power—then it is your war and you must fight it alone."

Sen. Charles E. Goodell (R., N.Y.) added a new dimension to the renewed war protest movement Sept. 25 by proposing legislation to require withdrawal of all U.S. troops from Vietnam by the end of 1970. Goodell's legislation would have barred the use of Congressionally appropriated funds after Dec. 1, 1970 for maintaining U.S. military personnel in Vietnam. The purpose of his proposal, Goodell told the Senate, was "to help the President and Congress develop a workable plan for ending American participation in the war—and the slaughter of American servicemen—in the very near future." "At present," he said, "there is no visible plan of this kind, and the assumptions under which the military is now operating will probably keep us fighting for years."

Goodell's plan was denounced by Nixon, who, at his Sept. 26 news conference, called it "defeatist" and appealed for national unity behind his Vietnam policy. An "arbitrary cutoff time—say the end of 1970 or the middle of 1971"—for a total U.S. pullout, Nixon said, "inevitably leads to perpetuating and continuing the war until that time and destroys any chance to reach the objective that I am trying to achieve of ending the war before the end of 1970 or before the middle of 1971." He said such proposals also "inevitably undercut and destroy" the U.S. bargaining position in Paris. Although there was no significant progress in those talks, he said, "any incentive for the enemy to negotiate is destroyed if he is told in advance that if he just waits for 18 months we'll be out anyway."

The President cited "some progress" in efforts to end the war—the withdrawal of 60,000 U.S. troops, the 50,000-man draft-call reduction, $2/_3$ less enemy infiltration since January, $1/_3$ fewer U.S. casualties and the "far-reaching and comprehensive" peace offer by the U.S. "Now is the time for Hanoi to make the next move, he said, and he emphasized that there was only one thing that was "not negotiable"—the right of the people of South Vietnam to choose their own leaders without outside imposition, either by us or by anybody else." In calling for national unity, Nixon said: "If we stay on this course and if we can have some more support in the nation—we have a lot of support—but even more support in the nation for this steady course . . . , the enemy then will have the incentive to negotiate, recognizing that it isn't going to gain time, that it isn't going to wait us out." "We're on the right course in Vietnam. We're on a course that is going to end this war. It will end much sooner if we can have to an extent—the extent possible in this free country—a united front behind very reasonable proposals. If we have that united front, the enemy then will begin to talk."

Republican Congressional leaders appealed Sept. 29 for a 60-day moratorium on criticism of the Administration's Vietnam policy to provide time and a "common front" for the negotiation of a peace settlement. The appeal was made amid signs of unrest among critics of the war. Democratic National Chairman Fred R. Harris said after a secret caucus of Democrats Sept. 26, "it's time to take the gloves off on Vietnam." Sen. J.W. Fulbright (D., Ark.), one of the foremost Vietnam critics, announced Sept. 25 that he was "ready to speak out" once more on Vietnam. He had muted his criticism of the war during the early months of the new Administration. Fulbright praised Goodell's proposal and said he hoped that his Senate Foreign Relations Committee could hold hearings on it.

The secret Democratic caucus in Washington Sept. 26 was attended by about 24 Congress members. It was reportedly called by Harris to discuss support for a planned nationwide student anti-war protest Oct. 15 and troop pullout legislation. Harris had hoped for a bipartisan antiwar effort, but some participants, including Sens. Edward Kennedy (Mass.) and Frank Church (Ida.), indicated concern over the partisan flavor of the meeting. Both Sept. 29 expressed opposition to making Vietnam a partisan issue. Sens. Hugh Scott (Pa.) and Robert P. Griffin (Mich.) Sept. 29 urged the 60-day moratorium on Vietnam criticism, and House GOP leader Gerald R. Ford (Mich.) denounced troop-withdrawal proposals as "tantamount to surrender." "Politics should stop at the water's edge," he said. Griffin said criticism would "only serve to prolong the war."

The Goodell proposal had been attacked Sept. 25 by New York Gov. Nelson A. Rockefeller (R.), who called it "ill-advised," and by Defense Secy. Melvin R. Laird, who said it would be "a grave error" to "project figures and set dates that we might not be able to deliver on." Laird hoped that "all Americans" would support the President's program. "That is the thing that Hanoi will understand," he said.

The President, Scott and Ford Sept. 30 made further appeals

for support of the war effort. Speaking at a White House ceremony—the presentation of a Presidential Unit Citation for bravery
to members of the First Marine Regiment of the First Marine
Division—Nixon said "the peace that we will be able to achieve will
be due to the fact that Americans, when it really counted, did not
buckle and run away, but stood fast."

Scott and Ford had commented after a lengthy meeting with
Nixon earlier Sept. 30. On the Goodell proposal, Scott said that
"the American people and the Congress clearly . . . oppose these
cut-and-run and bug-out resolutions." Ford said that Nixon, the
GOP leadership and the majority of the American people believed
that "there must not be capitulation or bug-out in our conflict in
Vietnam." Scott had told newsmen Sept. 22 that for the Republicans to make gains in the 1970 elections, the Administration
would have to reduce the number of troops in Vietnam by half,
substantially reduce draft calls and cut defense spending by more
than the $3 billion already pledged.

Scott reported Oct. 1 that Nixon had remarked to some
Republican Senators at a White House meeting the night before
that he did not intend to be "the first President to preside over
an American defeat." Sen. Eugene J. McCarthy (D., Minn.)
charged Oct. 2 that if Scott were correctly quoting the President,
it would mean Nixon "is willing to sacrifice almost anything to
preserve what he considers to be his role in history."

Speaking on TV Oct. 5, Scott said the U.S. and North Vietnam could be moving toward a *"de facto* ceasefire." "There may
be one more offensive," he said. "The enemy has about one
offensive left in him. After that, that enemy is a defeated enemy.
Now, it may take a long time for them to admit it. . . ."

Hints of new diplomatic activity, coming from Congressional
sources, were largely discounted by informed observers. The
most specific report—by Washington correspondent James Mc-
Cartney Oct. 4—was that secret overtures had been made to the
new Hanoi leadership for a negotiated settlement of the war and
that the secret effort was "directly related" to the plea for a
moratorium on criticism. The White House refused to confirm or
deny the report.

Objections to the call for a moratorium on criticism had
been voiced by several Senators. Foreign Relations Committee
Chairman J.W. Fulbright said Oct. 1 that "the time has come
now when, with the best of spirits, we should try to develop this

issue." "I object to the policy that we should all keep quiet and hope for the best," he said. "Rather than a moratorium on criticism, which kills no one, we who criticize continuation of the war seek, instead, a moratorium on killing." Sen. Edward Kennedy said Oct. 1 that he hoped others would join in urging prompt extrication of the U.S. from the war. "Rather than being disunified," he declared, "I think it helps to build a unity of purpose."

Senate Majority Leader Mike Mansfield (D., Mont.) called Oct. 2 for a ceasefire and stand-fast in Vietnam and an effort to get rival political groups, including the Communists, to work out the details for a coalition government and elections. "If the spirit is there," he asserted, "the details should not be too hard to overcome." Sen. Harold E. Hughes (D., Ia.) said Oct. 2 that if the Saigon government refused to join talks on a provisional government, the U.S. should "declare openly and officially the end of its commitment to the present government of South Vietnam." Sen. Charles H. Percy (R., Ill.) advocated Oct. 3 that the U.S. respond to the current lull in combat "by ending the bombing and shelling of South Vietnam and suspending ground offensive operations as long as the enemy takes no advantage of the situation." Sen. George S. McGovern (D., S.D.) Oct. 5 urged the withdrawal of all U.S. troops from the Asian mainland and an offer of asylum to South Vietnamese political leaders and others in Vietnam who felt their lives endangered if U.S. troops were withdrawn.

Ex-Vice Pres. Hubert H. Humphrey said Oct. 5 U.S. forces "must be removed from Vietnam and this costly, pitiful war . . . ended." But he opposed "nit-picking from the Democratic Party" and said he was prepared "to support the President in any way I can if he is really pursuing a plan to withdraw." He said Nixon should call in Congressional leaders and war critics and explain, "in confidence if necessary, exactly how he expects to end the war." "He cannot expect the Congress, or the people either, to stop their criticism unless they are confident he is really using every means he has to end this war," Humphrey declared.

Congressional preoccupation with the Vietnam issue resulted in a flurry of Vietnam resolutions Oct. 8-13. There was also a move to force the House into an all-night session Oct. 14-15 in support of nationwide demonstration then taking place. *The resolutions being offered included these:*

Oct. 8—From Sens. Harold E. Hughes (D., Ia.) and Thomas F. Eagleton (D., Mo.), to end U.S. commitment to the Saigon government unless that government made reforms necessary for a provisional government within 60 days. From Sens. Frank Church (D., Ida.) and Mark O. Hatfield (R., Ore.), to accelerate the U.S. troop withdrawal and U.S. disengagement.

Oct. 9—From 3 Democratic Senators and 14 Congressmen, a concurrent resolution calling for immediate withdrawal limited only by the need to protect U.S. forces. From 4 Democratic Congressmen, to create a joint committee to study the U.S. role in Vietnam.

Oct. 13—From Sen. Robert J. Dole (R., Kan.) and 35 co-sponsors, 31 of them Republicans, to support the Administration policy and urge Hanoi to negotiate seriously (called the "White House Resolution").

Sen. Henry M. Jackson (D., Wash.) objected Oct. 10 to the rash of antiwar proposals, saying they would give off "confusing signals" to Hanoi. He recommended a joint meeting of the Senate's Armed Services and Foreign Relations Committees to develop a common Vietnam troop withdrawal plan with the Administration.

Sen. George D. Aiken (R., Vt.) proposed Oct. 11 that the U.S. "adopt a 'live and let live' attitude toward the rest of the world." But he said "the President needs time" on Vietnam and was making progress toward correcting a basic policy problem: namely, that "we have prevented self-determination through the weight of our intervention, even while proclaiming the preservation of self-determination as our goal."

Sen. Thomas J. McIntyre (D., N.H.) Oct. 13 revealed his conclusion, after a "confrontation" with himself, that it was time "to get out of Vietnam with all due speed." Another former supporter of Vietnam involvement, Sen. Frank E. Moss(D., Utah), also announced Oct. 13 his conclusion that the Administration's policy was "not working." He proposed that the U.S. end offensive action and begin to withdraw its combat forces "as swiftly as as can be done without endangering American lives."

A bipartisan group of 17 Senators and 47 Congressman Oct. 9 expressed support for a planned demonstration called the Vietnam Moratorium by telling its organizers that they shared the "commitment toward ending the war in Vietnam . . . as soon as possible." Rep. Wayne L. Hays (D., O.) Oct. 13 denounced "the designs of a few self-appointed emissaries of Hanoi to keep the House in session and make it appear the House is on the side of Hanoi."

Ex-Vice Pres. Humphrey indorsed the Administration's Vietnam stand after a meeting with the President Oct. 10. Nixon was "proceeding along the right path" in Vietnam, Humphrey declared, and "we have to give the President time to carry out his proposals, to carry out his plan and his policies." While there were "honest differences" in the nation over Vietnam and "the American people are not going to be hushed," Humphrey said, "we only have one President at a time" and "the worst thing we can do is try to undermine the efforts of the President."

Ex-State Secy. Dean Acheson, in a *N.Y. Times* interview published Oct. 10, objected to "the attempt being made from so many sources to destroy Nixon." "I think we're going to have a major constitutional crisis if we make a habit of destroying Presidents," Acheson warned. He was predisposed "to support the President whatever the issue."

A letter urging a "stepped-up timetable for withdrawal from Vietnam" was sent to the President Oct. 11 by the presidents of 79 private colleges and universities. The war, they asserted, "stands as a denial of so much that is best in our society."

'Ceasefire' Proposals Discussed

The subject of a ceasefire in Vietnam was debated by Nixon Administration leaders Oct. 22-27. Senate Republican leader Hugh Scott (Pa.) suggested Oct. 22 it might be time for the U.S. to act boldly "and proclaim an end to the shooting." "One side has to take the initiative, and to that extent it would be a unilateral action," he said. "But ceasefires can't happen unless they are mutually observed. If the enemy then attacks us, we would have to defend ourselves and it would bust up the cease-fire." Scott stressed the personal nature of his comments and said he was not floating "a trial balloon" for the Administration. Speaking later Oct. 22 and in reference to Scott's comments, Defense Secy. Melvin R. Laird opposed a unilateral ceasefire by the U.S. —on the ground that it would not be "a successful approach"— and cautioned against entering into any ceasefire "without some firm indication from the other side of assurances that they would go forward" with political and other military steps to end the war. A ceasefire was "a matter up for negotiation," he said, and the proper place for that was "in Paris" at the peace talks. House GOP Leader Gerald R. Ford (Mich.) reinforced Laird's position Oct. 23 by stating his opposition to any "unilateral" ceasefire in Vietnam.

After conferences with White House advisers, including Dr. Henry A. Kissinger, Pres. Nixon's national security adviser, a cabinet official and 2 Pentagon generals, Scott clarified his comments

Oct. 27. He was expressing the hope, he said, "that a ceasefire will become possible under the policy the President is pursuing. . . . I don't know what the President will say on Nov. 3 [the previously announced date for a Presidential statement on Vietnam], but I do hope a mutually observed ceasefire will result." Asked why he was making a clarification, Scott said he had "given some thought to the fact that initially a unilateral ceasefire perhaps would not be observed by the other side."

(Pres. Nguyen Van Thieu had said Sept. 19 that his government would "not agree to a ceasefire without first arranging" an over-all political settlement. Thieu expressed opposition to the 3 truce plans most frequently discussed in Saigon: [1] a ceasefire in place observed by Communist and allied forces; [2] the gradual widening of the demilitarized zone to pave the way for a halt in the fighting; [3] the ceding of South Vietnam's 2 northernmost provinces to North Vietnam in exchange for an end to the combat. Thieu said Saigon would "allow the enemy to participate" in proposed elections to decide South Vietnam's future form of government, "but we will not accept a Communist Party in South Vietnam.")

Senate Democratic Leader Mike Mansfield (Mont.) spoke Oct. 22 of the "decided shift" away from the past Vietnam tactics of "search and destroy" and "maximum pressure." Referring to the new "protective reaction" policy cited by Administration spokesmen recently, he said the Administration had "moved a long distance in the direction of a 'ceasefire and stand-fast' policy."

In his comments Oct. 22, Laird cautioned against equating the "protective reaction" strategy with a halt in combat. The new strategy, he said, was designed "to keep casualties at a minimun" and "does not mean we are just going to stand still and be fired upon." Reports had been published and broadcast that U.S. field commanders in South Vietnam were unaware of any basic changes in their orders on strategy.

A Laird comment Oct. 22 about reduced war costs drew repercussion in a Congressional hearing Oct. 23. Laird predicted that the overall Vietnam war cost—which totaled $30 billion in fiscal 1969—would be reduced to an annual level of $17 billion in fiscal 1970. Paul W. McCracken, chairman of the President's Council of Economic Advisers, questioned about the figures at a session of the Joint Subcommittee on Fiscal Policy, said he was "not aware" of the Pentagon's plans for a $13 billion reduction in war costs.

'War Crime' Issue Emerges

Questions concerning military conduct in Vietnam began to emerge during the latter part of 1969. The first of these arose from allegations against members of the U.S. Special Forces (the "Green Berets").

The U.S. Army command in Saigon Aug. 6 announced the arrest of the commander of a U.S. Special Forces group and 7 members of his unit on suspicion of premeditated murder in the fatal shooting of a missing Vietnamese national near Nhatrang June 20. U.S. authorities refused to disclose further details of the case on the ground that it would jeopardize the rights of the accused. But American press reports indicated that the Vietnamese had been a spy for the "Green Berets" and was slain after it was discovered that he was a double agent, also in the employ of the North Vietnamese. The U.S. Central Intelligence Agency (CIA) was said to have ordered the execution.

The Army identified the accused Green Berets as Col. Robert B. Rheault of Vineyard Haven, Mass., commander of the 5th Special Forces Group (Airborne), with headquarters at Nhatrang, 160 miles north of Saigon; Maj. David E. Crew, Cedar Rapids, Ia.; Maj. Thomas C. Middleton Jr., Jefferson, S.C.; Capt. Leland J. Brumley, Duncan, Okla.; Capt. Robert F. Marasco, Bloomfield, N.J.; Capt. Budge E. Williams, Athens, Ga.; Chief Warrant Officer 2d Cl. Edward M. Boyle, New York; Sgt. First Cl. Alvin L. Smith Jr., Naples, Fla. The Army announcement said the 8 men were confined under guard at Longbinh, 12 miles northeast of Saigon, to await possible trial. Col. Rheault had taken command of the Fifth Special Forces May 29 and was relieved of his post July 21 after Army investigation of the case.

The body of the alleged spy, known as Thai Khac Chuyen, was said to have been thrown into the South China Sea at Nhatrang harbor after he was shot. A U.S. Navy team started a hunt for the body Aug. 4 but abandoned the search Aug. 10. The Special Forces, which trained Vietnamese in counter-guerrilla warfare, had put Chuyen in charge of a team of Vietnamese to observe the movement of Communist troops on both sides of the Cambodian border. He was said to have informed the North Vietnamese of his activities in late May or June. The betrayal was said to have resulted in the killing by Communists of several of the U.S.-directed agents. U.S. intelligence established Chuyen's identity as a double agent on the basis of a photo of him taken secretly while he met with North Vietnamese agents in Cambodia. After subsequent interrogation confirmed his links with the North Vietnamese, the CIA was reported to have ordered Chuyen's death. According to press accounts, the CIA rescinded the order a few days after June 20, unaware that the Special Forces had already slain Chuyen that day. Gen. Creighton W. Abrams, commander of U.S. forces in Vietnam, was said to have reviewed the case.

Attorney George Gregory, of Cheraw, S.C., defense counsel for Maj. Middleton, told newsmen in Saigon Aug. 11, after visiting his client, that the missing Vietnamese had been a "dangerous Communist double agent," working simultaneously for the CIA and North Vietnamese intelligence. The CIA, Gregory charged, "was gravely involved" in the case. U.S. government officials in Washington denied Aug. 11 that the CIA had any connection with the affair.

A *N.Y. Times* report Aug. 28 gave the CIA's version of its role in the incident. The newspaper said its report was based on private talks that high CIA officials had held with newsmen in Washington the previous 2 days. According to the CIA's account: The Special Forces officers informed the CIA June 12 that an agent in their employ whom they did not identify by name at that time was under suspicion as a possible double agent for the North Vietnamese. They asked whether the CIA would take the suspect off their hands and confine him in "some safe haven," possibly outside Vietnam. The CIA refused and suggested instead that the double agent not be killed. The CIA June 18 again urged the Special Forces not to kill Chuyen but to wait until the agency traced his background to determine whether he could be fitted into the CIA's operations. By this time the CIA's office in Saigon had alerted Army authorities about the case. The Special Forces men June 21 assured the CIA and Army authorities that Chuyen had been sent on a "high-risk, sensitive mission to North Vietnam." One of the 8 Green Berets involved in the controversy, Sgt. Alvin L. Smith Jr., informed the CIA office in Nhatrang June 30 that Chuyen had been killed by the Special Forces, and Smith asked for protection.

The Army Sept. 29 dropped the murder charges against the

6 Special Forces men. The announcement, made in Washington by Army Secy. Stanley Resor, said the scheduled courts-martial of the Green Berets had to be ruled out because the CIA, "though not directly involved in the alleged incident, has determined that in the interest of national security it will not make available any of its personnel in connection with the pending trials." "Under these circumstances," Resor explained, "the defendants cannot receive a fair trial. Accordingly, I have directed today that all charges be dismissed immediately. The men will be assigned to duties outside Vietnam." Resor emphasized that "the acts which were charged, but not proved, represent a fundamental violation of Army regulations, orders and principles." He concluded: "The Army will not and cannot condone unlawful acts of the kind alleged. Except in the rare cases where consideration of national security and the right to a fair trial cannot be reconciled, proceedings under the Uniform Code of Military Justice must take their normal course. . . . The determination of guilt may be made only by a court which has access to all information with respect to the alleged offense." (7 of the 8 left South Vietnam for the U.S. Sept. 30. The 8th departed alone Oct. 1.) In the first public statement on the specifications of the charges, the Army in Saigon had said Sept. 27 that Capt. Robert F. Marasco, one of the 6 suspects in the case, had shot Chuyen to death with a pistol on or about June 20 in Nhatrang. According to the Army statement: 2 other suspects in the case, Capt. Leland J. Brumley and Chief Warrant Officer Edward M. Boyle, had taken Chuyen from the Special Forces headquarters in Nhatrang; Bromley had obtained a boat and injected morphine into Chuyen to render him unconscious before he was shot; Chuyen's body was later dumped into Nhatrang harbor from the boat and was never recovered.

White House Press Secy. Ronald L. Ziegler said Sept. 29 that, contrary to reports, Pres. Nixon had not been involved in the original decision to prosecute the Green Berets and the subsequent decision to drop the charges. Ziegler Sept. 30 again denied Nixon's role in the case, but he qualified his disclaimer by saying that to the best of his knowledge the President had not taken part in the decision to drop the case. Rep. L. Mendel River (D., S.C.) said Sept. 30 that he had urged Nixon to review the situation and "not to have the trial." Sen. Stephen M. Young (D., O.) said the order to withdraw the case "came, as far as I know, from the White House."

Robert B. Rheault, head of the Green Berets group accused of Chuyen's murder, denied Oct. 1 that there was a killing. Rheault, speaking for his colleagues, made the statement on arriving for reassignment from Vietnam at Travis Air Force Base, Calif. with 6 others involved in the case. When asked whether Chuyen was "a close political ally of [South Vietnamese Pres. Nguyen Van] Thieu" and whether he thought "this resulted in the case that was brought against you," Rheault replied: "No, there is no conclusive evidence that the individual ever was killed, and there is certainly no indication anywhere that the alleged victim was connected with Thieu." At a separate news conference, Sgt. Smith denied that he had informed Gen. Abrams of the alleged murder. "There was no murder," he said. Capt. Robert Marasco, accused by the Army as the "triggerman," denied the charges as "ridiculous" on arriving at Newark, N.J. later Oct. 1. (A year and a half later, however, Marasco, no longer in the service, said Apr. 2, 1971 that he had shot and killed Chuyen on CIA orders.)

In a reversal of previous denials, the White House acknowledged Oct. 1 that Pres. Nixon had been involved in the decision to drop the charges against the Green Berets. Press Secy. Ziegler said CIA director Richard Helms had "made the decision that, in the light of national security interests, CIA personnel should not appear as witnesses" in any trial of 6 of the 8 accused. (A trial for the 2 others, Sgt. Smith and Chief Warrant Officer Edward M. Boyle, had been ordered held in abeyance pending the other trials.) Ziegler added: "The CIA informed the White House, and the President approved this decision." The CIA's refusal to provide witnesses influenced the decision to abandon the case. Ziegler said he "did not know" of Nixon's review of the CIA position when he issued denials of the President's involvement Sept. 29 and 30.

The U.S. government announced Oct. 5 that it had paid a "missing person gratuity" of $6,472 to Chuyen's widow the previous day. The statement said: "We have no evidence that Chuyen is dead. He is in the missing category. The man has not been legally proved dead in a court of law. Therefore, it can only be assumed that he is missing."

Mylai Massacre

First Lt. William Laws Calley Jr. of Miami was charged by

the U.S. Army Sept. 5 with murder and Staff Sgt. David Mitchell of St. Francisville, La. was charged Oct. 28 with assault with intent to kill in connection with the slaying of more than 100 South Vietnamese civilians during a military operation in Mar. 1968 against an alleged Viet Cong stronghold,Mylai 4,in northern Quangngai Province. Mylai was one of several hamlets that comprised the village of Songmy. The number of civilians slain was said to range from 109, according to Calley's attorney, to 567, as claimed by surviving villagers. The charges against Calley were announced Nov. 12 and those against Mitchell Nov. 14.

Calley had commanded the unit that took part in the Mylai incident—the first platoon of Company C, First Battalion, 20th Infantry, 11th Infantry Brigade, Americal Division. Mitchell was the leader of the first squad of the platoon. Calley's attorney, George W. Latimer, said Nov. 12 that there were 6 specifications against his client and they alleged that he had killed "quite a number of people." Latimer asserted that Calley was not guilty, that he had acted "in the line of duty" against "Viet Cong villagers" who had "worked for the Viet Cong—carrying ammunition and so on." The Army charge against Mitchell accused him of "intent to commit an assault upon a group of 30 Vietnamese nationals, more or less, by shooting at them with an M-16 rifle."

The U.S. Army command had issued a routine communiqué following the operation. It had said that the actions by Company C, First Battalion, 20th Infantry, 11th Brigade were part of a 3-company task force. It reported "128 enemy soldiers" killed. 2 Americans were slain and 10 wounded. It did not mention civilian losses.

A group of the Vietnamese surviviors of the incident told American newsmen Nov. 16, in the presence of U.S. Army officers, that a U.S. infantry unit had killed 567 unarmed men, women and children in the village. According to an account provided by one of the villagers and confirmed by the others: The American soldiers entered the village following a one-hour artillery barrage and encountered no resistance. The soldiers dynamited or burned down all the houses, lined up the villagers in 3 sites about 200 yards apart and gunned them down. About 20 soldiers carried out the executions. The figure of 567 slain was arrived at by subtracting the number of survivors—132—from the total known population in the hamlet.

Ton That Khien, governor of Quangngai Province, said in a

separate interview Nov. 16 that the number of dead was possibly exaggerated. He said that the victims had been buried by the survivors within 3 days of the slayings and that no body count had been made. Khien conceded that most of those killed were not Communists. But he said there were Viet Cong cadres in the village who may have fired at the Americans. Khien said he had been notified of the slayings within a week but at first assumed they had resulted from an artillery barrage.

A former soldier stationed in Vietnam, Ronald Lee Ridenhour, 23, said Nov. 15 in Claremont, Calif., where he attended college, that his account of the incident, in letters sent in February to 30 U.S. officials, had prompted the Army investigation. Among those receiving the message were Pres. Nixon, Defense Secy. Melvin Laird and 4 or 5 Congress members. Ridenhour said he had relayed the report after learning about it from several members of Calley's company he had met in Vietnam and in Hawaii several months after the incident. Ridenhour, who had been discharged from the Army after returning to the U.S. in Dec. 1968, said he had been interviewed about the incident by an Army colonel at his home in Phoenix, Ariz. in Apr. 1969. (The Army confirmed Nov. 19 that a letter from a Vietnam war veteran had prompted the investigation of the incident. Although the Army did not name the writer, it apparently referred to Ridenhour.)

6 men involved in the operation provided eyewitness accounts of the incident in press and TV interviews:

● Sgt. Michael A. Bernhardt, who said he had refused to participate in the shooting of the villagers, reported in Ft. Dix, N.J. Nov. 19 that "most of the men" in his company had gunned down "women and childern and old men" in compliance with a company command order "that the village and the occupants were to be destroyed." He said he believed about 100 civilians were killed. Bernhardt said the commander had told them that "they were all VC [Viet Cong] and there were no innocent civilians in the area." Bernhardt reported that "I didn't notice any military-age males there." In a statement Nov. 20, Bernhardt said he had been ordered by the company commander not to talk about the incident. He refused to name the commander, who was subsequently identified as Capt. Ernest L. Medina. Bernhardt said he was "not aware" of any hostile fire encountered by the Americans as they moved into Songmy.

● In an interview published Nov. 20 in the *Cleveland Plain Dealer*, Ronald L. Haeberle, a former Army combat photographer who had accompanied the American unit, said he had seen "as many as 30 American soldiers murder as many as 100 South Vietnamese civilians, many of them women and babies." He said the killings were carried out with M-16 rifles and machineguns. No

Viet Cong were sighted, Haeberle declared, and there were no reports of Viet Cong fire. The interview was accompanied by photos taken by Haeberle, which showed 15 to 20 bodies in a ditch. The dead included babies, women and children. Haeberle said he had made the photos available to the Army's Criminal Investigation Division.

● In an interview with the *Washington Post* Nov. 19, Michael B. Terry, a former private first class, said he had seen 20 to 30 villagers machinegunned in a group lying in a ditch, "mostly women and kids and maybe a few old men." Terry, who had participated in the shootings, said that "some of them were still breathing. . . . They weren't going to get any medical help, and so we shot them. Shot maybe 5 of them. . . . I thought that was the best thing I could do."

● In a CBS-TV interview Nov. 24, Paul D. Meadlo, of Terre Haute, Ind. said he personally had killed 35 to 40 women with rifle fire after receiving orders from Lt. Calley and Sgt. Mitchell to slay the civilians. Meadlo, who had lost a foot when he stepped on a mine a day after the operation, estimated that 370 persons had been killed in the village. Meadlo said his participation in the slaughter "was the natural thing to do at the time. My buddies getting killed or wounded—we weren't getting no satisfaction from it, so what it really was, it was mostly revenge."

● Another veteran of the operation, Charles A. West, told the *Chicago Sun Times* Nov. 21 that his unit had been ordered "to destroy Songmy and everything in it." West, who had been discharged from the Army in Nov. 1968, reported that Capt. Medina, in an order read to the men before the attack, "said the village was considered heavily armed and held by the Viet Cong and the North Vietnamese were believed to be in underground tunnels."

● Varnado Simpson, 22, said at his home in Jackson, Miss. Nov. 26 that Medina told his men that the village was filled with Viet Cong and their sympathizers and instructed them to "kill or burn down anything in sight." Simpson admitted that he had killed 10 adult civilians but said he felt at the time he was only obeying orders.

Mrs. Nguyen Thi Binh, chief delegate of the Viet Cong's Provisional Revolutionary Government (PRG), had charged at the Paris talks Nov. 20 that the Mylai massacre was only one of "thousands and thousands of crimes perpetrated by the United States in Vietnam." After the meeting, PGR spokesman Duong Dinh Thao produced a Vietnamese "eyewitness" letter allegedly confirming the events that occurred at Mylai and disclosed another incident in Quangngai Province, in the coastal village of Balangan, in which 1,200 civilians were said to have been drowned by U.S. forces in the South China Sea in Mar. 1969. The letter asserted that the U.S. troops had moved into Songmy and attacked the villagers' underground shelters with machineguns and hand grenades. Thao said the letter had been disclosed in Hanoi shortly after Mar. 16, 1968, the day of the killings, but had gone unnoticed because of the excitement created by the Viet Cong's Tet offensive at the time. In the incident at Balangan, only miles from Songmy,

Thao said that 8,200 U.S., South Vietnamese and other allied troops had swept through the area between Jan. 11 and Feb. 19, killing 200 people and then rounding up more than 11,000 villagers in a concentration camp. According to Thao, 1,200 of these residents were placed aboard large boats that were towed out to sea and were sunk by warships "which veered sharply and quickly enough to tip" them over. Thao said the PGR delegation had published a document on the alleged incident in March.

Army authorities in Ft. Benning, Ga. announced Nov. 24 that Calley would be court-martialed on charges of premeditated murder in connection with the Mylai slayings. 6 specifications against Calley accused him of violating Article 118 of the Uniform Code of Military Justice, which stated that a person could be tried for "unlawfully" killing a human being "without justification or excuse." 2 of the counts accused him of killing at least 100 men, women and children. A new charge against Calley was announced by Army authorities in Ft. Benning Nov. 29. It accused him of "the murder of one adult male in Quangngai Province in an incident that preceded the alleged Mylai incident by approximately $1^1/_2$ months."

The Defense Department had announced Nov. 21 that 24 other men—9 soldiers and 15 former servicemen—were under investigation in connection with the alleged massacre. The announcement publicly confirmed for the first time that a large number of civilians had been killed at Songmy.

Army authorities in Washington Nov. 24 announced the appointment of Lt. Gen. William R. Peers to "explore the nature and scope" of an original Army investigation of the slayings in Apr. 1968. The initial probe, conducted by members of the 11th Infantry Brigade, the unit involved in the affair, apparently concluded that no massacre had occurred and that no further action was warranted.

A White House statement issued Nov. 26 by Press Secy. Ronald Ziegler said the Army investigation would make certain that "appropriate action" would be taken "to assure that illegal and immoral conduct, as alleged, be dealt with in accordance with the strict rules of military justice." "This incident should not be allowed to reflect on the . . . Americans who have now returned to the United States after having served in Vietnam with great courage and distinction," Ziegler added. He described as "regrettable" the delay of a year between the occurrence of the alleged incident and the beginning of the Army investigation. He said Pres. Nixon had been aware of the episode "for several months" before the report was made public. This was the only such incident that Nixon had been informed of, Ziegler said.

In his first public statement on the matter, Nixon said at his news conference Dec. 8 that it was "an isolated incident" and that he would "see to it that what these men did—if they did it—does not smear the decent men that have gone into Vietnam in a very, in my opinion, important cause." The American soldiers' "record of generosity, of decency" in Vietnam "must not be allowed to be smeared and slurred because of this kind of an incident. That's why I'm going to do everything I possibly can to see that all the facts . . . are brought to light and that those who are charged, if they are found guilty, are punished." "What appears was certainly a massacre, and under no circumstances was it justified," the President said. Nixon said he was opposed to the idea of a civilian commission to investigate the matter on the ground that it might prejudice the rights of the accused. He indicated he would consider such a commission only if military justice proved inadequate "in bringing the incident completely before the public."

Sen. John C. Stennis (D., Miss.), chairman of the Senate Armed Services Committee, had urged Nixon Dec. 7 to appoint a civilian panel, "outside the government, outside the military," to conduct an impartial investigation and then report to the President. Stennis suggested that the panel first hold private hearings and "after they are satisfied they have the facts . . . they might have an open hearing to bring it out and to let people judge the witnesses."

Army Secy. Stanley S. Resor had briefed members of the Senate and House Armed Services Committees Nov. 26 and showed color slides of the civilian victims of the massacre. The photos had been taken by Army photographer Ronald Haeberle. Some of the Congress members later expressed shock at what they had seen and were critical of the Army's handling of the case. Sen. Daniel K. Inouye (D., Hawaii) said he was "a bit sickened"; "it is apparent that noncombatants were shot." Sen. Richard S. Schweiker (R., Pa.) said he was "convinced" there had been a cover-up of the incident. Sen. Stephen Young (D., O.) called it "an abominable atrocity—murder at point-blank range." House Republican leader Gerald Ford said that "responsi-

ble people of the Department of the Army in Vietnam knew
all about this shortly after it occurred." He did not reveal their
names. Resor had said in his testimony to the committees: "It
is difficult to convey to you the feelings of shock and dismay
which I and other civilian and military leaders of the Army have
experienced as the tragedy of Mylai unfolded before us." No one
in the Defense Department or in the Army's top command in
Vietnam knew of the episode until Apr. 1969. One of the prime
critical issues Army investigators were trying to determine was
whether the soldiers involved "were acting pursuant to orders
from their company commander or higher headquarters when
they destroyed Mylai's buildings and fired upon its unresisting
inhabitants."

A U.S. Army board of inquiry began closed hearings in
Washington Dec. 2 into the Mylai massacre. The 8-member board,
composed of Army officers and civilians working for the Army,
had been appointed Nov. 24 by Army Secy. Resor and Army
Chief of Staff William C. Westmoreland to determine whether
the Army investigation in Mar. 1968 was inadequate and whether
there was an attempt by it to suppress the facts.

The Army board Dec. 2 questioned Col. Oren K. Henderson,
the former commander of the 11th Brigade, who had conducted the
original inquiry 2 days after the incident. Henderson was asked
to testify on the contents of his original report, which he had submitted to the Americal Division headquarters Apr. 24, 1968. Henderson had said Nov. 25 that "up until 2 weeks ago, I would have
sworn" that the incident "could not happen without me knowing
about it." "But when I start seeing TV broadcasts and hearing
soldiers speak about this subject who were eyewitnesses, I begin
to wonder," he said.

Medina, accompanied by his attorney, F. Lee Bailey, said at
a news conference during a recess Dec. 4 that he had not ordered
a massacre of civilians and did not see any mass slayings of civilians in the village. His statement refuted a charge by a former
rifleman in the unit, Richard Pendleton, who had told the press
the previous week that he had seen Medina shoot a Vietnamese
child to death, "the only one alive among a lot of dead people."
Pendleton had said Nov. 27 that the American troops that had
moved into Songmy began to slaughter the civilian population and
that Medina made no effort to stop it until he received "a phone
call." Pendleton said he surmised that the call was the result of U.S.

helicopter observers who flew over Songmy and "could see what was going on." Medina acknowledged that he had killed a Vietnamese woman but said he had fired at her instinctively when it appeared that she was about to attack him. Medina said his outfit had been ordered to move into Songmy to engage the 48th Viet Cong Battalion, which was suspected of being in the village. "We had been told by intelligence sources that there would be no women or children or innocent civilians in the village after 0700 hours," that they would be gone to market, he said. Medina reported seeing the bodies of about 20 to 28 civilians who had been shot, but he said they had apparently been killed during the course of the fighting. In a CBS-TV interview Dec. 5, Medina said he had not gone through the entire village during the clash. "If I had been there and had known that any such thing [the alleged massacre] was taking place, I would have stopped it," he said.

The Army board Dec. 4 also questioned Chief Warrant Officer Hugh C. Thompson Jr., 27, said to have piloted one of the reconnaissance helicopters that radioed the task force command that "unnecessary killings" had been seen in the village. Thompson had been awarded the Distinguished Flying Cross Oct. 19 for evacuating 16 children from Songmy during the operation. Thompson's report was said to have prompted the original Army investigation.

Medina said in a N.Y. Times interview Dec. 9 that "it is possible that it [the atrocity] could have taken place." But he repeated his Dec. 4 statement that "I did not see any massacre take place, and I did not order any massacre." Medina said he would have taken precautionary measures to prevent the slaying of civilians if "I had any reason to believe that there would be . . . any innocent noncombatants in that village." Medina said he did not know whether any such precautions as warning civilians of an impending attack had been taken before his troops moved into Mylai. Medina said he had remained outside the village with his command group during the assault and entered it only once to meet troops on the other side of the hamlet. Following the action, Medina said, he had asked his platoon leaders if any civilians had been killed, but "I received negative indications from all platoon leaders." The South Vietnamese Defense Ministry Nov. 22 had denied as "totally untrue" press reports and other accounts that U.S. troops had massacred civilians in Mylai. It was "a purely military matter, not a massacre in any sense," the ministry said. The ministry communiqué was issued after Pres. Nguyen Van Thieu had received a confidential report on the alleged incident from Gen. Hoang Xuan Lam, South Vietnamese commander of the 5 northern provinces. The communiqué said that U.S. troops had moved into Songmy Mar. 16, 1968 to destroy "an important Communist force there." The statement insisted that "this hamlet was organized as a fortified Viet Cong hamlet with bunkers and was under the administration of the Viet Cong." During the encounter, the Americans had slain 125 Viet Cong, and 20 civilians were inadvertently killed by air and artillery strikes, the communiqué said. The civilians had been "forced by the Communists to stay in their places," according to the ministry.

The South Vietnamese government reaffirmed Nov. 29 that its inquiry into the massacre was "definitely closed" despite a call by Vice Pres. Nguyen Cao Ky that it be reopened. Ky had said earlier Nov. 29 that "the government must carry out a further investigation . . . so as to know what exactly happened and how." The government's account was disputed by 2 committees of the National Assembly, which conducted informal investigations of their own in the Songmy area Dec. 1–3. A joint Senate Defense & Interior Committee group was led by Sen. Tran Van Don, an avowed opponent of Pres. Thieu and chairman of the Defense Committee, and by a committee of the House of Representatives. The legislators' findings of widespread killings was based on discussions with survivors of the Songmy incident. The Senate committee said Dec. 8 that its preliminary inquiry in Quangngai Province, in which Mylai was located, had confirmed the mass slayings of civilians. Don said a massacre had occurred, but the committee document, yet to be issued, avoided any such characterization. The Senate committee had met Dec. 3 with Maj. Gen. Hoang Xuan Lam, commander of the I Corps area in which Songmy was located. One committee member said Lam "knows nothing" about the incident "but the government communiqué [of Nov. 22] is based on his report." The House of Representatives fact-finding committee was reported Dec. 6 to have concluded that a large number of women and children had been needlessly killed by American troops at Mylai. The report said the fatality figure was higher than the 125 claimed by the government to have been killed.

The Senate committee said in a report Dec. 15 that at least 43 civilians had been killed by American troops at Songmy. The report was based on interviews the committee had held with 9 survivors Dec. 10-13. The House of Representatives concluded in a report released Dec. 17 that there was no evidence to prove that American troops had mercilessly killed a large number of civilians during their sweep of Songmy. But it noted that the attack had "caused casualties and property damage beyond military needs" in violation of military rules.

The National Salvation Front, an opposition political group, criticized the Saigon government Dec. 17 for "declining its responsibility and guilt" in the massacre by ordering the case closed. The front's declaration said it condemned "the guilty criminals at Songmy, although the massacre represents an isolated case."

The U.S. House Armed Services Committee had held closed hearings in Washington Dec. 8-11 on Mylai. In ending the preliminary investigation, Chairman L. Mendel Rivers (D.,S.C.) Dec. 12 announced the formation of a 4-member subcommittee to delve further. He said that "at this point in our record, there is no evidence sufficient to convict anybody of massacres." But enough evidence had been introduced in the committee hearings to warrant "the subcommittee to go further into this matter in depth," he said. After the Dec. 9 hearings, Rivers took issue with Pres. Nixon's Dec. 8 statement that "what appears was certainly a massacre." Rivers told newsmen that if the President "knows that, he knows more than I do."

The Army announced Dec. 31 that it would courtmartial Staff Sgt. David Mitchell on charges of assault with intent to murder 30 South Vietnamese civilians in connection with Mylai. Mitchell had declared Dec. 12 that "the charges brought against me are an injustice and I am innocent." Speaking to newsmen at Ft. Hood, Tex., Mitchell said published photos of civilian casualties "were pictures of something that could have happened." But, he added, he had seen nothing out of the ordinary during the operation.

U.S. commanders in South Vietnam had been directed by the American high command in Saigon Dec. 5 to reindoctrinate their men on the treatment of civilians and warned that "actions of the sort being reported in the press in recent days will not be condoned." The directive made no reference to Mylai. It reaffirmed a revised guideline on the treatment of civilians and called on officers to see that they were being "fully complied with." The new guidelines had been issued in Mar. 1969, about the time U.S. and South

Vietnamese authorities began to investigate the Mylai incident. But a military spokesman said Dec. 6 there was no connection between that probe and the new regulations. The guidelines specified that U.S. troops were to "avoid all use of unnecessary force and the indiscriminate employment of weapons that will lead to noncombatant casualties." It urged "commanders at all echelons to establish a balance between the force and weapons necessary to establish their missions and the safety of the noncombatant populace. This requires the exercise of restraint beyond that usually required of soldiers on the battlefield."

Hue Massacre Recalled

In what some observers described as an attempt to divert at least part of the criticism the U.S. was enduring over Mylai, U.S. military authorities in Saigon Nov. 24 made public a captured enemy document saying that nearly 2,900 South Vietnamese had been "eliminated" during the Communists' seizure of Hué during the 1968 Tet offensive. A U.S. source said the paper had been captured near Hué by U.S. soldiers Apr. 25, 1968. The document was said to have gone unnoticed in U.S. military files until the previous week when a writer asked to see it. The Communist leaflet read: "We eliminated 1,892 administrative personnel, 38 policemen, 790 tyrants, 6 captains, 2 first lieutenants, 20 second lieutenants and many noncommissioned officers." Allied officials had estimated that more than 3,000 people had been slain in Hué. Of this number 2,737 bodies had been recovered. The *Washington Post* had reported Nov. 7 that a new mass grave containing about 600 bodies had been unearthed in Phu Thu District, 10 miles southeast of Hué. 809 bodies had been recovered in mass graves in the same area earlier in 1969. The victims were said to have been seized and slain by Communist forces.

Defense Department officials Dec. 8 showed pictures to Congress members of South Vietnamese civilians identified as having been slain by the Communists in Hué during the 1968 Tet offensive. Rep. Richard H. Ichord (D., Mo.) said he had asked that the photos be shown "so that this whole matter may be placed in the proper perspective." "We know the alleged acts [of American troops] are in violation of official directives," while the photos and captured Viet Cong documents "present . . . evidence that the Viet Cong and North Vietnamese pursue assassination and torture in South Vietnam as an official policy," he said.

Prisoners of War

The status of Americans captured during the war, particularly those who had been taken prisoner in the air war over North Vietnam, began to emerge as an important issue during 1969. Some Americans were released, occasionally for what appeared to be political reasons and occasionally under circumstances that were, in the published accounts, unclear. The U.S. gave increasing prominence to this issue, raising it both at the Paris talks and in the UN.

The Viet Cong released 3 U.S. Army POWs (prisoners of war) in South Vietnam Jan. 1. The freed men were Pfc. Donald G. Smith of Akron, Pa., captured May 13, 1968 near Phukhuong, about 50 miles northwest of Saigon, Spec. 4 Thomas N. Jones of Lynnville, Ind., last seen driving a truck about 20 miles east of Saigon Aug. 25, and Spec. 4 James W. Brigham of Ocala, Fla., who had disappeared in the Phukhuong area during an operation Sept. 13. (Brigham died Jan. 17 at Walter Reed Army Medical Center in Washington. He had been unconscious since undergoing brain surgery Jan. 9. Brigham had suffered a head wound before his capture and had been operated on by the Viet Cong while a prisoner.) The soldiers were turned over to 5 U.S. Army officers in an open field in Thuathien Province 51 miles northwest of Saigon. The officers had negotiated their release earlier Jan. 1 at a meeting in the field with Viet Cong representatives. A special one-mile-wide and 6-mile-long corridor "free of military action" had been established for the meeting.

The Viet Cong had offered Dec. 19, 1968 to free the 3 Americans and had suggested that an unarmed U.S. military delegation discuss the arrangements with Viet Cong representatives. A meeting was held Dec. 25, but a National Liberation Front broadcast asserted Dec. 28 that the discussions had broken down because of the Americans' refusal to accept the "necessary procedures" for the release of the captives. The NLF proposed another meeting, which led to the release of the GIs Jan. 1.

U.S. Army Maj. James N. Rowe, 31, of McAllen, Tex., held prisoner by the Viet Cong since his capture near the Mekong delta's U Minh Forest Oct. 29, 1963, had escaped Dec. 31, 1968. Rowe was rescued by a U.S. helicopter during a South Vietnamese troop sweep near the forest.

Cambodia Mar. 11 freed 4 U.S. airmen who had been captured by Viet Cong in South Vietnam Feb. 12. They had been seized after their observation plane was shot down near the Cambodian-Vietnamese border. The Viet Cong turned them over to Cambodia. The account of their capture was confirmed by the airmen when they arrived in Bangkok, Thailand Mar. 12. Pres. Nixon had asked for the men's release in a letter sent Mar. 9 to Prince Norodom Sihanouk, Cambodian chief of state. The airmen were identified as Maj. Querin Hurlik of Savannah, Ga., Chief Warrant Officer Laird Osburn of Webster Springs, W. Va., Spec. 5 John Fisher of Gainsville, Fla. and Spec. 5 Rob Pryor of Oak Ridge, Tenn.

Defense Secy. Melvin R. Laird called on the Viet Cong and North Vietnam May 19 to immediately release all sick and wounded American prisoners, to permit impartial inspection of their POW camps and to allow all prisoners to send and receive mail on a regular basis. According to Administration officials, more than 1,300 American fighting men were listed as missing in action. Of this number, 400 to 800 were believed held by North Vietnam and 100 to 500 by the Viet Cong. Laird charged that Communist refusal to identify these men was contrary to the 1949 Geneva convention on prisoners of war. He contended that "there is clear evidence" that North Vietnam was not treating the captives "humanely." North Vietnamese negotiator Xuan Thuy in Paris May 19 rejected Laird's appeal. Thuy said Hanoi would not identify the captives as long as the U.S. continued the war. Thuy refused to state how many Americans were in North Vietnamese captivity on the ground that the figure "is connected with other questions" involved in the Paris talks.

State Secy. William P. Rogers complained July 17 that North Vietnam was "lacking in humanity" for refusing the names of U.S. prisoners and for denying permission for international observers to inspect their camps. Appearing before the House Foreign Affairs Committee, Rogers asserted that the "wives of these men don't even know if they are alive. This is clearly in violation of the Geneva convention on the treatment of prisoners of war."

3 U.S. servicemen held by North Vietnam were released Aug. 4. The men were flown the following day from Hanoi in an International Control Commission plane to Vientiane, Laos and they finally reached the U.S. Aug. 7. Defense Secy. Laird said

that although he was pleased with their release, the U.S. "cannot be content with propaganda-planned releases of a few prisoners at infrequent intervals." The 3 were returned in the custody of 7 members of a U.S. pacifist group, the National Mobilization Committee to End the War in Vietnam. The chairman of the committee, David T. Dellinger, had negotiated their release with members of the North Vietnamese delegation to the Paris conference in July. The Americans were identified as Air Force Capt. Wesley L. Rumble, 26, Oroville, Calif., captured Apr. 28, 1968 in North Vietnam's southernmost Quangbinh Province; Lt. Robert F. Frishman, 29, Santee, Calif., a pilot from the aircraft carrier *Coral Sea*, captured Oct. 24, 1967 north of Hanoi; and Navy Seaman Douglas Hegdahl, 22, Watertown, N.D., a crewman of the cruiser *Canberra*, captured at sea Apr. 5, 1967 after he fell overboard. The 3 were the first American captives freed by North Vietnam since Aug. 2, 1968.

North Vietnam had announced July 9 that the 3 men would be released as a goodwill gesture in observance of American Independence Day. Dellinger, at the request of the North Vietnamese delegation, flew to Paris July 9 to arrange for the prisoners' release. The U.S. government had lifted a travel ban against Dellinger to permit him to go to Paris. The ban stemmed from a federal indictment against Dellinger in connection with the demonstrations at the Democratic National Convention in Chicago in Aug. 1968. The 7 members of Dellinger's committee, led by Rennard C. (Rennie) Davis, arrived in Hanoi July 18 to escort the 3 U.S. prisoners home. (Davis also was under federal indictment in connection with the Chicago demonstrations, and the government had lifted his travel ban.)

The U.S. Defense Department Aug. 14 published the names of 42 U.S. Air Force men previously listed as missing in Vietnam but confirmed as prisoners in North Vietnam. 5 other American airmen also were listed as prisoners of North Vietnam, but their names were not released pending notification of next of kin. The Defense Department said the names of the captives came from the 3 men released by Hanoi Aug. 4 and from other sources.

U.S. Army prisoners, whose release had been announced by the Viet Cong Oct. 27, walked into a South Vietnamese militia outpost near Danang Nov. 5. 2 of the men, Pfc. James H. Strickland of Dunn, N.C. and Spec. 4 Willie A. Watkins of Sumter, S.C., had been missing since Jan. 8 and 9, 1968, respectively. The 3d man, Pfc. Coy R. Tinsley of Cleveland, Tenn., had been captured in March. Another American prisoner, Pfc. Jesse B. Harris Jr., of Port Chester, N.Y., was released by the Viet Cong and made his way back to a U.S. base 51 miles south of Danang Oct. 20 Harris had been captured June 8.

The U.S. brought the issue of North Vietnam's treatment of American prisoners before the UN General Assembly's Economic & Social Committee Nov. 11. Mrs. Rita Hauser, the U.S. delegate, criticized Hanoi for refusing access to or information about the captives. She called this a violation of human rights and the Geneva convention on prisoners.

Mrs. Hauser said the U.S. would "welcome the intervention of any organization or group of concerned people who may be able to reduce the anguish of the prisoners and their families." 2 private U.S. civilian groups Nov. 12 released separate lists purporting to confirm the prisoner-of-war status of missing Americans in Vietnam, but they were discounted by the Defense Department as meaningless. One of the lists, released by the Chicago Veterans for Peace in Vietnam, an antiwar group, was accompanied by photographs of 74 captured U.S. fliers in North Vietnamese clothing. Deputy Assistant Defense Secy. Richard G. Capen Jr. said it contained only "the most dated information." An official of the Chicago group, Leroy Wollins, said the prisoner list and the photos had been received several months previously by mail from Hanoi, by way of Toronto, but had then become "lost in our files in Chicago until now." The 2d list, containing 97 names, was made available to military authorities at Fort Sheridan (near Chicago) by the Rev. Paul D. Lindstrom, the national director of the Remember the Pueblo Committee. A Defense Department official said that all but one of the names were "utterly meaningless to us—they are not the names of missing people we are trying to locate."

A 3d roster of U.S. captives was to have been "hand delivered" in Chicago Nov. 12 to David Dellinger and Rennard Davis, who were on trial in connection with the violence at the 1968 Democratic National Convention. William J. Kunstler, the 2 defendants' lawyer, had conferred with members of the North Vietnamese delegation in Paris Oct. 25-26. He said on his return to the U.S. Oct. 27 that North Vietnam was ready to hand over a list of U.S. prisoners through an office that was to be established by Dellinger's and Davis' National Mobilization Committee to

End the War in Vietnam. The committee's link to Hanoi on the captive question was assailed by Capen Oct. 28. He said that "once again North Vietnam appears to be dealing with dissident elements in the United States in an effort to abuse United States prisoners and their families for propaganda purposes."

Wives and other relatives of missing American soldiers had held a series of meetings with North Vietnamese delegates to the Paris conference in September-October but did not learn whether the men were prisoners. 2 of the visiting Americans were informed by the North Veitnamese Oct. 15 that Hanoi would not release any captives until the U.S. withdrew its troops from Vietnam and the war ended. (Xuan Thuy in Paris Nov. 6 rejected a South Vietnamese offer to return to Hanoi 62 ill and wounded North Vietnamese prisoners of war. Thuy and Mrs. Nguyen Thi Binh of the Viet Cong's provisional government called instead for the liberation of "all political prisoners" in South Vietnam.)

Texas billionaire industrialist H. Ross Perot said in Bangkok Dec. 26 that North Vietnam had refused to allow him to deliver 2 plane-loads of gifts to U.S. prisoners in North Vietnam. He said that North Vietnamese officials with whom he met in Vientiane, Laos, had told him that the prisoners could receive the gifts if the parcels were in the custody of Soviet postal authorities by Dec. 31. But in Copenhagen Dec. 31, Perot announced that the USSR would not permit him to enter the country. An estimated $1¹/₂ million had been spent on this effort. Perot's group, called United We Stand, also sponsored a trip to Paris Christmas Eve for 152 wives and children of servicemen believed to be prisoner in North Vietnam. On their arrival in Paris, they were told that the North Vietnamese delegation to the Paris talks would not receive them.

PROTEST MOVEMENTS

Antiwar protests escalated in 1969 and reached peaks in massive demonstrations Oct. 15 and Nov. 15.

Early Protest Activities in 1969

300 to 400 youthful antiwar demonstrators hurled rocks, bottles and obscenities at Richard M. Nixon's limousine in Washington Jan. 20 as the President-elect rode to his inauguration. This

was said to have been the first time that a group of this size had attempted to disrupt a Presidential inauguration. The youths were part of a larger group, numbering up to 6,000, which had been assembled in Washington by the National Mobilization Committee to End the War in Vietnam for an orderly, nonviolent, 3-day "counter-inaugural." The smaller group of ultramilitants had decided Jan. 19 to ignore the nonviolent plans of the committee's leaders. About 80 protesters were arrested, most of them on charges of disorderly conduct. The disruption reportedly was led by members of Students for a Democratic Society (SDS) and Co-Aim, the Committee for an Anti-Imperialist Movement. (The SDS National Council, meeting in Ann Arbor, Mich. Dec. 31, 1968, had rejected a resolution calling for inauguration demonstrations.)

The Mobilization Committee, called "the Mobe," had staged a symbolic counter-inaugural parade Jan. 19 in which thousands of youths marched the reverse of the official inaugural parade route. The protesters, estimated by the police to number 5,000 and by demonstration leaders at 10,000 to 12,000, waved banners and chanted slogans denouncing American "racism" and "fascism" and demanding peace in Vietnam. The parade was reportedly led by 4 "active duty GIs" opposed to the war. Following the parade, an estimated 8,000 persons attended a counter-inaugural ball in a circus tent. At least 22 demonstrators were arrested during the day, most of them for scuffles that erupted at the end of the parade. The Youth International Party (Yippies) Jan. 19 "inhogurated" their presidential candidate, a pig.

Members of Clergy & Laymen Concerned About Vietnam, a 3-year-old national organization of churchmen opposed to the war and the draft, held its 3d annual 3-day "mobilization" in Washington Feb. 3-5. The 25,000-member organization sponsored workshops and issued a 3,000-word position paper. Representatives of the group, including Mrs. Martin Luther King Jr. and the Rev. William Sloane Coffin Jr., Yale University chaplain, met Feb. 5 with Henry A. Kissinger, Pres. Nixon's special assistant for national security affairs. More than 800 paying participants attended the conference, the first national antiwar meeting during the Nixon Administration. Opening day speeches Feb. 3 included an address by Sen. George S. McGovern, who repeated proposals he had made at the Democratic National Convention in 1968 to

confine U.S. offensive operations in Vietnam to defendable en-
claves.

Prescriptions for peace offered by the Clergy & Laymen group
in its position paper Feb. 4 included calls for (a) military disengagement of U.S. troops in South Vietnam, including a halt in the
bombing and the transfer home of U.S. soldiers stationed in Vietnam; (b) U.S. pressure on the South Vietnamese government to
free "thousands of political prisoners" and to guarantee rights of
free expression; (c) abolition of compulsory military service and
grants of executive amnesty to Americans jailed for draft refusal
or self-exiled to escape military service in Vietnam; (d) vigorous
pursuit of U.S. programs to aid poor nations. The statement condemned the "failure of bishops and other religious leaders to follow
through on their support of conscientious objection." At a press
conference Feb. 4, the group introduced the Rev. Thomas L.
Hayes, executive director of the Episcopal Peace Fellowship (who
in March began a mission sponsored by the organization as min-
ister-at-large to American deserters living in Sweden).

Representatives of the group who met with Kissinger at the
White House urged amnesty for draft resisters and for soldiers
who refused to fight in Vietnam. After the 40-minute meeting,
Coffin said that the delegation was "very grateful for a very re-
spectful hearing from Mr. Kissinger." The members of the delegation, besides Mrs. King and Coffin, were Rabbi Abraham J.
Heschel, professor at the Jewish Theological Seminary of America
(New York), the Rev. Richard J. Neuhaus, pastor of the Lutheran
Church of St. John the Evangelist in Brooklyn (New York), and
the Rev. Richard R. Fernandez, 34, national director of the organization.

Federal District Judge Frank M. Johnson Jr. ruled in Mont-
gomery, Ala. Feb. 4 that Auburn University officials would have
to allow the Rev. Coffin to speak on the campus. His scheduled
Feb. 7 address had been banned by Auburn Pres. Harry M. Philpott, who had cited Coffin's conviction of conspiring to urge draft
resistance. Johnson's ruling, that Philpott's ban "is illegal ...
censorship in its rawest form," was handed down in a suit brought
by members of the faculty-student Human Rights Forum, which
had invited Coffin. Alabama Gov. Albert Brewer, backing Philpott's decision Jan. 29, had said Coffin was a "self-appointed nut,
who perhaps would cause discord and dissension" on the campus.

After Philpott's request for a stay of the court order was refused, Coffin appeared on the campus Feb. 7 and spoke to some 2,000 students. He criticized U.S. involvement in Vietnam but made no mention of resistance to the draft.

Antiwar demonstrators interrupted a speech by Sen. J. William Fulbright (D., Ark.) Mar. 5 during a New York luncheon meeting of what was called a first National Convocation on the Challenge of Building Peace. About 2,000 participants attended the luncheon and panel discussions, sponsored by the Fund for Education in World Order, a national peace organization. Fulbright's talk was halted by demonstrators, some disguised as hotel waiters, who placed pigs' heads on platters on the speakers' table, unfurled Viet Cong flags and chanted: "Ho, Ho, Ho Chi Minh, NLF is gonna win!" The heckling continued even after Fulbright gave up his efforts to resume his speech. The Senator said that nothing he could say "would be nearly as eloquent about the difficulties of achieving peace as what you have seen here today." The leader of the demonstrators was identified as Robin Palmer of the Veterans & Reservists to End the War in Vietnam. Palmer was finally arrested for disorderly conduct as Sen. Jacob K. Javits (R., N.Y.) took over the floor from Fulbright. Javits said that the "cause of peace" was not served by those who would employ violence and that it was "violence to try to destroy a meeting." He criticized Stewart R. Mott, co-chairman of the conference, for allowing one of the demonstrators to speak. Sen. George McGovern, who also addressed the luncheon meeting, also assailed the hecklers.

Scientists at some 30 U.S. campuses had participated in a one-day "research stoppage" Mar. 4 in protest against what they called government misuse of science in defense-oriented projects. The movement had begun at the Massachusetts Institute of Technology (MIT), where a "Union of Concerned Scientists" had issued a statement that said: "Misuse of scientific knowledge presents a major threat to the existence of mankind. Through its actions in Vietnam, our government has shaken our confidence in its ability to make wise and humane decisions." Scientists should "express our determined opposition to ill-advised and hazardous projects such as the ABM [anti-ballistic missile] system, the enlargement of our nuclear arsenal, and the development of chemical and biological weapons." Other scientists at MIT had said they welcomed constructive discussion but opposed a work stoppage as a "prejudgment."

The work-stoppage plans had spread to Yale and Cornell and to the University of Pennsylvania, where the provost cancelled all undergraduate classes at the request of administration and faculty members to permit discussions of "the relationship between science and society" and "the uses and misuses of knowledge." Some opposition to the protest had developed at MIT from faculty members who felt that scientists had a legitimate concern over government "misuse" of knowledge but that a stoppage was an inappropriate means of expressing that concern. Support of government projects was voiced at the Argonne National Laboratory outside Chicago, where researchers sponsored an overtime-work counter-movement. Institutions where programs similar to the MIT stoppage were held included: Stanford; the University of California at Berkeley, San Francisco and Irvine; San Francisco State; the University of Washington at Seattle; New York University; Fordham; Columbia; Rockefeller University; Brooklyn Polytechnic Institute; New York State University at Stony Brook; Rensselaer Polytechnic Institute; the University of Maryland; Dartmouth; Case Western Reserve and the University of Wisconsin.

About 1,300 women, some clad in black and carrying antiwar posters and helium-filled, black balloons, picketed the White House and marched single file to the Capitol Mar. 26 in a protest sponsored by the Women Strike for Peace. After arriving at the Capitol, they were seated in shifts in the House gallery, where they heard 4 hours of antiwar speeches, many of them by representatives from New York commenting on this first large-scale antiwar demonstration in Washington since Pres. Nixon's inauguration. Bella Abzug, spokesman for the marchers, said that the "moratorium on war criticism is over." On the House floor, Rep. Shirley Chisholm (D., N.Y.), in her maiden speech, said that she would vote against every defense money bill before the House "until the time comes when our values and priorities have been turned right side up again." Rep. Paul Findley (R.,Ill.) had inserted into the *Congressional Record* Mar. 25 the names of 31,-379 U.S. soldiers killed by hostile action in Vietnam through the end of Jan. 1969. Speaking before the House, Findley said that by listing the names, he hoped to offer a reminder of the "precise width, breadth and depth of the war Mr. Nixon has inherited." Findley pointed out that if the death toll continued at the same level, in a few days the number of Americans killed in Vietnam "will surpass Korea" and in 11 months "will surpass our losses in World War I." (The cost of printing the 121-page list totaled more than $10,000.)

A 3-year-old Lawyers Committee on American Policy Towards Vietnam charged the Nixon Administration Mar. 31 with failing to follow its "clear mandate to make peace in Vietnam." It called on Congress to "reverse the disastrous [Vietnam] policy that has been and is being pursued." The committee, comprising both legal authorities and political scientists, announced at a press conference in New York (and in a letter to Congress members) a proposed program for ending the war. Dr. Hans J. Morgenthau, director of the University of Chicago Center of Foreign Affairs, and Dr. Richard J. Barnet, co-director of the Institute for Political Studies in Washington, told newsmen that their proposals had been sent to Nixon and to the State Department Mar. 7 but that they had received no acknowledgement. Their program called for an end to U.S. offensive operations, the withdrawal of American troops and the formation of a provisional South Vietnamese government that would be genuinely representative of the country's political, social, religious and ethnic groups. The committee offered Congress the help of committee members who had established contacts with leaders of North Vietnam or of the National Liberation Front (NLF). Barnet, a former aide of Pres. Kennedy's, had met in March with Hanoi and NLF negotiators in Paris. Dr. Richard A. Falk of Princeton, a committee member, had conferred with North Vietnamese Premier Pham Van Dong in Hanoi in June 1968.

Gen. David M. Shoup, former Marine Corps commandant and member of the Joint Chiefs of Staff, warned in the April issue of *The Atlantic* that the military leadership of the U.S. was turning the U.S. into "a militaristic and aggressive nation." "Many ambitious military professionals truly yearn for wars and the opportunities for glory and distinction afforded only in combat," Shoup charged in the article. Shoup declared that "the relationship between the defense industry and the military establishment is closer than many citizens realize. Together they form a powerful public opinion lobby." Shoup cited the deep U.S. involvement in Vietnam and the 1965 invasion of the Dominican Republic. The U.S. bombing in Vietnam was described by Shoup as "one of the most wasteful and expensive hoaxes ever to be put over on the American people" since, he charged, most of it served no purpose aside form support of ground troops and the reporting of the bombing by the rival Navy and Air Force groups was "misleading . . . propaganda." He characterized the ground action in Vietnam as an Army-Marines "race to build forces" that did "not slow down until both became over-extended, overcommitted and depleted at home." Shoup asserted that "if the Johnson Administration suffered from lack of credibility in its reporting of the war, the truth would reveal that much of the hocus-pocus stemmed form schemes in the military services, both at home and abroad."

Protesters' Convictions Reversed

The First Circuit Court of Appeals in Boston July 11 reversed the 1968 conviction of Dr. Benjamin Spock on charges of conspiring to counsel evasion of the draft. The 3-judge panel ruled that there was insufficient evidence of a conspiracy to warrant a case against Spock, The court also reversed the conviction of Michael Ferber, a Harvard graduate student who had been convicted with Spock, but it ordered the cases of 2 other Spock co-defendants, Yale University chaplain William Sloane Coffin Jr. and Mitchell Goodman, a New York teacher, returned to a lower court for retrial. The court's ruling was partly split. Chief Judge Bailey Aldrich and Judge Edward M. McEntee held that Spock and Ferber should be acquitted but Coffin and Goodman should be retried because of an "error" by Judge Francis J. W. Ford in submitting 10 special questions to the jury. Aldrich and McEntee held that the antiwar activities of Coffin and Goodman could have led a "properly instructed jury" to return a guilty verdict. They set aside a defense contention that the First Amendment's guarantee of free speech justified the acquittal of all the defendants. The 3d judge, Frank M. Coffin, agreed with the majority on releasing Spock and Ferber but dissented from the decision to retry the other 2. Judge Coffin said all the defendants should be released on the ground that applying a doctrine of conspiracy to the case was "not consistent with First Amendment principles."

Federal District Judge Charles E. Wyzanski Jr. in Boston Apr. 1 had declared unconstitutional provisions of the 1967 Selective Service Act that exempted as conscientious objectors only those whose objections to war were religious. Wyzanski held that "Congress unconstitutionally discriminated against atheists, agnostics and men who are motivated by profound moral beliefs which constitute the central convictions of their beings." Sen. Eugene J. McCarthy (D., Minn.) said in a congratulatory letter to the judge Apr. 3 that the ruling was a "great service to the responsible, conscientious young people of America who have been forced more than any others in our society to face up to the moral issue of the war in Vietnam." The ruling overturned the Mar. 21 conviction of John Heffron Sisson Jr., 22, a Harvard University graduate who had refused induction in Apr. 1968. In his 21-page opinion, Wyzanski said that Sisson's objections to war were based on "moral and ethical" values that were unrecognized in the draft law because of "religious prejudice." He argued that the law was therefore in violation of the First Amendment of the Constitution prohibiting laws "respecting an establishment of religion." Even the "granting [of] exemption on religious grounds is, I believe, unconstitutional," Wyzanski asserted. He held that when the law "treats a reasonable, conscientious act as a crime, . . . it subverts its own power. It invites civil disobedience." Wyzanski said that his ruling was in no way a judgment on the war in Vietnam, but he indicated that his decision might have been different if a war involving "a defense of the homeland" had been at issue.

(In an earlier decision involving the draft, U.S. District Judge Jack Roberts in Austin, Tex. Jan. 27 had granted an injunction against Selective Service Director Lewis B. Hershey and the El Paso, Tex. draft board. Roberts ruled that Albert Armendariz Jr., a law student at the University of Texas, had a statutory right to finish his academic year. Armendariz had brought the suit as a class action on behalf of all graduate students, but Roberts said that the ruling applied to Armendariz alone. A similar ruling was delivered by U.S. District Judge William B. Bryant in Washington, D.C. Mar. 11 in favor of Mark A. Kravik, 24, an American University graduate student in psychology.)

Dissidents in the Forces

Spec. 4 Harold Muskat, an organizer of an antiwar coffeehouse for Fort Dix, N.J. soldiers, was sentenced by a court-martial Aug. 8 to 6 months' hard labor for unauthorized distribution of an underground newspaper, *Shakedown*, critical of the Vietnam war. He had been fined $25 and reprimanded after conviction on a similar charge in April. The American Civil Liberties Union (ACLU) had accused the New Jersey State Police July 17 of "harassment and intimidation" of the staff of the coffeehouse, which Muskat had helped set up in Wrightstown. The ACLU had filed suit on behalf of the owners of the coffeehouse, which was the center of Fort Dix antiwar activities and the editorial quarters for *Shakedown*.

The U.S. Court of Military Appeals Aug. 15 upheld the conviction of Capt. Dale F. Noyd, 34, on charges of refusing to train pilots for Vietnam duty. The court rejected Noyd's claim that he was entitled to separation from the Air Force because he opposed the war in Vietnam but not all wars. The court said it believed Noyd's convictions to be sincere, but it held that a serviceman could not be granted the right to a "selective conscience." The court said that if a serviceman did not claim exemption for conscientious objection before induction, he lost his right to CO status, although the military could grant such status as "a government-conferred privilege." Noyd had served all but 2 days of his one year sentence while awaiting action on his appeal.

Military policemen raided 3 Honolulu churches Sept. 12 and arrested 12 antiwar servicemen who had claimed sanctuary in the churches during the past 6 weeks. A military spokesman said that 8 or 9 other allegedly AWOL servicemen had not been arrested because "they weren't around." 8 men were seized at the Church of the Crossroads, 3 at the Unitarian Church of Honolulu and one at a Quaker meetinghouse. The meetinghouse had opened its doors to a Navy man Sept. 11. The military spokesman said the armed forces had decided on the raids after "deliberation on the varied aspects of the situation and careful consideration of the rights of the individuals concerned." The Church of the Crossroads' executive board announced Sept. 15 a moratorium on granting sanctuary to AWOL servicemen. 2 who escaped the raids were arrested at Honolulu International Airport Sept. 17, and 2 other surrendered by Sept. 12. A military spokesman said Sept. 22 that 10 of the serviceman who escaped were still at large. Airman Louis D. Parry, 21, the first of the servicemen to seek sanctuary, had been admitted to the Church of the Crossroads Aug. 7. The protest reportedly was coordinated by The Resistance, a national antiwar group, which first used the tactic of sanctuary in May 1968 to protect protesters in Boston.

The Army Sept. 12 made public the rules under which military personnel were permitted to express their disagreement with national policies. The rules were disclosed in a memo, entitled "Guidance on Dissent," which had been issued May 28 to all Army commanders in the U.S. and abroad. According to the memo, it was Army policy "to safeguard the servicemember's right of expression to the maximum extent possible." A similar directive was issued by the Defense Department Sept. 15 in an effort to standardize rules on dissent for all branches of the armed forces. The Army memo, authorized by Army Secy. Stanley R. Resor and signed by Maj. Gen. Kenneth G. Wickham, the adjutant general, dealt with the possession and distribution of political materials, demonstrations by soldiers and civilians, coffeehouses near Army posts, underground newspapers and servicemen's unions. *The memo's provisions:*

A commander could not outlaw the distribution of a publication "simply because he does not like its contents," and he could not prohibit possession of "an unauthorized publication." A commander could not prohibit distribution of a publication without specific approval by Army headquarters. Commanders were barred from dealing with "servicemen's unions" but were to recognize that membership in such unions and "the right of soldiers to complain and request redress of grievances against actions of superiors" were protected.

Commanders could not prevent soldiers from frequenting coffeehouses while off duty "unless it can be shown, for example, that activities taking place in the coffeehouse include counseling soldiers to refuse to perform duty or to desert or otherwise involve illegal acts with a significant adverse effect on soldier health, morale or welfare." Soldiers could not be disciplined for working on "underground newspapers" while off duty unless the newspaper contained material punishable under federal law. A commander could not deny civilians a permit to demonstrate "in an area to which the public has generally been granted access" unless he could show that the activity would present "a clear danger to loyalty, discipline and morale."

The memo said, however, that "the purpose of national defense justifies certain restraints upon the activities of military personnel which need not be imposed on civilians." The Pentagon's 5-page directive, announced by Assistant Defense Secy. Roger T. Kelley, said that activities such as underground newspapers should be allowed because "dissent in its proper sphere is healthy for the United States." It said protest activity should not be prohibited unless it presented a "clear danger" to morale, discipline or military "effectiveness."

The Defense Department Oct. 1 issued a directive defining the extent to which members of the armed forces could engage in political activity. The directive, signed by Deputy Defense Secy. David Packard, said servicemen could belong to political clubs and display political stickers but could not serve as club officers or march in political parades. The new regulations would also allow servicemen to express opinions on public issues in letters to the editor "provided those views do not attempt to promote a partisan political cause." According to an Oct. 4 report, the Army had withdrawn a ban on political stickers on autos owned by servicemen.

'Fall Offensive' Begins

Plans for massive antiwar demonstrations in the fall of 1969 got under way during September. A "fall offensive" was announced Sept. 18 by Dr. Benjamin Spock and 10 other spokesmen for the New Mobilization Committee to End the War in Vietnam, a group organized July 4. The "fall offensive" included a 36-hour March Against Death in Washington Nov. 13-15 combined with a Nov. 15 rally in San Francisco. (Spock announced Sept. 20 that SANE, the National Committee for a Sane Nuclear Policy, had passed a resolution demanding the immediate unilateral withdrawal of U.S. forces from Vietnam.)

·A "no peace for Nixon" campaign was announced Sept. 29 by Don Gurewitz, spokesman for the Student Mobilization Committee to End the War in Vietnam. Gurewitz declared that "Richard Nixon will no longer speak in this country without public opposition to his war policies."

A number of prominent professors and liberal and moderate Congressmen declared their support for a nationwide campus boycott Oct. 15 to protest the war. The protest was sponsored by the Washington-based Vietnam Moratorium Committee. Plans for the "moratorium" were outlined Sept. 21 in a *N.Y. Times* ad that said nearly 500 college student body presidents and editors of campus newspapers had signed a "Call for a Vietnam Moratorium." Participating students, according to the ad, would use the day "to ring doorbells and help organize our fellow Americans against the war in Vietnam." The plans called for a 2-day moratorium in November and a 3-day moratorium in December, with protests to continue until there was "a firm commitment to an early withdrawal of all American troops."

The idea for such a nationwide protest was attributed to Jerome Grossman, a Boston businessman and president of the Political Action for Peace organization in Massachusetts. He suggested organizing a "general strike" against the war. He consulted

Sam(uel Winfred) Brown (Jr.), 25, a former divinity student turned organizer (he had been youth coordinator for Sen. Eugene J.
McCarthy's Presidential campaign in 1968). Brown took the idea
to 2 friends—David Hawk, a former staff member of the National
Student Association, and David Mixner, a helper in the McCarthy
campaign. They changed the "strike" call to a call for a "moratorium." An office for a Vietnam Moratorium Committee was set
up in Washington, where the details were disseminated, originally through Brown's organizing lists, for Moratorium Day observance as an "educational experience"—a day for a pause in normal activity to protest against the Vietnam war.

24 professors announced their support of the protest Sept. 22.
They included John Kenneth Galbraith, former U.S. ambassador
to India; Noam Chomsky, linguist from the Massachusetts Institute of Technology; and Hans Morgenthau, political scientist
from the University of Chicago. The professors said that the President's "gradual and partial displacement of American troops is
not the substantive change in policy needed to end the war." Sam
Brown said Sept. 22 that the moratorium was being financed by
"the same sources that supported the McCarthy and [Robert F.]
Kennedy campaigns." He said support for the protest had "mush-
roomed" since Nixon's announcement of a withdrawal of 35,000
troops from Vietnam and temporary draft suspension. During a
secret Democratic caucus called Sept. 26 by Sen. Fred R. Harris
of Oklahoma, Democratic national chairman, and 2 dozen Senators and Representatives agreed to support the moratorium.

Pres. Nixon said at his Sept. 26 news conference: "Now, I
understand that there has been and continues to be opposition to
the war in Vietnam on the campuses and also in the nation. As
far as this kind of activity is concerned, we expect it. However,
under no circumstances will I be affected whatever by it." Brown
said Sept. 27 that the President's statement was "the kind of rigid
stance which contributed so much to the bitterness of debate
during the last days of the Johnson Administration." David Hawk
said "the evident cynicism of Pres. Nixon's policies" had generat-
ed "a new and growing constituency for the antiwar movement."
The moratorium committee released statements of support from
Sens. McCarthy, George S. McGovern, Charles E. Goodell
(R., N.Y.) and Mark O. Hatfield (R., Ore.). The Columbia University Senate Sept. 26 adopted a resolution that authorized members of the university community to participate in the moratorium.

The senate, which Columbia Pres. Andrew W. Cordier said "does speak for the university," also resolved: "The university senate expresses its opposition to the war in Vietnam. While as individuals we differ in detail, this body agrees that the most reasonable plan for peace is the immediate withdrawal of all U.S. troops." (Cordier said Oct. 6 that senate members "meant simply to go on record as expressing their own opinion.")

4 more Senators and 5 Representatives gave their support to the protest Oct. 6. The group urged all Americans to join the students and to continue to protest until all troops returned home. Rep. Donald W. Riegle Jr. (R., Mich.) said the group's encouragement of the Oct. 15 moratorium was "not a challenge to the President. He seeks to end the war, so do we. But clearly we have to move faster." Others in the group were Sens. Frank Church (D., Ida.), Mark Hatfield, Alan Cranston (D., Calif.) and Charles Goodell and Reps. Allard Lowenstein (D., N.Y.), Ogden R. Reid (R., N.Y.), Abner J. Mikva (D., Ill.) and Paul N. McCloskey Jr. (R., Calif.). Sen. Edmund S. Muskie (D., Me.) had announced his support of the protest Oct. 3. Muskie urged everyone to engage in "constructive discussion of the war" in order to avoid discussion "on a confrontation basis."

The central faculty of Harvard University Oct. 7 urged a "prompt, rapid and complete withdrawal of United States forces" from Vietnam and supported a "united and sustained national effort to bring our troops home." The resolution was passed 255-81 with 150 abstentions by the university's Faculty of Arts & Sciences. The antiwar resolution was passed after leading members of the faculty—including sociologists Seymour Martin Lipset and David Riesman, historian H. Stuart Hughes and Edwin O. Reischauer, former ambassador to Japan—cautioned their colleagues against becoming involved as a body in a political debate. The wording of the resolution, however, noted that the war in Vietnam was an extraordinary issue: "With full recognition that this is not a precedent-setting action but one occasioned by the unique importance of the Vietnam conflict, be it resolved that it is the sense of this faculty that the war in Vietnam must not continue."

Vice Pres. Spiro T. Agnew Oct. 9 called the moratorium "ironic and absurd" and aimed at "the wrong target." The right target, he said, was Hanoi.

State Secy. William P. Rogers commented on TV Oct. 12 that "there is so much dissent here and . . . so many voices" that the enemy must feel "that the President doesn't have the . . . support . . . necessary to carry on for a long time." Rogers said he doubted that any progress would be made in the Paris talks unless it were clear that the President's policy had the public's support. He saw the war "being de-escalated" by the enemy as well as the allies and evidence of "tremendous progress" for the President's policy. His remarks drew rebuttal from Sens. Frank Church and Charles E. Goodell in a broadcast later Oct. 12. Church said that "if we fall silent now, we take the pressure off," and "it was under the pressures of dissent that Pres. Johnson finally reversed the policy of acceleration." Goodell said that under Rogers' reasoning, if the enemy escalated the war, presumably the U.S. would "rethink" its policy and "once again dedicate ourselves to staying there 6, 8, 10 years."

(A Gallup Poll reported Oct. 11 that 57% of a sampling of 1,500 persons favored passage of Goodell's resolution to withdraw all U.S. troops from Vietnam by the end of 1970.)

Concessions to Protests?

2 days before the planned Vietnam "Moratorium Day," Pres. Nixon Oct. 13 reaffirmed his refusal to be swayed by street demonstrations and announced his intention to make a nationwide address Nov. 3 on the Vietnam situation. But indications appeared increasingly that the Administration was yielding to at least some of the protesters' demands.

Nixon Oct. 1 had ordered the Selective Service System to allow graduate students eligible for the draft to complete the school year before being inducted. (Deferments for graduate students had been discontinued in Feb. 1968. 9 months later, after complaints from universities citing the effect of the ruling on students' careers, Selective Service had allowed graduate students to complete their semester before induction.) An estimated 10,000 young men were affected by the new ruling. The ruling, in the form of a National Security Council recommendation to Selective Service, stated: "In courses of graduate study, an interruption at the end of a term, other than the final term of the academic year, is costly to the student in terms of expenses and academic progress and therefore contrary to the national interest." Observers suggested that the President's action, like his suspension of the draft Sept. 19, was an attempt to lessen student dissent. Sam Brown had said the draft suspension only added to student distrust and dissatisfaction with Nixon's war policy. Brown said Oct. 1: "The same holds true for this announcement."

Gen. Lewis B. Hershey, target of youthful war dissenters, was relieved Oct. 10 as director of the Selective Service System. Hershey, 76, relieved effective Feb. 16, 1970, was promoted to the rank of 4-star general and became an adviser to the President on manpower mobilization. Nixon said the nation owed Hershey, who had served as draft director for 28 years, "a hearty 'well done.'" The President also held a series of publicized strategy sessions on Vietnam policy—meeting Oct. 9 with Ellsworth Bunker, ambassador to South Vietnam; Oct. 11 with Gen. Earle G. Wheeler, chairman of the Joint Chiefs of Staff, recently returned from his 2d Vietnam inspection tour (Oct. 4-7) in $2^1/_2$ months*; Oct. 13 with the U.S. delegates to the Paris talks, Henry Cabot Lodge and Philip C. Habib.

Defense Secy. Melvin Laird Oct. 9 had indicated a shift of emphasis in combat orders from the "maximum pressure" of the Johnson Administration to "protective reaction." Vietnamization of the war had the "highest priority," he said. Speaking at a press conference, Laird said the overall policy emphasis was on the "dual approach" of "negotiations in Paris and Vietnamization" of the war.

Nixon's comments on antiwar demonstrations were made in a letter, released Oct. 13 by Georgetown University student Randall J. Dicks, 19, who had written to protest what he called Nixon's "ill-considered" Sept. 26 statement that "under no circumstances will I be affected whatever" by the moratorium. Dicks contended that it "is not unwise for the President of the United States to take note of the will of the people." Nixon replied that "there is nothing new we can learn from the demonstrations" and that he had to consider the consequences of a Vietnam withdrawal "in both human and international terms" or history "would rightly condemn" him. He was against permitting "government policy to be made in the streets," for this would "invite anarchy." "There

---

*In summing up his inspection tour prior to departure from Saigon Oct. 7, Wheeler said "progress in Vietnamization—that is improvement and modernization of the Republic of Vietnam armed forces—is being steadily and realistically achieved," but U.S. forces would have to assist the South Vietnamese for "some time to come" and "Vietnamizing" of the war should not be rushed.

is a clear distinction between public opinion and public demonstrations," he said, and it would be "an act of gross irresponsi-
bility on my part" to abandon his Vietnam policy because of a
demonstration.

'Moratorium' Observed Throughout U.S.

The "moratorium" took place Oct. 15. It turned out to be
one of the most massive antiwar protests in U.S. history as demonstrators throughout the country took part in an effort to demonstrate to Pres. Nixon what protesters held was a broad public
mandate to end the war in Vietnam. The event—planned and
coordinated by the Vietnam Moratorium Committee—drew support from thousands of students and other youths, professors and
clerics and many representatives of the middle class who generally had remained aloof from public opposition to the war effort.

The Moratorium Day activities were as diverse as the elements of support—rallies, speeches, church aud synagogue services,
memorial readings of the names of the Vietnam war dead, the toll-
ing of bells, candlelight marches, teach-ins, seminars, folk-song
concerts, vigils, leaflet distributions, petition-signings, wreath-
layings and door-to-door canvassing. A nationwide symbol of sympathy with the moratorium was the wearing of a black armband.
Another was the flying of the flag at half-staff. Opposition to the
moratorium, which was also manifested, was signaled by proper
display of the flag and the driving of vehicles during the day with
headlights on. But the extent of the opposition, like the support
for the moratorium, was difficult to assess.

Only a few incidents of confrontation between protesters and
hecklers occurred—in Detroit, where some 12,000 persons had assembled and some stones, bottles and insults were exchanged; at
the University of Indiana, where Clark Kerr, former University
of California president, was hit in the face with a custard pie
while delivering a moratorium speech. There were other bizarre incidents: 2 Blackwood, N.J. high school classmates, both 17, committed suicide in a car strewn with their personal notes urging
peace and brotherhood; 2 skydivers parachuted into New York's
Central Park with large U.S. flags flying; a veterans' group in Spear-
fish, S.D. sent a plane aloft to shower some 2,000 antiwar protesters with "America—Love It Or Leave It" leaflets; Boy Scouts in
Franklin, Ky. affixed small flags to parking meters. One incident

of violence took place at the White House, when a group of young black militants carrying a Viet Cong flag were kept from entering the grounds by police authorities swinging clubs (3 youths were arrested).

The dominant tone of the Moratorium Day protests was illustrated by Mrs. Martin Luther King Jr., who led an estimated 45,000 persons from the Washington Monument to the White House, where she lit a candle for peace. "The only solution to the problem is to bring the boys home and to bring them home now," she told the demonstrators. It took the marchers, 10 to 12 abreast, about 2 hours to pass the White House.

One of the largest antiwar rallies took place in Boston, where an estimated 100,000 persons gathered on Boston Common. 20,000 had marched there from Cambridge. Sen. George S. McGovern was a speaker. Another speaker in Boston, Sen. Edward M. Kennedy, announced his "hard compromise" to advocate a U.S. withdrawal of its combat forces from Vietnam within a year and its air and support units by the end of 1972. Ex-Supreme Court Justice Arthur J. Goldberg, addressing a meeting of lawyers in Washington, called for a "straightforward" Presidential statement that the U.S. would "accept the principle" of "a prompt withdrawal of all American forces" and that it was "prepared to discuss in Paris a timetable for their prompt and systematic withdrawal."

In New York, there were many gatherings—the largest in Bryant Park, midtown Manhattan, where it was estimated that 40,000 persons gathered to hear Mayor John V. Lindsay, who had decreed a day of mourning for the city, and Sens. Charles Goodell, Jacob Javits and Eugene McCarthy, who described the event as "a kind of moral testament." Other New York rallies took place on Wall Street (7,000 persons attended), where Trinity Church opened its pulpit to business and professional leaders taking turns reading the names of the war dead; UN Plaza (3,000 people attended); Central Park Mall (5,000 high school students); the garment district (1,000); Gracie Mansion, the mayor's residence (a candlelight vigil); St. Patrick's Cathedral (8,000 for a 3-hour, ecumenical, candlelight service outside); and Times Square. Mayor Lindsay, visiting 10 rallies during 12 hours, embraced the moratorium with fervor in the midst of an intense mayoral campaign. (An opponent, State Sen. John J. Marchi, called the moratorium situation in the city "a New York version of Dunkirk.") Lindsay had ordered the U.S. flags on city property to be flown half-staff and City Hall to be draped with dark bunting. But many police stations flew flags at full staff, and many patrol cars and buses were driven during the day with lights on. All schools remained open Oct. 15, but the Board of Education estimated that absenteeism reached 90% in the high schools, 75% in the elementary and junior high schools, and up to 67% of the teachers.

Other antiwar rallies (speakers in parentheses) were reported to have been attended by: 20,000 people at the University of Michigan in Ann Arbor (Sen. Philip A. Hart [D., Mich.]); 1,200 in Los Angeles (the Rev. Ralph Abernathy, head of the Southern Christian Leadership Conference); 15,000 at the University of Wisconsin in Madison; 6,000 in Chicago (David Dellinger, chairman of the National Mobilization to End the War in Vietnam); 30,000 in New Haven, Conn. (Malcolm Baldridge, chairman of the 1968 state Citizens for the Nixon-Agnew group); 9,000 in Pittsburgh, where the city council Oct. 14 passed a resolution urging a complete U.S. troop withdrawal by the end of 1970; 10,000 at Rutgers University in New Brunswick, N.J. (Sen. McCarthy); 5,000 in Minneapolis; 3,500 in Berkeley, Calif.; 3,500 in Denver, Colo.; 1,200 in Albuquerque, N.M.; 1,000 in Lewiston, Me. at Bates College (Sen. Edmund S. Muskie [D., Me.]); 15,000 in East Meadow, Long Island, N.Y. (where W. Averell Harriman, former chief delegate to the Paris talks, told the protesters: "Now you've started something and nobody can stop you. Pres. Nixon said he wouldn't pay attention to your voices. Now he's going to have to pay attention").

The city council of Miami Beach, Fla. approved a call for a quick and drastic reduction of U.S. forces in Vietnam. Crosses were planted on the ROTC grounds at Louisiana State University in Baton Rouge. University of Miami (Fla.) students engaged in a 24-hour reading of the list of war dead; a similar reading at the University of Tennessee in Nashville evoked taunts from a group wearing white arm-bands. A representative town meeting in Westport, Conn. Oct. 8 had adopted a resolution urging the U.S. to take "immediate action" to withdraw from the war.

Among organizations and individuals backing the moratorium were: The American Friends Service Committee, Americans for Democratic Action, the Alliance for Labor Action, the Southern Christian Leadership Conference, the National Association of Black Students, the National Welfare Rights Organization, the Democratic Coalition, Servicemen's LINK to Peace, Women Strike for Peace; Govs. Kenneth M. Curtis (D., Me), Frank Licht (D., R.I.) and Francis W. Sargent (R., Mass.); Whiney M. Young Jr., executive director of the National Urban League; and more than a dozen leading Protestant, Roman Catholic and Jewish leaders (in a statement issued at the Interchurch Center in New York Oct. 10). Mayar Richard C. Lee of New Haven, Conn. and Pres. Kingman Brewster Jr. of Yale Oct. 9 issued a joint statement urging an unconditional withdrawal of U.S. forces from Vietnam.

An attempt to keep the House of Representatives in an all-night session in conjunction with the Moratorium Day observance was blocked by a 112-110 adjournment vote at 11:15 p.m. Oct. 14. The attempt, organized by Reps. Benjamin S. Rosenthal (D., N.Y.) and Andrew Jacobs Jr. (D., Ind.), resulted in the most extensive debate (2 to 3 hours) on Vietnam in the House since the U.S involvement began. The all-night session was sought by 23 members, 22 of them Democrats, who had been granted unanimous consent earlier to speak for an hour each. Only 2 of the scheduled speakers had spoken when the debate was cut off. A bipartisan resolution introduced in the Senate Oct. 14 by Sens. Jacob K. Javits and Claiborne Pell urged a pullout of all combat troops from Vietnam by the end of 1970 and the withdrawal of all other U.S. troops "in a reasonable time thereafter."

A Hanoi letter backing the moratorium had been injected into the U.S. political scene Oct. 14. Hanoi Radio broadcast an open appeal from North Vietnamese Premier Pham Van Dong to his "Dear American Friends." Dong acclaimed the U.S. antiwar demonstrators and their effort, which, Dong said, reflected the American people's desire to save their sons "from a useless death in Vietnam." Vice Pres. Spiro Agnew, emerging from a meeting with Pres. Nixon later Oct. 14, denounced the Hanoi letter as a "shocking intrusion into the affairs of the American people." He called on moratorium leaders to repudiate the letter. But the Moratorium Committee's reply later Oct. 14 was to call it "regrettable" that the Administration "would seize this straw in an attempt to discredit the patriotism of the millions of Americans who sincerely desire peace." The White House later Oct. 14 distributed copies of the Hanoi letter to Republican Congressional leaders, and an effort was made Oct. 15 to have a resolution offered in the House and Senate deploring the "insolent" attempt of Hanoi "to associate those Americans who demonstrate for peace with the cause of our enemy." The resolution was introduced in the House by Democratic leader Carl Albert (Okla.) and GOP leader Gerald R. Ford (Mich.), but their call for immediate consideration was blocked by an objection from Rep. Robert W. Kastenmeier (D., Wis.). In the Senate, the resolution was introduced by Hugh Scott but, after Democratic leader Mike Mansfield joined in its sponsorship, the resolution was delayed, as was another upholding the "right of all Americans to responsible and peaceful dissent." Moratorium Day protests extended to Vietnam and to some major world capitals. Black armbands were worn by 15 members of a platoon of the Americal Division on patrol south of Danang in South Vietnrm (4 of these soldiers were wounded by Viet Cong booby traps while on the patrol). At Tansonnhut airbase near Saigon, half a dozen airmen wore black wrist bands while on duty. Some 20 American civilians working for private organizations in South Vietnam kept a vigil at the U.S. embassy in Saigon. There were marches, demonstrations or petitions by Americans, usually at U.S. embassy buildings, in Copenhagen, London, Paris, Dublin, Tokyo, Sydney and Australia.

The moratorium protests sparked varied reactions within the Nixon Administration. But the Administration emphasized Oct. 21 that its officials did not always agree on public issues such as the antiwar protests and that all officials had a right to express personal feelings. The differences surfaced when Vice Pres. Agnew said at a Republican fundraising dinner in New Orleans Oct. 19 that the moratorium was "encouraged by an effete corps of impudent snobs who characterize themselves as intellectuals." Agnew warned that "hardcore dissidents and professional anarchists" within the antiwar movement were planning "wilder, more violent" demonstrations Nov. 15.

State Secy. William P. Rogers offered a more conciliatory view in an address at the "Family of Man" awards dinner in New York Oct. 20. Rogers said many who participated in the demonstrations "wished principally to register dramatic but dignified expression of their deep concern for peace in Vietnam." Rogers added that "we listened to those voices with respect, because we, too, have a deep concern for peace in Vietnam." The State Department revealed that Rogers had sent the White House an advance text of his remarks. A spokesman for the State Department said Oct. 21 that Rogers appeared at the New York dinner as the President's representative.

White House Press Secy. Ronald L. Ziegler reported Oct. 21 that the White House had not cleared an advance text of Agnew's speech. Ziegler added, however, that Agnew's speeches were not customarily reviewed by the White House for advance clearance. Ziegler confirmed that the White House had received an advance copy of Rogers' speech but said the speech "was not cleared" by the White House. Ziegler told newsmen that both Agnew and Rogers were "expressing personal feeling" in their remarks.

As antiwar groups continued planning for massive demonstrations is Washington and San Francisco Nov. 13-15 and for local activities against the war Nov. 13-14, Agnew asserted in a speech in Philadelphia Nov. 10 that antiwar demonstrations were a "carnival in the streets," performed by a "strident minority" who raise "intolerant clamor and cacophony." Transportation Secy. John A. Volpe said in New York Nov. 10 that the majority of the organizers of the planned November protests were "Communist or Communist-inspired" who did "nothing but break down our democracy." He added, however, that a "great number of these people who support the demonstrations do so conscientiously."

Several thousand people ralled in Washington, D.C. on Veterans Day Nov. 11 to proclaim their support of the President's Vietnam policy and their opposition to antiwar demonstrators. Rep. L. Mendel Rivers (D., S.C.), chairman of the House Armed Services Committee, told a crowd of perhaps 10,000: "There are more of us patriotic Americans than those pro-Hanoi-crats. Keep up the fight. Spiro Agnew is helping us. You back up Spiro, and he will continue to throw it on." Others who spoke included Rep. D.E. Lukens (R.,O.), Rep. John Buchanan (R., Ala.) and Sen. John G. Tower (R., Tex.). The rally was sponsored by the American Legion and the Veterans of Foreign Wars. Other Veterans Day demonstrations in support of the President took place in New York City, where 2,000 to 5,000 people marched down 5th Avenue; in Pittsburgh, where Gen. William Westmoreland, Army chief of staff, appeared in the reviewing stand before a crowd of 100,000 people; and in numerous other major cities and smaller communities.

Maj. Gen. Winston P. Wilson, chief of the National Guard Bureau, Nov. 3 urged the nation's 500,000 Guardsmen to counter-demonstrate against antiwar activity to show North Vietnam that the nation was determined "to follow a prudent course in

Vietnam." Wilson, in a letter to all state adjutant generals, urged that between Nov. 11 and Nov. 16 Guardsmen drive their autos with headlights turned on, fly the American flag and leave their porch lights burning. The Pentagon said Nov. 4 that Wilson was expressing "his personal view" in the letter and had acted without Defense Department knowledge.

At the Paris talks on Vietnam, Chief U.S. Negotiator Henry Cabot Lodge had said in his formal statement Nov. 6 that his delegation's position would not "crumble" because of dissent "of a vocal minority of the American people." Lodge again raised the matter of domestic dissent at the Nov. 13 session. He asserted that "the great majority of the American people supports" Pres. Nixon's policy on Vietnam. Lodge said it was "vital" that the Communists should not misjudge or miscalculate the President's efforts to seek a just peace. Lodge incorporated into his statement the text of a resolution sponsored and signed Nov. 12 by 300 members of the U.S. House of Representatives supporting Nixon on Vietnam. In reply, Nort¹, Vietnamese Negotiator Xuan Thuy expressed confidence that "the American people will certainly with increasing vigor oppose the Nixon Administration's policy of aggression in Vietnam."

Some Congress members who had supported the Oct.15 moratorium hesitated to back the November demonstrations sponsored by the New Mobilization Committee to End the War in Vietnam. Rep. Lester Wolff (D., N.Y.) had said Oct. 27 that he would back the November marches only when the New Mobilization Committee acted to "purge from its ranks those elements that have the avowed goal of destroying our society." Sam Brown, spokesman for the Vietnam Moratorium Committee, said Oct. 21 that he and other moratorium leaders would participate in the Nov. 15 march in Washington. But he said his group would stress local activities against the war.

The Nixon Administration agreed Nov. 11 to allow the Nov. 15 demonstrators to march down Pennsylvania Avenue in Washington to within a block of the White House. Earlier, Deputy Attorneys Gen. Richard G. Kleindienst and John W. Dean 3d had said Nov. 6 that protesters would not be allowed to march on Pennsylvania Avenue because "militant" groups planned to try to turn the demonstration into a violent confrontation. A number of antiwar leaders and members of Congress charged that the Administration was stressing possible violence to intimidate potential marchers. The Justice Department Nov. 10 had issued a permit for a Nov. 13-15 March Against Death from Arlington National Cemetary past the White House to the Capitol. Both marches were planned by the New Mobilization Committee to End the War in Vietnam. The agreement on the route for the Nov. 15 march was announced jointly by Kleindienst and Washington Mayor Walter E. Washington. The announcement followed days of negotiation with the New Mobilization Committee, which insisted that the Pennsylvania Avenue route was of symbolic importance.

Nov. 15 March Draws Record Crowd

More than 250,000 protesters gathered in Washington, D.C. Nov. 15 to participate in the largest antiwar demonstration in the nation's history. The New Mobilization Committee to End the War in Vietnam (the "New Mobe"), which sponsored the Washington demonstration, also sponsored a parallel San Francisco protest drawing, according to varying estimates, 60,000 to 175,000 demonstrators and a Nov. 13-15 March Against Death in Washington involving 46,000 persons.

In anticipation of possible violence during the Nov. 15 demonstration in the capital, the Pentagon had announced Nov. 12 that 9,000 troops had been moved to special posts in the Washington area ready to help metropolitan police and National Guardsmen control the demonstrators. The only incidents of violence, however, came not during the New Mobe marches but during 2 demonstrations Nov. 14 and 15 by a splinter minority of militant protesters. In order to control the crowd, the New Mobe had organized thousands of parade marshals to advise demonstrators and to help the 3,000-man District of Columbia police force keep the peace. Ex-Atty. Gen. Ramsey Clark had announced Nov. 12 that about 200 lawyers and 75 clergymen would monitor the demonstrations.

During the March Against Death, which began at 6 p.m. Nov. 13 and lasted for about 40 hours, each participant carried the name of an American soldier killed in Vietnam or of a Vietnamese village allegedly destroyed by American troops. Leading off the march from a point a near the Arlington National Cemetery were demonstrators who carried the names of close relatives killed in Vietnam. The march led past the White House, where each protester called out the name of the soldier or village repesented, and on to the Capitol, where the placard bearing the name was deposited in one of 40 black, wooden coffins. Some protesters were drenched with freezing rain by the time they finished the march.

1,000 to 2,000 militant radicals clashed with Washington policemen Nov. 14 near the South Vietnamese embassy. The trouble grew out of a rally held at Washington's Dupont Circle by factions of Students for a Democratic Society, the Mad Dogs, the Crazies and the Youth International Party (Yippies). As police threw tear gas to block the marchers from the embassy, the militants hurled rocks that broke some 50 store windows and damaged about 40 police cruisers. A number of policemen received minor injuries, and at least 20 demonstrators were arrested.

Demonstrators poured into Washington by bus, train and car Nov. 15 to join the protesters already there. Washington Police Chief Jerry V. Wilson said that 250,000 people was a "moderate" estimate of the crowd. New Mobe leaders claimed that 800,000 protesters participated at one time or another. Thousands marched down Pennsylvania Avenue beginning at 10:15 a.m., and after the parade permit for the avenue expired at 12:30 p.m., thousands more poured down the Mall near the Capitol to gather near the Washington Monument for the rally. Speakers included Sens. George McGovern, Eugene McCarthy, and Charles Goodell, welfare rights leader George Wiley and pacifist-radical David Dellinger, who introduced 2 codefendants at his current Chicago conspiracy trial, Jerry Rubin and Abbie Hoffman. Among other participants were Mrs. Martin Luther King Jr., Dr. Benjamin Spock, comedian Dick Gregory, conductor Leonard Bernstein and ex-Commerce Undersecy. Howard Samuels. The speeches were interspersed with performances by folksingers Arlo Guthrie, Pete Seeger and Peter, Paul and Mary. Sens. Harold E. Hughes and Stephen M. Young and a number of Representatives also participated in the march. Other Congress members opened their offices to let demonstrators come out of the cold during the weekend and to serve sandwiches to protesters. 23 Senators signed a statement calling on Washington residents to assist participants in the demonstrations. Observers characterized the crowd as generally young, white and middle-class. During the rally the crowd was generally relaxed and cheerful despite temperatures ranging in the 30s.

Of the 3 major television networks, only the National Broadcasting Co. (NBC) had a live camera present. The camera was used 3 times for a total of 5 minutes of live coverage. *Washington Post* columnist Nicholas von Hoffman commented Nov. 17 that the coverage amounted to a "television blackout" of the event.

During the march, Pres. Nixon met with aides at the White House and watched the televised Ohio State-Purdue football game. The White House was cut off from the line of march by a thin line of police and a barricade of 57 city buses parked end to end.

At about 4.30 p.m. radicals split off from the main rally to march on the Justice Department in a demonstration led by Yippies and supporters of defendants in the Chicago conspiracy trial. The crowd, numbering about 6,000, carried banners reading "Stop the Trial" and "Free [Black Panther leader] Bobby Seale." Several young demonstrators ran up a Viet Cong flag on the main flagpole of the Justice Department building, but police replaced it with a U.S. flag. The police began using tear gas when demonstrators threw rocks and bottles at the building. Most of the demonstrators began to retreat, but radicals urged them on to a confrontation. Parade marshals placed themselves between police and the crowd, pushing the protesters back and urging calm as police released wave after wave of tear gas. One policeman told reporters Nov. 16: "Those marshals tried real hard. . . . I'm sorry some of them got caught in the gas." At about 7 p.m. police and Guardsmen swept across the Washington Monument grounds, dispersing the remaining youths. Windows in some 50 buildings were broken during the melee, but little looting occurred. The police reported Nov. 16 that 135 arrests had been made, nearly all for disorderly conduct. Only minor injuries were reported.

Atty. Gen. John N. Mitchell said Nov. 16 that overall the demonstration could not be characterized as peaceful. He blamed march leaders for allowing the crowd to be urged on to the Justice Department and said flatly that New Mobe leaders "expected violence to occur and that was the result." Herbert G. Klein, Pres. Nixon's director of communications, dismissed the rally Nov. 16 as "small" and contended that a large majority of Americans supported the President's policies. He said that had it not been for police, Guardsmen and federal troops in reserve, the danger to the city "would have been far greater than it was at the time of the previous riots after the death of Martin Luther King." But White House Press Secy. Ronald L. Ziegler said Nov. 17 that it was "generally the White House view" that the demonstrations were "generally peaceful."

In San Francisco, police agreed that the thousands of antiwar protesters who marched to a peaceful rally at Golden Gate Park's polo field constituted the largest protest demonstration ever assembled in the city. The crowd heard speeches by the Rev. Ralph D. Abernathy, ex-Sen. Wayne Morse and Rennard C. Davis, a defendant in the Chicago conspiracy trial. When Black Panther leader David Hilliard told the rally: "We ain't here for no goddam peace, you gotta fight for it," youthful protesters shouted "Peace! Peace!" More than 1,000 parade marshals controlled the crowd along the march route. Rain interrupted the rally midway through the program, and thousands left the park or turned back before reaching it.

Other rallies organized by the Vietnam Moratorium Committee took place around the nation Nov. 13-14, but turnouts were small compared to the mass protests at Washington and San Francisco. 4 moratorium leaders served on the 16-member New Mobe executive committee.

In Paris Nov. 15, 2,651 persons were arrested and at least 20 persons were injured as 20,000 antiwar protesters demonstrated in defiance of a government ban and clashed with police. All but 19 of the protesters were released without charges Nov. 16. Protests took place in 42 cities around France. In Frankfort, West Germany, several thousand demonstrators, including U.S. servicemen in civilian clothes, clashed Nov. 15 with police during a demonstration that had been banned. More than 8,000 people, including the son of West German Chancellor Willy Brandt, marched through West Berlin Nov. 15 carrying red banners and Viet Cong flags. In Stuttgart, police subdued 2,000 demonstrators after windows had been smashed at the U.S. Information Center. About 1,200 London protesters demonstrated Nov. 15 near the U.S. embassy and later held a torchlight vigil. Some 400 Americans in Rome also demonstrated. In Canada, students demonstrated in Montreal and Halifax Nov. 15; 1,000 people had protested in a candlelight procession in Vancouver Nov. 14. Antiwar demonstrations were held before U.S. embassies in Belgium Nov. 14 and in Denmark and Spain Nov. 15. Antiwar protesters and counterdemonstrators confronted each other in Auckland, New Zealand

Nov. 16 and in Argentina Nov. 15. Peaceful marches supporting the U.S. demonstrators took place in each Australian state capital Nov. 15, and 2,000 demonstrators marched through Vienna Nov. 14. Peace Corps volunteers protested the war Nov. 15 in Manila and in Ethiopia (before the U.S. embassy in Addis Ababa). In Africa, 100 antiwar demonstrators paraded before the U.S. embassy in Lusaka, Zambia.

Local demonstrations sponsored by the Vietnam Moratorium Committee were held across the nation Dec. 12, 13 and 24. A spokesman for the Committee said Dec. 12 that its December plans were for "low-keyed, grass-roots, locally oriented protests." The Moratorium Committee and the Coalition on National Priorities & Military Policy, which included such national leaders as ex-Supreme Court Justice Arthur J. Goldberg and ex-Sen. Joseph S. Clark of Pennsylvania, had joined Dec. 6 to back a series of local "town meetings" scheduled Dec. 13-14 to discuss military expenditures and domestic needs.

DOMESTIC EVENTS IN SOUTH VIETNAM

Politics

A new political party opposed to communism and critical of Pres. Nguyen Van Thieu's regime was formed in Saigon Apr. 20. The party, the Progressive Nationalist Movement, was headed by Dr. Nguyen Ngoc Huy, a member of South Vietnam's delegation to the Paris talks. The movement's manifesto blamed the "Communists and the colonialists" for the country's ills. It assailed "feudalistic and reactionary elements who flocked together behind a facade of anti-communism in order to exploit their fellow countrymen."

Pres. Thieu assumed the leadership of a new pro-government 6-party coalition group whose formation he announced at its inaugural meeting in Saigon May 25. The new organization, the National Social Democratic Front (NSDF), was composed largely of conservatives, centrists and Roman Catholic refugees from North Vietnam. Among the prominent southern political groups absent from the front were the new anti-government Progressive Nationalist Movement and the militant An Quang faction of the Buddhists. The 6 major parties comprising the NSDF were: the

Greater Union Force, composed largely of militant Roman Catholic refugees from North Vietnam; the Social Humanist Party, successor to the Can Lao party, which had held power under the Diem regime; the Revolutionary Dai Viet, formerly the Dai Viet, created to fight the French; the Social Democratic Party, a faction of the Hoa Hao religious sect; the Unified Vietnam Kuomintang, originally formed as an anti-French party; the People's Alliance for Social Revolution, a pro-government bloc formed in 1968.

In an address to 2,000 NSDF delegates, Thieu said the creation of the new party was "the first concrete step in unifying the political factions in South Vietnam for the coming struggle with the Communists." The NSDF would not be "totalitarian or despotic," Thieu said. He added: It was "not a party aimed at seizing power. This front has no intention of putting its leaders in the cabinet." Alluding to the possible broadening of NSDF's base, Thieu said: "This is just the beginning. The door is still wide open to any political group that agrees with our methods and our ideology. The front can become a large front." Thieu pledged that South Vietnam would "do everything necessary to prevent a hasty peace solution in Paris and to prevent the country from falling into the hands of the Communists. If necessary we shall form into resistance groups and continue fighting."

(Elections for village councils had been held throughout South Vietnam Mar. 3, 9, 16 and 23. The balloting, the first of its kind since 1956, involved more than 3 million people in nearly 3,500 villages, or 24% of South Vietnam's villages. Elections also were held for 2,882 hamlet chiefs. Previously these officials had been appointed; the communities taking part in the elections were considered safe enough for elected administrations. Tran Thien Khiem, deputy prime minister and interior minister, said Apr. 1 that 90% of the eligible voters had cast ballots in the elections.) Thieu's office Mar. 12 had announced the creation of 5 new cabinet posts that stressed civil and postwar problems. The move was interpreted by critics of the regime as another act to consolidate Thieu's political power and a further diminution of Vice Pres. Nguyen Cao Ky's influence in government. One of Ky's followers, Truong Thai Ton, was ousted as minister of agriculture and land reform. The new cabinet posts and their ministers: *Deputy premier in charge of pacification and reconstruction*— Lt. Gen. Tran Thien Khiem, who was to retain his post as interior minister; *Veterans Affairs*—Nguyen Thach Van, a former assistant to the premier for judicial affairs; *Deputy Minister of Finance*—Nguyen Anh Tuan, another assistant to the premier; *National Assembly Affairs*—Vo Huu Thu, a former mayor of Hué and member of the Assembly; *Secretary of State for Postwar Planning*—Vo Quoc Thuc, an economist and law professor. The post of minister of revolutionary development was revived by Thieu, and Nguyen Van Vang, a former official in the government of the late Pres. Ngo Dinh Diem, was named to it. Premier Tran Van Huong had been responsible for the functions of the ministry, whose aim was to win the political support of the Vietnamese people. Truong Thai Ton, the pro-Ky cabinet minister ousted from the Agriculture & Land Reform Ministry, was replaced by Cao Van Than, a publisher and employe of the Foreign Ministry. Le Minh Lien was appointed education minister, succeeding Dr. Le Minh Tri, who had been assassinated in January.* Nguyen Van An was confirmed as head of the Information Ministry and of Chieu Hoi, the "open arms" program for defectors, posts in which he had been serving for several months.

Thieu was reported Mar. 20 to have replaced or transferred 12 of the country's 44 province chiefs the previous week. A spokesman said the order was signed "to rotate functions in the army and increase job efficiency." Most of the province chiefs were army colonels. With the new appointments, Thieu had changed more than half the province chiefs in a year. Half of those dismissed in 1968 had been charged with corruption.

Premier Replaced

Tran Van Huong resigned as premier of South Vietnam Aug. 22 and was replaced Aug. 23 by Gen. Tran Thien Khiem, 43, deputy premier and interior minister and a close associate of Pres.

---

*Le Minh Tri, 43, was killed in Saigon Jan. 6 by a grenade tossed at his car. Tri, dragged from the car after it burst into flames, died of his injuries 10 hours later. His chauffeur was killed immediately; his bodyguard and 2 passersby were injured. The police called the assassination an act of terror but did not specifically blame the Viet Cong. Tri had made many enemies by fighting corruption in the educational system and had received letters and phone calls threatening him with death. A discharged serviceman was arrested as a suspect. In a move to protect government officials from attack, combat police were assigned Jan. 6 to guard each cabinet minister. (Dr. Tranh Anh, a friend of the late Tri and acting dean of Saigon University's medical college, was shot to death by a terrorist in Saigon's Cholon District Mar. 4.)

Nguyen Van Thieu. A new cabinet was presented by Khiem and Thieu Sept. 1. Huong had been under pressure for months to resign. Thieu was said to have urged Huong several times to leave office but to have refrained from dismissing him because it would be considered bad politics. Huong was charged with inefficiency and was assailed by some legislators for instituting a new tax schedule while inflation was spreading. The Saigon House of Representatives had proposed June 16 to debate in joint session with the Senate the replacement of Huong. Huong threatened June 17 to shut down any Saigon newspaper reporting that he planned to resign. 92 of the 135 deputies in the House of Representatives sent a letter to Thieu July 2 urging him to dismiss Huong, and the pro-government 6-party National Social Democratic Front had called on Thieu Aug. 8 to appoint a new premier "who has the prestige to carry out any measure introduced by the president."

(Huong had escaped unhurt when 2 men fired at his car in Saigon Mar. 5. A pedicab carrying an explosive charge had been wheeled toward Huong's car, but the explosive failed to detonate. The assailants then opened fire but were captured by Huong's armed escorts. 2 other men were later arrested in connection with the assassination attempt. One of them reportedly confessed to police that he was a Viet Cong member. The attack took place about 50 yards from the U.S. embassy.)

Thieu had been planning a cabinet revision for several months but did not announce his intentions until early in July. He said then that his goal was to broaden the base of the government. In explaining his decision to appoint Khiem, Thieu said Aug. 26 that "the fact that the cabinet is headed by a general does not mean that it will be a warmongering cabinet." But Thieu reiterated the view that "there will never be any kind of coalition or reconciliatory government as the enemy wishes. South Vietnam will not be sold out."

The cabinet announced Sept. 1 included 4 generals, 2 other military officers, 17 technicians and civil servants and 9 members of Huong's cabinet. The post of premier and the key Ministries of Interior, Defense and Rural Development were held by military men. The country's non-Communist opposition and the leaders of the dominant religious groups were not represented. Among those absent were representatives of the National Social Democratic Front. Several of its members had rejected offers of minor cabinet positions. Thieu said Huong had agreed to remain in the government as his special adviser. In addition to getting the premiership, Khiem retained his post as interior minister.

The new cabinet: *Premier & Interior*—Khiem; *Deputy Premier & Education*—Nguyen Luu Vien; *Secretary of State for Cultural Affairs*—Mai Tho Truyen; *Secretary of State for Reconstruction & Development*—Prof. Vu Quoc Thuc; *Ministers of State Without Portfolio*—Nguyen Tien Hy, Phan Quang Dan; *Foreign Affairs*—Sen. Tran Van Lam; *Defense*—Gen. Nguyen Van Vy; *Justice*—Le Van Thu; *Economy*—Pham Kim Ngoc; *Finance*—Nguyen Bich Hue; *Revolutionary Development & Pacification*—Maj. Gen. Tran Thanh Phong; *Information*—Ngoc Khac Tinh; *Open Arms*—Ho Van Cham; *Land Reform, Agriculture & Fisheries*—Cao Van Tham; *Public Works* —Duong Kich Nhuong; *Transportation & Communications*—Tran Van Vien; *Health*—Tran Minh Tung; *Social Welfare*—Tran Nguon Phieu; *Labor*—Dam Si Hien; *War Veterans*—Gen. Pham Van Dong; *Ethnic Development*—Paul Nur; *Secretary at the Premier's Office*— Nguyen Van Vang; *Secretary of State for Liaison with the National Assembly*—Cao Varn Tuong; *Undersecretary at the Economy Ministry* —Pham Minh Duong; *Undersecretary at the Finance Ministry*—Ha Xuan Trung; *Undersecretary at the Interior Ministry*—Le Cong Chat; *Undersecretary at the Education Ministry*—Tran Luu Cung; *Undersecretary at the Information Ministry*—Le Trong Quat; *2d Undersecretary at the Economy Ministry*—Tran Cu Nong; *2d Undersecretary at the Education Ministry*—Nguyen Danh Dan.

Viet Cong Cordial to Minh Proposal

The chief delegate of the Viet Cong's Provisional Revolutionary Government at the Paris conference, Mrs. Nguyen Thi Binh, declared Nov. 14 that if Gen. Duong Van Minh, a major non-Communist opposition leader in Saigon, became head of a "peace" cabinet, "we are ready to begin conversations with him." Mrs. Binh gave qualified approval of a proposal made by Minh Nov. 13 for a national referendum in South Vietnam "to help the government gain enough strength in demanding that our American ally step into the background and let the Vietnamese negotiate directly with the Vietnamese." Minh said he agreed "with those who have proposed that the government should consult the aspirations of the people through a popular referendum or through the convening of a national people's congress or through some other formula." (Ending a year-long political seclusion, Minh

Nov. 2 had called for a national convention to work for "a truly representative government" in South Vietnam.)

Mrs. Binh said any referendum should be limited to Vietnamese cities and not be held in Viet Cong-held areas, which, she claimed, totaled "4/5 of South Vietnamese territory and 11 of its 14 to 15 million citizens." There was no need to hold a referendum in those areas because the people there were "resolutely opposed" to the Saigon regime, she said. (The South Vietnamese government said Nov. 14 that its control extended to 92% of the country's population, a record high. According to Saigon's figures, 563,200 persons lived in areas dominated by the Viet Cong, while 841,400 resided in "contested" areas, where both the government and the Viet Cong were competing for control.)

Asserting that the Viet Cong would settle for representation in a provisional coalition government, Mrs. Binh said, "We are not in a position understand all Gen. Minh's policy. But we are ready to start conversations with anyone having the urban population's support to head a peace government." The South Vietnamese delegation in Paris Nov. 15 denounced Mrs. Binh's proposal.

Economic Problems

A joint team of U.S. and South Vietnamese economists and consultants concluded that South Vietnam's war-shattered economy could be restored within 10 years after the fighting ended at a cost of 2^{1}/_{2}$ billion. The assessment was contained in a report made public May 10 and submitted to Pres. Nguyen Van Thieu. The report was delivered to Pres. Nixon May 15. The 70-member team, headed by David Lillienthal, had been asked to investigate South Vietnam's postwar prospects by Pres. Johnson in 1966. *Among the report's major recommendations:*

● The recovery program should be carried out under a free-enterprise economy, financed mainly by private investments, rather than by a centrally directed system.
● Interest rates should be increased immediately to encourage savings and reduce the amount of money in circulation; the piaster should be devalued to restore its position in the foreign-exchange markets.
● The current "inequitable and inefficient" tax structure should be revamped.
● Members of the armed forces should be used in economically productive enterprises, such as road building.
● The Directorate General of Planning and the National Planning Council should be replaced by a central institute of planning and development.

● Agricultural and industrial production should be increased. (The report warned, however, that the current land-reform program, if pursued too vigorously, could have an adverse effect on the growth of certain crops that cannot be grown economically on a small scale.)
● South Vietnam "must take effective measures to limit population growth or accept reduced standards of living."

A major economic problem was inflation. The *N.Y. Times* reported June 9 that the U.S. had withheld $40 million in aid to Saigon during April and May in order to apply pressure on the government to control inflation. Prices reportedly rose 10% during March, April and May. The Saigon government agreed at the end of May to take measures against inflation. These included curbs to reduce luxury imports and to increase imports of essentials such as fertilizers and machinery.

The U.S. and South Vietnamese governments signed 2 economic agreements June 27. The first provided for U.S. allocation of $10 million in support of a program to give land to more than 800,000 rice farmers. Under the program, proposed by Land Reform Min. Cao Van Than to the National Assembly June 20, 3.2 million acres of land would be taken from landlords, local governments and religious groups, who would be paid 20% of the land value in cash and the remainder in 5% bonds over the next eight years. The 3-year program was expected to cost $400 million. Saigon hoped to receive 10% of the sum from the U.S. Under the 2d agreement, the U.S. agreed to provide 150,000 tons of rice, valued at $25.5 million, before the end of 1969. The new rice pact raised U.S. rice imports by South Vietnam to 1.8 million tons, valued at more than $300 million, since 1965. The agreements were signed by U.S. Amb. Ellsworth Bunker and Foreign Min. Tran Chanh Thanh.

Pres. Thieu Oct. 24 decreed a severe economic austerity program aimed at reducing a huge budget deficit and at avoiding the need to devalue the piaster. He announced extensive new taxes on imported goods that resulted in sharp increases in their prices. By Oct. 30 the price index had jumped 10 points. Thieu met with National Assembly leaders Oct. 24 to urge them not to challenge his austerity program and to ask for special powers to impose other austerity measures, such as revising business and personal tax schedules. The legislature had denied Thieu a similar request in 1968. The National Assembly Oct. 27 voted to adjourn in protest against the imposition of the new taxes. The Senate had asked the Supreme Court to consider the constitutionality of the

government's decree. In a nationwide radio and TV address Oct.
31, Thieu defended his austerity program and vowed to resign if
a majority of the people opposed it. Noting that South Vietnam
had spent $600 million on imports during the past year while
earning only $20 million from exports, Thieu said "this absurd
spending must stop." He called on the South Vietnamese "to
accept more efforts, more sacrifices than anyone else." "We must
carry our responsibilities in every field, political, military and
social," he said.

Police Action

Militant Buddhist leader Thich Thien Minh and 50 to 60
young followers were arrested Feb. 23, at the start of the Viet
Cong's post-Tet offensive, at the headquarters of the Buddhist
Youth Association in Saigon. Government authorities said Feb. 25
that action was taken against Thien Minh, chairman of the association, because a branch of the Viet Cong was using the youth
headquarters as a political base. Police arrested 3 or 4 youths Feb.
24 as they were entering the headquarters, and 50 others were said
to have been picked up in the vicinity of the Anquang Pagoda,
headquarters of the militant Buddhists. The government said an
arrested Viet Cong civil leader had supplied the information about
the youth headquarters. Police searching the center were said to
have found a Chinese pistol, explosives and several Communist
documents, including a Tet greeting signed by Ho Chi Minh.
Thien Minh's deputy, Thich Huyen Dieu, denied the government's implication that Thien Minh was either a Communist or
pro-Communist. Huyen Dieu Feb. 25 said he suspected that the
incriminating evidence found at the youth center had been planted by government agents. Thien Minh, long a critic of the Saigon
government, had been accused by the Interior Ministry Feb. 4 of
"distorting the truth" and "libelling the government" in a recent
Buddhist sermon.

A South Vietnamese military court in Saigon Mar. 15 convicted Thien Minh on charges of "harboring [Viet Cong] rebels and
concealing weapons and illegal documents." He was sentenced to
10 years at hard labor. The court Mar. 17 found Thien Minh
guilty of 2 additional counts—providing aid and support to army
draft dodgers and deserters—and sentenced him to another 5 years
in prison. A court officer said that the sentences would be served

concurrently and that the maximum term would not exceed 10 years. 3 of Thien Minh's arrested followers were convicted at the Mar. 17 trial of desertion from the army. One man was sentenced to 5 years in prison; the others received 2-year terms.

The Buddhists conceded that the Youth Center was used by the Viet Cong, but they denied that Thien Minh was involved. The government confiscated the center. The Saigon regime's action against Thien Minh was assailed at a meeting of the Anquang faction Mar. 16. The gathering, attended by 500 persons in Saigon's Anquang Pagoda, heard an anti-government statement that called Pres. Nguyen Van Thieu "a loyal Catholic faithful who relies on the power of the foreigner [the U.S.] to carry out the program of the late Pres. [Ngo Dinh] Diem of repressing Buddhists under many wicked and cruel forms." The statement blamed the U.S. for Thien Minh's "brutal" sentence, which it called "a serious provocation by the government against the [Buddhist] church."

The government released Thien Minh from detainment Oct. 30 as part of National Day observances Nov. 1. About 700 common-law prisoners were freed Nov. 1 and another 500 had their sentences reduced. In a previous amnesty gesture, the government Oct. 29 had released 88 Viet Cong prisoners, 63 of them women, and had announced that 310 political prisoners would be freed or be given reduced sentences. Pres. Thieu Aug. 26 had ordered the release of 51 common-law and political prisoners and had reduced the sentences of 470 others. The action was taken in observance of a Buddhist festival the following day. (Thieu had been reported May 24 to have signed a decree reducing the long-term sentences of Thien Minh and about 20 other prisoners, both political and civil.)

The government had carried out punitive measures in March and April against several Saigon newspapers and their editors and publishers for articles critical of the Saigon regime. The government had announced Mar. 25 that it had extended for the 2d time (from one month to 3 months) the suspension of the daily newspaper *Tin Sang (Morning News)*. The journal originally had been forced to stop publication for 6 days in punishment for printing an article implying that Pres. Thieu had compelled Premier Tran Van Huong to accept cabinet changes. The government Mar. 27 lifted a one-month suspension of the daily *Hoa Binch (Peace)*, published by a Vietnamese Roman Catholic priest. It had been disciplined for allegedly distorting the truth and denying the legal status of several government agencies.

Pham Viet Tuyen, publisher of the daily *Tu Do (Freedom)*, was sentenced to 4 months in prison in a Saigon court Apr. 3 on charges of slandering Foreign Min. Tran Chanh Thanh. Tuyen also was fined the equivalent of $930 and was ordered to pay Thanh one piaster (less than 1 cent) as "honor indemnity." Tuyen had published a letter of a South Vietnamese senator calling Thanh a "Communist cadre." Thanh had sued Tuyen and the senator.

The government Apr. 17 announced the arrest of 26 intellectuals and professional people on charges of having maintained private contacts with Viet Cong political agents. A prime suspect in the case, Nguyen Lau, arrested Apr. 12, confessed at a news conference at national police headquarters in Saigon that he had been in contact with one of 3 enemy agents present at the conference. Police said that the man, Tran Ngoc Hien, had passed "strategic information" to Lau. Lau was publisher of the English-language *Saigon Daily News*. Another newspaper publisher arrested on charges of having Communist ties was Pham Van Nhon of the French-language weekly *Le Vietnam Nouveau*. Lau was sentenced July 4 to 5 years in prison for "actions detrimental to the national order." But a military tribunal, which had tried Lau and the others arrested with him, found Lau innocent on a charge of rebellion against the Saigon government. Tran Ngec Hien and Nguyen Chuong Cung, alleged Viet Cong captains, were sentenced to life in prison; 5 defendants were acquitted, and the others received sentences of up to 5 years. The Vietnamese daily newspaper *Chinh Luan* was reported Apr. 17 to have been temporarily suspended for allegedly reprinting a North Vietnamese newspaper article. The item had called South Vietnamese Pres. Thieu's position on ending the war "a plot." The govenment suspended 3 newspapers Apr. 19 and another 3 May 20. This brought to 30 the number of newspapers forced to halt publication since the government had eased press censorship in 1968. One of the newspapers suspended May 20, *The Morning Bell*, was accused of printing a headline asserting that Pres. Nixon had secretly agreed to install a neutral government in Saigon and had arranged for the secret withdrawal of North Vietnamese troops from South Vietnam. The Information Ministry said the headline had "caused much apprehension of public opinion and to the fighting spirit of the South Vietnamese armed forces." Saigon's *Tin Sang (Morning News)* was shut down July 2 for printing articles the government said were "offensive to the allied forces and undermined the fighting spirit of the country." The articles reportedly dealt with unnatural deaths caused by "B-52 raids, defoliant chemicals and consorting with Americans."

A 5-man military tribunal in Saigon May 8 had sentenced Le Doan Kim, 40, to one year in prison on charges of subversive activities. Kim, a professor and politician, had been arrested Mar. 26 after advocating a "truly neutralist government" to bring peace to South Vietnam and social and economic reforms. The government prosecutor conceded that Kim's "neutralist solution is different from that of the Communists, but it creates misunderstanding and confusion among the people."

A private 8-member study group of American church officials and civil rights advocates that visited South Vietnam May 29–June 5 charged in a report released June 10 that the South Vietnamese government employed widespread "torture and brutality" to govern and suppress opposition. The statement said the regime depended "more upon police state tactics and American support to stay in power than upon true representation and popular support." One of the group's members, United Methodist Bishop James Armstrong, said that 67% of the 45,000 imprisoned South Vietnamese were jailed for political reasons, "because of some suspicion that they belong to or sympathize with the Viet Cong." The group reported June 6 that it had sent a cablegram informing Pres. Nixon that it had found in South Vietnam "a climate of political and religious suppression" incompatible "with representative or stable government." "Speaking for peace or in any other way opposing the government easily brings the charge of Communist sympathy and subsequent arrest," the statement said.

The Americans had met with Thieu June 5 and had urged him to release 2 jailed opponents of his regime—Truong Dinh Dzu, "peace candidate" in the 1967 presidential elections, and the militant Buddhist monk Thich Thien Minh (who was freed Oct. 30). The head of the group, Allan Brick, of the Fellowship of Reconciliation, said later that Thieu had made no response to the request. The other members of the study team were Rep. John J. Conyers Jr. (D., Mich.); the Rev. Robert F. Drinan, Roman Catholic dean of the Boston College Law School; John Pemberton, executive director of the American Civil Liberties Union; Rabbi Seymour Siegal of the Jewish Theological Seminary; Mrs. John C. Bennett, wife of the president of Union Theological Seminary (New York), and retired Adm. Arnold E. True.

David Truong, son of the imprisoned Truong Dinh Dzu, accused the Saigon government June 28 of starving his father "to eliminate him from the political scene." Truong said at a news conference in New York that his father was suffering from malnutrition. A Saigon government spokesman June 30 denied Truong's allegations. He said Dzu had been transferred from a prison island to Saigon May 31 for treatment of a heart condition.

The South Vietnamese government Aug. 2 confirmed that nearly 50 persons had been arrested in the past 10 days on suspicion of belonging to "an international Communist spy network." Among those reported rounded up were Huynh Van Trong, Pres. Thieu's special assistant for political affairs; Vu Ngoc Ruat, who had served as an assistant in the office of Nguyen Van Huong, secretary general of the president's office; and 3 officials at the Chieu Hoi Ministry, which screened Viet Cong defectors. Saigon police sources charged that the spy ring, with contacts in Cambodia, Hong Kong, Laos and France, had passed "strategic military and political intelligence" to the Communists. Trong was described as the central figure in the network. Police had first questioned him July 26 about unauthorized contacts with the Viet Cong. (Trong had fled to Cambodia in 1960 after participating in an unsuccessful *coup d'état* against the late Pres. Ngo Dinh Diem. He returned from exile after Diem's overthrow. Trong was appointed Thieu's assistant in Mar. 1968. He reportedly had been sent to Paris in 1968 to prepare for Saigon's participation in peace talks.) Thieu said in a TV interview Sept. 20, however, that Trong could not have transmitted secret information to the Communists because during the time he had "worked for me, he did not handle any important political or strategic information."

A Saigon military court Nov. 29 convicted Trong and 3 other men of high treason and sentenced them to life in prison. 37 other defendants, including 13 women, were found guilty of lesser charges of espionage and received sentences ranging from 6 months to 20 years. All were accused of links with the Viet Cong. The 4 who received the stiffer penalties included Vu Ngoc Nha and Le Huu Thuy. Nha was the confessed leader of the group accused by the prosecution of passing political and military information to the Viet Cong. Nha admitted that he was a member of the Communist Party and had infiltrated into South Vietnam in 1955 to establish an intelligence network. Trong denied that he was a Communist or had aided the enemy.

The South Vietnamese House of Representatives Dec. 31 approved a motion concurring with the findings of a special investigating committee, accusing 3 of its members of having engaged in pro-Communist activities. The accused were Tran Ngoc Chau, Pham The Truc and Hoang Ho, 69 of the 135 House members approved the resolution against Truc, 70 against Chau and 68 against Ho. About 50 opposition representatives walked out of the chamber, denouncing the vote as "illegal and unconstitutional." Pres. Thieu had asked the House to strip the 3 representatives of their immunity to prosecution. The House vote did not affect the legislators' immunity. Pham Duy Tue, secretary general of the National Assembly, had said Nov. 17 that Thieu had asked the lower house to impeach Truc, who had been in Tokyo for the past year, and Hoang Ho, former assistant information minister, who was linked to Trong. According to Thieu's accusation, there was photographic evidence to prove that Truc had met with a senior Communist official in Tokyo and had burned effigies of Thieu and Pres. Nixon in Tokyo. Truc had demanded the withdrawal of U.S. troops from Vietnam and the establishment of a neutral government in Saigon. House procedures had been disrupted Dec. 20 when a mob of several hundred persons invaded the building, demanding action against the 3 legislators. A resolution adopted by a majority of the National Assembly Dec. 22 charged that the demonstration had been fomented by Thieu.

12 members of the House of Representatives declared at a news conference Dec. 22 that Thieu was planning a military dictatorship, and they demanded that he be tried for high treason. One deputy, Nguyen Van Phuong, charging that Thieu wanted to abolish the National Assembly, said the president "advocates a policy of assassination and sabotage towards deputies, newsmen and the people with the purpose of setting up a dictatorial regime."

Terrorism

Government authorities reported Feb. 4 that the Viet Cong had carried out 981 terrorist attacks on civilians in January, had killed 501 civilians and had wounded 1,377. This compared with 703 Viet Cong terrorist incidents in Dec. 1968, when 393 civilians were killed and 844 wounded. The South Vietnamese Foreign Affairs Ministry had said Jan. 27 that it had filed a protest with the International Control Commission against "the new crimes committed by North Vietnamese against the South Vietnamese people" in December. The protest attributed the terrorist drive to the "complete failure" of the Communists' winter-spring campaign. The national police chief, Col. Tran Van Hai, had reported Jan. 18 that 516 Viet Cong agents had been arrested in Saigon in the previous 3 months. Their capture, plus the seizure of 107 pistols and rifles and 127 charges of dynamite, had thwarted a Viet Cong terrorist campaign in the capital, Hai said. The Viet Cong plans, Hai said, had come to light in the interrogation of prisoners and captured documents. He said that Viet Cong agents had penetrated Saigon labor unions, student groups and newspapers.

Index

Note: This index follows the Western usage in regard to most Vietnamese names. A Vietnamese individual, therefore, would be listed not under his family name but under the last section of his full name. *E. g.,* Nguyen Luong Bang would be indexed thus: BANG, Nguyen Luong (not NGUYEN Luong Bang). Exceptions are usually the cases of monks or others (*e. g.* Ho Chi Minh) who use adopted names; such persons are generally listed under the first sections of their names (HO Chi Minh, not MINH, Ho Chi).

A

ABERNATHY, Rev. Ralph D. —198, 206
ABRAMS, Gen. Creighton W.—25, 35, 54-5, 57, 78, 82, 90, 164. U.S. forces in Vietnam—32; troop withdrawal —4, 152
ABZUG, Bella—185
ACHESON, Dean—161
AERIAL Warfare—See also DEFOLI- ATION. Helicopter use—11, 83-4, 93, 96, 100. U.S. bombing halt —3, 11, 91—See also Ceasefires. U.S. bombing raids: Cambodia—106- 8, 99; Cambodia border—68, 77, 83, 94-5, 97; Ho Chi Minh Trail —105-6; Loation border—101; U.S. reconnaissance planes—31
AFRICA—207
AGNEW, Spiro T.—62. Antiwar protests—193, 199-201. News media —119-21
AIKEN, Sen. George D. (R., Vt.) —53, 64, 112-3, 160
AIR Force, U.S.: Casualties—105-6. Withdrawal—95, 110-1
AIRBASES, U.S.—32. See also specific base
ALBANIA—89, 142
ALBERT, Rep. Carl (D., Okla.)—200
ALDRICH, Chief Judge Bailey—187
ALGERIA—135
ALLIANCE for Labor Action—198

ALLIANCE of National Democratic & Peace Forces—130-2
AMERICAN Broadcasting Companies (ABC)—120
AMERICAN Civil Liberties Union (ACLU)—122, 188-9, 218
AMERICAN Friends Service Committee (Quakers)—118, 198
AMERICAN Legion—201
AMERICANS for Democratic Action —198
AN, Nguyen Van—209
ANH, Dr. Tranh—209
ANHOA, South Vietnam : U.S. airbase—75
ANKHE, South Vietnam—71. Camp Radcliffe (U.S. Army base)—100
AN Quang (Buddhists)—207
APBIA (Hamburger Hill) (South Vietnam)—70-3, 75
ARGENTINA—206
ARGONNE National Laboratory (Chi- cago)—185
ARMENDARIZ Jr., Albert—188
ARMSTRONG, Bishop James—217
ARMY, U. S. :
Antiwar Protest—200; arrests—189; guidelines for dissent—189-90; con- scientious objectors—189. Casualties —2, 10-3, 21-3, 26, 31-4, 36-7, 67-71, 74-85, 92, 94-101, 167. Draft calls— 152. Green Berets (U.S. Special Forces) —163-6. Strength—96. Troop with- drawals—60-1, 126, 151; Thailand

221